Don Burleson Series Editor

ORACLE
Database Automation

HIGH PERFORMANCE

Don Burleson **Series Editor**

ORACLE
Database Automation

HIGH PERFORMANCE

Jonathan Ingram

 **CORIOLIS GROUP BOOKS**

an International Thomson Publishing company I(T)P®

Albany, NY • Belmont, CA • Bonn • Boston • Cincinnati • Detroit • Johannesburg • London
Madrid • Melbourne • Mexico City • New York • Paris • Singapore • Tokyo • Toronto • Washington

Publisher	Keith Weiskamp
Project Editor	Toni Zuccarini
Production Project Coordinator	April Nielsen
Cover Artist	Gary Smith
Cover Design	Anthony Stock
Layout Design	Nicole Colón
Compositor	EriBen Graphics
Copyeditor	Mary Millhollan
Proofreader	Shelly Crossen
Indexer	Laura Lawrie
CD-ROM Development	Robert Clarfield

High Performance Oracle Database Automation
Copyright © 1997 by The Coriolis Group, Inc.

The Coriolis Group, Inc.
An International Thomson Publishing Company
14455 N. Hayden Road, Suite 220
Scottsdale, Arizona 85260

602/483-0192
FAX 602/483-0193
http://www.coriolis.com

Printed in the United States of America
ISBN 1-57610-152-5
10 9 8 7 6 5 4 3 2 1

Acknowledgments

Long ago I decided that my life would involve writing, but I never anticipated that my first book would be a technical book, but, lo and behold, here it is.

The wonderful people at The Coriolis Group exhibited vast amounts of faith and patience with me and were instrumental in completing this book. I hope that I've repaid that faith with a book that goes a long way towards my early goals of emphasizing design and testing skills as much as, if not more than, syntax. I certainly hope that you find this book useful for those purposes; I think that those skills are the meat and potatoes of any kind of application development.

Many people have helped me complete this project in one way or another; I want to take a few lines and thank them:

- My wife Sara has been patient, loving, and supportive throughout this project, understanding the pressures of deadlines and helping out in whatever ways I needed.

- My friend Mark Rife has served as a sounding board for ideas and has been an excellent technical editor. He also contributed ideas and snippets of code as well.

- My editor, Toni Zuccarini, has always been helpful and patient. Thanks Toni.

- My good friends and former coworkers Herald Williams and Doug Young were especially supportive throughout this project (albeit often in their own special ways).

- My co-workers have all provided support and opinions and are a constant inspiration, as well as a source of new and different perspectives. I don't think you can ever see something from too many sides.

There are many other people to whom I owe a debt of gratitude as well, but listing them all would take a book in itself. Suffice it to say that you are all very dear to me and that I couldn't have accomplished this monstrous undertaking without your friendship and support.

A Note From Donald Burleson

Today's Oracle professionals are standing at the turning point. As Oracle technology moves into the twenty-first century we are seeing the complexity of database systems becoming almost unfathomable. Today's Oracle professional must be an expert in database performance and tuning, database administration, data warehousing, using Oracle with the Web, using OLAP and spatial data, and many other areas. These robust new features of Oracle present unique challenges to anyone who must use Oracle technology to deliver solutions to complex data-oriented challenges.

Oracle, the world's leading database management system, provides a mind-boggling wealth of features and options—far more than one Oracle professional can easily digest. The Oracle market is filled with new possibilities as Oracle introduces the management of objects, data warehouses, and Web-enabled applications; Oracle professionals everywhere are struggling to understand how to exploit these new features.

It is no longer acceptable for Oracle professionals to be generalists—they must become intimately familiar with all facets of Oracle technology and understand how these technologies interoperate. Rather than simply breadth of knowledge, the Oracle professional must have enough depth to effectively apply the technology. To get this knowledge we must rely on experts to guide us through the labyrinth of complicated tools and techniques, and we do not have the luxury of wading through mundane technical manuals.

What we need is clear, concise advice from seasoned Oracle professionals. That is the purpose of The Coriolis Group's High Performance Oracle series. As you are challenged to keep pace with this exciting new technology, we are challenged to provide on-point books to help guide you through the myriad of Oracle features and ensure your success.

Don Burleson
Rochester, New York

Contents

Introduction   **xxi**

Chapter 1   Database Automation In The Real World   **1**

Scripting   **4**
Backup And Restoration   4
Creating And Maintaining Users   6
Dynamic Code Generation   7
Testing   10
Other Uses   12

Stored PL/SQL Objects   **12**
Procedures   13
Functions   14
Packages   15
Database Triggers   17

The Future Of Database Automation   **21**
The Business Rules Engine   22

Summary   **22**

Chapter 2   The Architecture Of The Oracle Database, SQL, And PL/SQL   **25**

The Architecture Of The Oracle Database   **27**
Constraints   28

Indexing   32
Privileges And Roles   34
Schemas   36
Sequences   36
Snapshots   36
Synonyms   37
Tables And Columns   37
Views   38
The System Global Area   39

What Is SQL?   41

Data Definition Language   41
Data Manipulation Language   42
COMMIT And ROLLBACK   42
Datatypes   43
Joins   44
Table Aliases   46
Locks   47
NULL Values   47
Operators   47
Subqueries   49

An Overview Of PL/SQL   49

Blocks   50
Cursors   51
Datatypes   53
Exceptions And Exception Handling   58
IF-THEN-ELSE Logic   62
The NULL Statement   62
Looping Constructs   62
Stored Objects   64
A PL/SQL Wish List   70

How Does The Database Parse SQL And PL/SQL?   72

Summary   74

Chapter 3   SQL And PL/SQL Scripting   75

The Many Faces Of Scripting   77
Backup And Restore   78
Dynamic Code Generation   79
Security And User Administration   80
Reporting   81
Testing   82
Other Tasks   87
Documenting Scripts   89

Scripting In SQL*Plus   90
SQL*Plus Commands   91
Connecting To SQL*Plus   103
Logging Out Of SQL*Plus   104
Script Parameters   105
Spooling Output To Files   105
Substitution Variables   106

PL/SQL In Scripts   106
Anonymous PL/SQL Blocks   106
Using DBMS_Output And UTL_File   107

Step-By-Step: Building A Report In SQL*Plus   107
Requirements   108
Pseudocode   108
Code   108

Summary   109

Chapter 4   Procedures   111

Advantages Of Procedures   113

Embedded SQL   113
Maintainability   114
Modularity   114
Performance Improvement   114
Reusability   116

Creating And Dropping Procedures   116

Recompiling Procedures   117
Local Procedures   117

Dependencies   121

Parameters   122

Datatypes   122
Parameter Types   123
Default Values   124

Calling Procedures   124

Anonymous PL/SQL Blocks   124
Stored PL/SQL Objects   126
Notation   127

Procedure Structure   129

The Procedure Declaration   129
Variable Declarations   131
Executable Declarations   132
The Procedure Body   134
Exception Handlers   135

Documenting Procedures   141

The Header   141
Pseudocode   143

Comments   144
Identifiers   145

Step-By-Step: Design A Procedure   145

Procedure Requirements   145
Design   146
Pseudocode   147
Code   148
Testing The Procedure   150

Summary   154

Chapter 5   Functions   155

Advantages Of Functions   157

Embedded SQL   157
Maintainability   158
Modularity   159
Performance Improvement   159
Reliability   159

Creating And Dropping Functions   160

Local Functions   160

Dependencies   163

Parameters   164

Datatypes   164

Return Values   164

Datatypes   165

Calling Functions   167

DML Statements   167
Anonymous PL/SQL Blocks   168

Stored PL/SQL Objects 169

The Structure Of A Function   169

The Function Declaration 170
Variable Declarations 172
Executable Declarations 173
The Function Body 175
Exception Handling 177

Documenting Functions   178

The Header 179
Pseudocode 180
Comments 181
Identifiers 182

Step-By-Step: Creating A Function   182

Function Requirements 182
Designing The Function 183
Pseudocode 184
Code 185
Testing 190

Summary   195

Chapter 6   Packages   197

The Package Spec   199

Global Variables 199
Procedures 202
Functions 204
Overloading Procedures And Functions 207

The Package Body   208

Procedures   209
Functions   210
Initializing A Package   211

Step-By-Step: Building A Package   212

Requirements   212
Pseudocode   214
Code   216
Testing   220

Summary   220

Chapter 7   Database Triggers   221

Features Of Database Triggers   223

Embedded DML Statements   223
Event-Driven Processing   225
Maintainability   228
Performance Improvement   228
Referencing Column Values   229
Reusability   229
The :old And :new Specifications   229
Boolean Functions   229

Creating And Dropping Triggers   231

Recompiling Database Triggers   232
Disabling And Enabling Triggers   233

Mutating Table Errors   233

Referencing A Trigger's Associated Table   234
Foreign Key References   236
Cascading Deletes   236
Working Around The Rules   237

The Data Dictionary And Trigger Source Code — 240

Typical Uses For Triggers — 241
Enforcing Complex Business Rules   241
Updating Relevant Data   241
Marking Rows For Processing   241
Signaling An Event   242

Trigger Structure — 242
Trigger Declaration   242
Triggering Event   243
Associated Table   244
Trigger Level   245
WHEN Clause   245
Trigger Body   246

Documenting Triggers — 247
Trigger Header   247

Step-By-Step: Creating A Trigger — 248
Trigger Requirements   248
Determining The Trigger's Level   250
Pseudocode   250
Code   251
Testing The Trigger   252

Summary — 253

Chapter 8   Debugging — 255

Compile Errors — 257
Listing Compile Errors   258
Fixing Compile Errors   259
Using Data Dictionary Tables   261

Line Numbers   262
When The Line Number Is Wrong   263

Runtime Errors   264

Using The DBMS_Output Package   265
Locating Runtime Errors   268
Handling Exceptions Cleanly During Execution   271
Useful Functions   276

Summary   277

Chapter 9   Special Packages   279

DBMS_Alert   281

The Register() Procedure   282
The Remove() Procedure   283
The RemoveAll() Procedure   283
The Set_Defaults() Procedure   283
The Signal() Procedure   283
The WaitAny() Procedure   284
The WaitOne() Procedure   285
Using Signals   285

DBMS_DDL   286

The Alter_Compile() Procedure   287
The Analyze_Object() Procedure   288

DBMS_Describe   288

DBMS_Job   290

The Broken() Procedure   291
The Change() Procedure   292
The Interval() Procedure   292
The ISubmit() Procedure   292

The Next_Date() Procedure   293

The Remove() Procedure   293

The Run() Procedure   293

The Submit() Procedure   293

The User_Export() Procedure   294

The What() Procedure   294

Scheduling A Job   294

DBMS_Output   295

DBMS_Pipe   295

The Create_Pipe() Function   297

The Next_Item_Type() Function   298

The Pack_Message() Procedure   298

The Purge() Procedure   299

The Receive_Message() Function   299

The Remove_Pipe() Function   299

The Send_Message() Function   300

The Unique_Session_Name() Function   300

The Unpack_Message() Procedure   301

Using Pipes   301

DBMS_SQL   302

The Bind_Variable() Procedures   304

The Close_Cursor() Procedure   305

The Column_Value() Procedures   305

The Define_Column() Procedures   307

The Execute() Function   307

The Execute_And_Fetch() Function   308

The Fetch_Rows() Function   308

The Open_Cursor() Function   308

The Parse() Procedure   308
The Variable_Value() Procedures   309
Using The DBMS_SQL Package   310

DBMS_Utility   311

UTL_File   312

The FClose() Procedure   312
The FClose_All() Procedure   313
The FFlush() Procedure   313
The FOpen() Function   313
The Get_Line() Function   313
The Is_Open() Function   314
The New_Line() Procedure   314
The Put() Procedure   314
The PutF() Procedure   315
The Put_Line() Procedure   315
Using The UTL_File Package   315

Summary   316

Chapter 10   Performance Tuning   317

Tuning SQL   319

Using The EXPLAIN PLAN Statement   320
Using TKPROF   322
Other Tuning Tips   326

Tuning PL/SQL   329

Using Cursors   330
Exception Handling   331

Summary   334

Appendix A Using Built-In SQL And PL/SQL Functions 335

Single-Row SQL Functions 337

Conversion Functions 338
Alphabetic Functions 340
Date Functions 346
Numeric Functions 347
Miscellaneous Functions 350

Multi-Row SQL Functions 351

avg() 351
count() 351
max() 352
min() 352
sum() 352

PL/SQL Functions 352

SQLCODE() 353
SQLERRM() 353

Special Functions Used To Convert Numbers 353

Converting Numbers Between Bases 353
Is_Number() 357

Summary 358

Appendix B DML Command Syntax And Examples 359

The DELETE Statement 361
The INSERT Statement 362

The SELECT Statement   362

The UPDATE Statement   363

Appendix C   Getting In Touch With Other Oracle Professionals   365

Frequently Asked Questions And White Papers   367

Newsgroups   368

Oracle On Linux   368

Oracle User Groups   369

Appendix D   SQL And PL/SQL Coding Standards   371

A Sample SQL And PL/SQL Coding Standard   375

The Development Environment And Processes   375

Programming Design Standards   376

Headers   377

Formatting Guidelines For SQL And PL/SQL Statements   378

SQL Statement Formatting Rules   389

PL/SQL Naming Conventions   392

Written Documentation   395

Taking Advantage Of Standardized Code   395

The Build_SUID_Matrix Package   395

Appendix E   What's New In Oracle8?   397

New Datatypes 399

The object Datatype   400
The varray Datatype   403
The Large Object Datatypes   404
The Nested Table Datatype   405
The New ROWID   405

Changes To SQL*Plus And PL/SQL 406

SQL Changes   406
PL/SQL Changes   407

Summary 407

Index 409

Introduction

When I first started using the Oracle relational database in 1991, I had no idea what I was doing or how important this tool would become to my future. Now, nearly six years later, I've written hundreds of thousands of lines of code in SQL and PL/SQL.

Oracle is an important product that drives a majority of the world's largest databases and runs on numerous operating systems, including most flavors of Unix. Oracle, perhaps more so than other relational databases, is a flexible tool that allows businesses to define their operations and build effective systems around them.

"Database automation" seems like a murky topic, but in reality it is very straightforward. Scripting is the very important first half of database automation, allowing database administrators and application developers to perform complex tasks on a regular basis with a minimum of fuss and a high level of confidence and repeatability.

The use of stored PL/SQL code to enforce business rules at the database level is the second half of database automation. Database triggers, procedures, functions, and packages can all play important roles when implementing a complex system, drastically reducing the amount of code that must be written for the system's front end.

The purpose of this book is not to teach the syntax of SQL and PL/SQL coding, but to emphasize the concepts behind the code. Toward this end, I've emphasized *designing*, *documenting*, and *testing* code as the most important duties of the application developer. If you need to know syntax, look at the manual. Technique is the most important weapon an application developer has against a dragon of a system.

Chapter 1 is an introduction to the central concepts of database automation. The chapter also discusses some long-term advancements that will make database automation even more powerful. Chapter 2 is a primer on Oracle, SQL, and PL/SQL for readers who are new to Oracle or to those who have limited experience with the database.

Chapters 3 through 7 emphasize the concepts behind designing, documenting, coding, and testing scripts, stored procedures, stored functions, packages, and database triggers. Emphasis is given to design, documentation, and testing over syntax.

Chapter 8 contains essential debugging skills for your code, with an emphasis on the best methods to locate runtime errors and write code that is easily debugged and maintained. Chapter 9 discusses the packages that are provided by Oracle and presents real-world examples of how to use these tools. Finally, Chapter 10 discusses tips and techniques that you can use to get the best performance out of your SQL and PL/SQL code. I've also included a look at some of Oracle8's new features, and a sample PL/SQL coding standard that can be customized for your place of business.

I've tried to cover the essentials first and then include whatever else seemed most useful, but with a project of this size you always feel that there's more to be done. If you would like to comment on the book, point out typos or inconsistencies, or simply add an encouraging word to the mix, I welcome your comments at **jingram@teleport.com.**

HIGH PERFORMANCE

Database
Automation In
The Real World

CHAPTER

1

Database Automation In The Real World

With the release of Oracle7 into the relational database world, Oracle Corporation changed the direction of system development based on Oracle. Once forced to rely on Oracle*Forms to include procedural logic that enforced complex business rules, developers could now enforce these rules inside stored PL/SQL objects.

This was a paradigm shift for Oracle Corporation and for systems based on Oracle databases. Code stored within the Oracle7 database enforced system logic, reducing redundant code spread over multiple applications. This has led to an era of systems development in which the use of database triggers and other stored PL/SQL objects are planned in the design phase of systems development.

Despite the importance of this paradigm shift, the use of stored PL/SQL objects is only one half of database automation. The other half of database automation, predating even prepackaged software, involves the use of scripts to accomplish a variety of tasks, such as:

- Backup and restoration
- Creating/maintaining users
- Dynamic code generation
- Testing
- Other miscellaneous purposes

This chapter provides numerous detailed examples of scripts that accomplish a variety of purposes, as well as numerous examples of stored PL/SQL objects. Familiarity with the actual tasks performed in the examples is useful, but not absolutely necessary.

Scripting

The oldest form of system automation involves the use of scripts and other mechanisms to batch jobs. Every major operating system provides some capacity to develop scripts, from the simple DOS batch programming to the potentially unlimited applications of awk, sed, and perl on Unix systems. On Oracle systems, the developer can utilize both SQL*Plus and PL/SQL in addition to any scripting languages supported by the operating system.

Within the context of an Oracle database, scripting usually follows one of several predominant types. More detailed information about the development of scripts using SQL and PL/SQL can be found in Chapter 3.

Backup And Restoration

Of all the tasks accomplished with scripts in an Oracle database, the automation of system backups (and to a lesser extent recovery of a database) is probably the most important. Most Oracle installations (especially those IS shops that use hot backups) automate the process of performing system backups.

Listing 1.1 is a generic script for a cold backup of an Oracle database. The OS-level commands that perform the backup of files have been excluded.

Listing 1.1   A generic cold backup script for an Oracle database.

```
#
# Set up the environment variables.
#
ORACLE_SID=registrar_db; export ORACLE_SID
ORACLE_HOME=/dbhost/database/oracle/v722; export ORACLE_HOME

#
# Shutdown the database.
#
svrmgrl
connect internal
shutdown immediate

#
# Backup the database control files, redo logs, and dbf files.
#
<OS commands to backup files here>
```

```
#
# Restart the database.
#
svrmgrl
connect internal
startup
```

Listing 1.2 is a generic script for a hot backup of an Oracle database. Again, the OS-level commands that perform the backup of files have been excluded.

Listing 1.2   A generic hot backup script for an Oracle database.

```
#
# Set up the Oracle environment variables.
#
ORACLE_SID=registrar_db; export ORACLE_SID
ORACLE_HOME=/dbhost/database/oracle/v722; export ORACLE_HOME

#
# Shut down the database.
#
svrmgrl lmode=Y
connect internal

#
# Back up each tablespace individually.
#
alter tablespace SYSTEM begin backup;
<OS command to backup the.dbf files containing the SYSTEM tablespace>
alter tablespace SYSTEM end backup;

alter tablespace ROLLBACK begin backup;
<OS command to backup the .dbf files containing the rollback tablespace>
alter tablespace ROLLBACK end backup;

alter tablespace APPLICATION begin backup;
<OS command to backup the .dbf files containing the application
tablespace>
alter tablespace APPLICATION end backup;

alter tablespace INDEXES begin backup;
<OS command to backup the .dbf files containing the application
tablespace>
alter tablespace INDEXES end backup;
```

```
#
# Turn off archive log and back up the archive log files.
#
archive log stop
exit

#
# Store a list of existing archive log files for export.
#
<OS command to generate a list of files>
svrmgrl lmode=y
connect internal
archive log start
exit

#
# Make sure the archive log files also get backed up.
#
<OS command to backup the archive log files>
<OS command to remove the archive log files that were backed up>

#
# Make a copy of the controlfile to be backed up.
#
svrmgrl lmode=y
alter database backup controlfile to <path for controlfile backup>
exit
<OS command to backup the controlfile copy>
```

Creating And Maintaining Users

Before Oracle7 introduced roles, Oracle DBAs had to grant rights on every table within a database to every user. Simply creating a new user was an arduous task, even with customized scripts that emulated the functionality that would come later with roles. Updating and maintaining grants was also a time-consuming task for DBAs. Listing 1.3 shows a sample script used to create a new user in an Oracle database.

Listing 1.3   A sample script to create a new user in an Oracle database.

```
GRANT CONNECT TO '&&1' IDENTIFIED BY '&&1';
GRANT RESOURCE TO '&&1';
GRANT SELECT ON STUDENTS TO '&&1';
```

```
GRANT SELECT ON STUDENT_FINANCIAL_AID TO '&&1':
GRANT SELECT ON ENROLLED_COURSES TO '&&1';
GRANT SELECT ON DEGREE_PLANS TO '&&1';
```

Obviously, this is a very simple example. In systems that contained hundreds of tables, these scripts often took hours to write and debug; executing the scripts for just one user took a significant amount of time. Furthermore, direct user grants had to be stored in the data dictionary, consuming storage space and memory and thereby using resources that can now be better used to improve performance.

An alternate method of handling this problem was to create an application that stored the privileges for each user inside one or more tables. Once the data was entered (usually via Oracle*Forms), an SQL script could generate the proper grant statements. Unfortunately, someone had to come up with a way to populate this table.

Dynamic Code Generation

Dynamic code generation is the meat and potatoes of script development, allowing a developer or DBA to write a single script to perform one task against many different data sources. An excellent example of this type of application is the HTMLCODE.SQL script, which uses multiple SQL statements to generate HTML documentation of source code by querying the Oracle7 data dictionary. The HTMLCODE.SQL script generates HTML code by selecting tags as text from the database, thus generating a document in HTML format. Listing 1.4 shows the HTMLCODE.SQL script.

Listing 1.4   The HTMLCODE.SQL script.

```
SELECT '<H2>'
FROM   DUAL;

SELECT rtrim (object_type) || ': ' || '<A NAME=>' ||
       rtrim (upper (object_name)) || '"</A>' ||
       rtrim (upper (object_name))
FROM   ALL_OBJECTS
WHERE  owner       = upper ('&&2')
AND    object_name = upper ('&&1');

SELECT '</H2>'
FROM   DUAL;
```

```
SELECT ' '
FROM    DUAL;

SELECT '<P> The ' || rtrim (object_name) || ' ' ||
        rtrim (object_type) ||
        ' calls these procedures owned by ' ||
        upper (&&2) ||
        '</P>'
FROM    ALL_OBJECTS
WHERE   object_name = upper ('&&1')
AND     owner       = upper ('&&2')
AND     object_name IN
        (SELECT DISTINCT name
         FROM    ALL_DEPENDENCIES
         WHERE   owner = upper ('&&2')
         AND     name  = upper ('&&1')
         AND     (type = 'PROCEDURE'
         OR       type = 'FUNCTION'
         OR       type = 'PACKAGE BODY');
         AND     referenced_owner = '&&2'
         AND     (referenced_type = 'PROCEDURE'
         OR       referenced_type = 'FUNCTION'
         OR       referenced_type = 'PACKAGE BODY');

SELECT ' '
FROM    DUAL;

SELECT '<CENTER>'
FROM    DUAL;

SELECT '<LI><A HREF="#' || rtrim (referenced_name) || '">' ||
        rtrim (referenced_name) || '</A>'
FROM    ALL_DEPENDENCIES
WHERE   owner            = upper ('&&2')
AND     name             = upper ('&&1')
AND     referenced_owner = '&&2'
AND     (referenced_type = 'PROCEDURE'
OR       referenced_type = 'FUNCTION'
OR       referenced_type = 'PACKAGE BODY');

SELECT '</CENTER>'
FROM    DUAL;

SELECT ' '
FROM    DUAL;
```

```
SELECT '<PRE>'
FROM   DUAL;

SELECT rtrim (replace (text, chr (9), '     '))
FROM   ALL_SOURCE
WHERE  name  = upper ('&&1')
AND    owner = upper (rtrim ('&&2'))
ORDER BY line;

SELECT '</PRE>'
FROM   DUAL;

SELECT '<HR>'
FROM   DUAL;
```

Another example of dynamic code generation is a script that recompiles all the invalid procedures, functions, and packages in the Oracle database. Listing 1.5 shows a script that recompiles stored, invalid objects.

Listing 1.5   A script to recompile stored objects that are marked as invalid.

```
set pagesize 0
set feedback off
set head off

spool recompile.sql

SELECT 'ALTER ' ||
       decode (object_type, 'PACKAGE BODY', 'PACKAGE', object_type) ||
       ' ' ||
       object_name ||
       ' COMPILE ' ||
       decode (object_type, 'PACKAGE BODY', 'BODY', NULL) ||
       ';'
FROM   ALL_OBJECTS
WHERE  status = 'INVALID'
ORDER BY decode (object_type, 'FUNCTION',  'A',
                              'PROCEDURE', 'B',
                              'PACKAGE',   'C', object_type);

exit
```

The code shown in Listing 1.5 generates SQL commands by first selecting strings of text from the database. Then, appropriate portions of the command are selected as literals and real data is concatenated in the right spots, generating a valid SQL command. The use of the **decode**() function in the script forces the query to return commands to recompile functions first, then procedures, and finally package specs. The output of the script is shown in Listing 1.6.

Listing 1.6   Generated code to recompile invalid PL/SQL objects.

```
ALTER FUNCTION Feet_To_Inches COMPILE ;
ALTER PROCEDURE Calculate_GPA COMPILE ;
ALTER PACKAGE Student_Addresses COMPILE BODY;
```

Testing

For an application developer, one of the most important uses of scripting is the ability to create and later re-create conditions for testing pieces of code. A good unit test defines a set of test data, documents the conditions established by the test data, predicts the output of the code being tested, and allows the developer to compare (or automatically compares) the predicted results with the actual results. Listing 1.7 displays a simple script that allows testing of a function.

Listing 1.7   A simple script that allows testing of a function.

```
set serveroutput on
set timing on
set verify off
set pause off
set linesize 80
set pagesize 0
set feedback off

spool test_out.txt
--
-- Set up some state abbreviations.
--
INSERT
INTO   STATE_CODES
       (state_name,
        state_code)
VALUES ('MISSISSIPPI',
        'MS');
```

```
--
-- Calling the function Get_State_Name() with a parameter of 'MS'
-- will return the value 'Mississippi'.
--
DECLARE
   vFullStateName    varchar2 (20);

BEGIN
   vFullStateName := Get_State_Name (vStateAbbr => 'MS');
   DBMS_Output.Put_Line ('The function returned ' ||
                         vFullStateName);

EXCEPTION
   WHEN OTHERS THEN
       DBMS_Output.Put_Line (SQLERRM);
END;


--
-- Calling the function Get_State_Name() with a parameter of 'AK'
-- will not return 'Mississippi'.
--
DECLARE
   vFullStateName    varchar2 (20);

BEGIN
   vFullStateName := Get_State_Name (vStateAbbr => 'AK');
   DBMS_Output.Put_Line ('The function returned ' ||
                         vFullStateName);

EXCEPTION
   WHEN OTHERS THEN
       DBMS_Output.Put_Line (SQLERRM);
END;

spool off
```

This script can be re-executed at any point in the future when the function **Get_State_Name()** is changed. While this is a very simple example, this type of script can be used to automate testing of almost any piece of code. The ability to easily repeat a test of complex code easily offsets the time required to develop a test for the same code—a 200 line procedure that drives part of a major application is not something that should rely on ad hoc testing.

Other Uses

The potential use of scripts to automate a task inside an Oracle database is limited only by the imagination of the developer. For instance, a developer might need to write a simple script that changes area codes to keep up with the rapid growth of the nation's phone system, as shown in Listing 1.8.

Listing 1.8 A simple script to update area codes inside phone numbers.

```
UPDATE STUDENTS
SET    home_phone = to_number ('&&1') ||
       substr (to_char (home_phone, 4, 7))
WHERE  substr (to_char (home_phone), 4, 3) = '&&2'
AND    substr (to_char (home_phone), 1, 3) = '&&3'
/
```

This script replaces the area code prefixes for all phone numbers in the area code specified by **&&3** and the local calling area **&&2** with the area code specified in **&&1**. The script concatenates the last seven digits of the phone number (the local calling area and extension) with the new area code.

Stored PL/SQL Objects

Stored PL/SQL allows you, the application developer, to write code once and enforce your business logic inside the database. This provides a tremendous advantage in an environment where business rules are regularly subject to change. The modular nature of these objects allows business rules to be enabled and disabled quite easily.

All stored PL/SQL objects have certain common traits, including:

- Their source code is stored within the **ALL_SOURCE** view (with the exception of database triggers, whose source code is stored in the **ALL_TRIGGERS** view).

- They execute with the authorities of the user who created the object.

- They incorporate both SQL and PL/SQL statements.

- Their access is controlled like all other objects in the database. The ability of an individual user to execute a specific stored object (or all stored objects) must be granted to a user.

Table 1.1 The three types of procedure and function parameters.

Parameter Type	Functionality
IN	IN parameters pass a value to the procedure. This value cannot be modified by the procedure.
OUT	OUT parameters are used to pass a value back to a calling block of PL/SQL code. The value in this parameter can never be read by the procedure.
IN OUT	IN OUT parameters are used to pass a value to the procedure. This value can then be modified by the procedure and the resulting value passed back to the calling PL/SQL block.

Procedures

A well-designed stored procedure is written to achieve one purpose and perform only the actions necessary to achieve that purpose. Procedures can accept and return values to their calling application with ease through the use of parameters. Table 1.1 shows stored procedure parameter types and functionality.

Listing 1.9 presents a typical stored procedure. This procedure accepts a social security number as a parameter, queries the **ENROLLED_COURSES** table to determine the total number of credits and credit hours for the student, calculates the student's grade point average by dividing the total number of credits by the total number of credit hours, and updates the student's master record in the **STUDENTS** table.

Listing 1.9 A typical stored procedure.

```
PROCEDURE Calculate_GPA (nSSN IN      integer)

IS

    nOverallGPA    number  := 0;
    iSumCredits    integer := 0;
    iTotalHours    integer := 0;
    iLogicStep     integer := 0;

BEGIN
    SELECT sum (credit_hours),
           sum (decode (course_grade,
                    'A', 4,
                    'B', 3,
```

```
                      'C', 2,
                      'D', 1, 0))
    INTO    iTotalHours,
            iSumCredits
    FROM    ENROLLED_COURSES
    WHERE   ssn = nSSN;

    iLogicStep := 1;
    nOverAllGPA := iSumCredits / iTotalHours;

    iLogicStep := 2;
    UPDATE STUDENTS
    SET     overall_gpa = nOverAllGPA
    WHERE   ssn = nSSN;

EXCEPTION
    WHEN OTHERS THEN
        SYSTEM_LOG.Log_Error (obj_name  => 'Calculate_GPA',
                              obj_step  => iLogicStep,
                              ora_error => substr (SQLERRM, 1, 65));
END Calculate_GPA;
```

Functions

The most common use of functions is to hold both simple and complex mathematical equations that are performed frequently by an application, but other simple tasks can also be accomplished. Well-designed functions, like well-designed procedures, are coded to perform one task. Like procedures, functions can accept and return values to calling objects via parameters, but returning values from a function via parameters is typically viewed as a poor coding practice. Listing 1.10 presents a typical stored function.

Listing 1.10 A typical stored function.

```
FUNCTION Calculate_GPA (nSSN IN      integer)

RETURN NUMBER

IS

    nOverallGPA      number  := 0;
    iSumCredits      integer := 0;
    iTotalHours      integer := 0;
    iLogicStep       integer := 0;
```

```
BEGIN
   SELECT sum (credit_hours),
          sum (decode (course_grade,
                        'A', 4,
                        'B', 3,
                        'C', 2,
                        'D', 1, 0))
   INTO   iTotalHours,
          iSumCredits
   FROM   ENROLLED_COURSES
   WHERE  ssn = nSSN;

   iLogicStep := 1;
   nOverAllGPA := iSumCredits / iTotalHours;

   iLogicStep := 2;
   RETURN nOverAllGPA;

EXCEPTION
   WHEN OTHERS THEN
        SYSTEM_LOG.Log_Error (obj_name  => 'Calculate_GPA',
                              obj_step  => iLogicStep,
                              ora_error => substr (SQLERRM, 1, 65));
END Calculate_GPA;
```

This function closely resembles the procedural implementation of **Calculate_GPA( )**, but the function does have one advantage that the procedure doesn't—the function can be called inside an SQL statement, as shown in Listing 1.11.

Listing 1.11 Use of the **Calculate_GPA( )** function in an SQL statement.

```
UPDATE STUDENTS
SET    overall_gpa = Calculate_GPA (nSSN => ssn);
```

Packages

The ability to group related procedures and functions into a single object is useful when building applications because the grouping process leads to a very modular application. A package consists of procedures, functions, global variables, constants, and type definitions.

Packages have two component pieces, a *package specification* (or *package spec*) and a *package body*. The package spec is generally used for the definition of constants, global variables, and user-defined datatypes for the package (although these declarations can also exist in the package body).

In addition to these declarations, the package spec defines the interfaces for procedures and functions that can be executed by applications. All declarations in the package spec are **public** and can be referenced or called by other stored PL/SQL objects and applications.

Listing 1.12 presents code for a typical package specification. This package spec defines two functions. The spec also asserts a purity level for each function, which allows the packaged functions to be called inside an SQL statement.

Listing 1.12 A typical package spec.

```
PACKAGE Conversions

IS

    FUNCTION Inches_To_Centimeters (nInches IN    number) RETURN number;
    PRAGMA restrict_references (Inches_To_Centimeters, NDWS, NPWS);

      FUNCTION Centimeters_To_Inches (nCentimeters IN    number)
      RETURN number;
      PRAGMA restrict_references (Centimeters_To_Inches, NDWS, NPWS);
END Conversions;
```

Any objects defined in a package body without having been first declared in the package spec are private objects, which can only be referenced by objects defined within the package. Global variables, user-defined datatypes, constants, procedures, and functions can all be declared inside a package body without being declared in a package spec. In a system where security is paramount, private objects are quite common. Listing 1.13 shows the code for a typical package body.

Listing 1.13 A typical package body.

```
PACKAGE BODY Conversions

IS

FUNCTION Inches_To_Centimeters (nInches IN    number)

RETURN number
```

```
IS

BEGIN
   RETURN (nInches * 2.54);
END Inches_To_Centimeters;

--

FUNCTION Centimeters_To_Inches (nCentimeters IN     number)

RETURN number

IS

BEGIN
   RETURN (nCentimeters / 2.54);
END Centimeters_To_Inches;

--

FUNCTION Inches_To_Meters (nInches IN     number)

RETURN number

IS

BEGIN
   RETURN (100 * Inches_To_Centimeters (nInches));
END Inches_To_Meters;

--

END Conversions;
```

In this example, the function **Inches_To_Meters**( ) is private and can only be called by other procedures and functions defined within the package body. The functions **Inches_To_Centimeters**( ) and **Centimeters_To_Inches**( ) are public objects and can be called by any user or application with the appropriate privileges.

Database Triggers

Database triggers are the ideal tool for enforcing business rules that relate directly to data. Each database trigger is associated with a single table in the database and is configured to fire at a certain point when data is modified. Typical uses of database triggers include the following:

- Checking columns for conformity to complex rules that cannot be enforced with check constraints.

- Updating relevant data in other tables.

- Marking newly created or recently modified rows for another process to analyze.

- Ensuring that columns are populated.

- Signaling that a particular event has occurred.

The real strength of database triggers is that a trigger always fires when a defined action is performed on the trigger's associated table. Even statements executed via the command line in SQL*Plus will fire a trigger, making triggers the perfect method for enforcing business rules. Triggers can be written to fire at both statement level and row level.

Statement-level triggers fire once for each statement (or transaction) that affects the associated table. For instance,

```
UPDATE STUDENTS
SET    overall_gpa = 4.0;
```

would fire a statement-level trigger once, no matter how many rows of data were affected by the statement.

Row-level triggers fire once for each row affected by a statement that affects the trigger's associated statement. For instance,

```
UPDATE STUDENTS
SET    overall_gpa = 4.0;
```

would fire a row-level trigger once for each row in the **STUDENTS** table.

Triggers are cued by specific events. A trigger that fires when its associated table is updated does not fire when a new row is inserted into the associated table, unless the same trigger is coded to fire for both updates and inserts on the associated table. Triggers can be written to fire when **DELETE**, **INSERT**, and **UPDATE** statements affect the trigger's associated table.

Furthermore, triggers can be written to fire either after or before a specified event occurs. A before insert row-level trigger fires once before each row is inserted into the associated table; if an **INSERT** statement creates six new rows in the table, the trigger will fire six times (once before each individual row is created).

All told, there are 12 types of database triggers, which are listed in Table 1.2.

Triggers do not have to be triggered by a single type of DML statement on the table. It's quite common to combine the functions of any two or all three triggering DML statements inside the trigger. The most common example of this is a trigger that fires when a new row is created using the **INSERT** statement or when one or more rows is modified using the **UPDATE** statement.

Listing 1.14 displays a typical database trigger. In this example, the trigger attempts to validate a social security number when a new student is added. If the social security number cannot be validated, the trigger raises an exception and prevents the creation of a new record in the **STUDENTS** table. If the social security number is valid, the procedure guarantees that the student record has a financial aid ID and that the grade point average values for the new student don't contain any data.

Table 1.2   The twelve types of database triggers.

Trigger Type	Functionality
before delete statement level	Fires once before each **DELETE** statement affects the trigger's associated table, no matter how many rows are deleted from the table.
before delete row level	Fires once for each row affected by a **DELETE** statement, before each row is deleted.
after delete row level	Fires once for each row affected by a **DELETE** statement, after each row is deleted.
after delete statement level	Fires once after each **DELETE** statement that affects the trigger's associated table, no matter how many rows are deleted from the table.
before insert statement level	Fires once before each **INSERT** statement affects the trigger's associated table, no matter how many rows are inserted into the table.
before insert row level	Fires once for each row inserted into the table, before each row is inserted.

continued

Table 1.2 The twelve types of database triggers (Continued).

Trigger Type	Functionality
after insert row level	Fires once for each row inserted into the table, after each row is inserted.
after insert statement level	Fires once after each **INSERT** statement affects the trigger's associated table, no matter how many rows are inserted into the table.
before update statement level	Fires once before each **UPDATE** statement affects the trigger's associated table, no matter how many rows in the table are updated.
before update row level	Fires once for each row updated in the table, before each row is updated.
after update row level	Fires once for each row updated in the table, after each row is updated.
after update statement level	Fires once after each **UPDATE** statement that affects the trigger's associated table, no matter how many rows in the table are updated.

Listing 1.14   A typical database trigger.

```
CREATE OR REPLACE TRIGGER STUDENTS_BRI
before INSERT on STUDENTS
FOR each row

IS

   bValidSSN           boolean := TRUE;
   xInvalid_SSN_Given  EXCEPTION;

BEGIN
   bValidSSN := Validate_SSN (:new.ssn);

   IF (!bValidSSN) THEN
      RAISE xInvalid_SSN_Given;
   END IF;

   :new.financing_num   := Finance_seq.NEXTVAL;
   :new.overall_gpa     := NULL;
   :new.most_recent_gpa := NULL;
END;
```

UPDATE triggers can be made to fire even more specifically through the use of a WHEN clause in the trigger definition, as shown in Listing 1.15.

Listing 1.15 An **UPDATE** trigger using a **WHEN** clause.

```
CREATE OR REPLACE TRIGGER STUDENTS_BRU
before UPDATE on STUDENTS
FOR each row
WHEN (overall_gpa > 4.0)

IS

   xInvalid_GPA      EXCEPTION;

BEGIN
   RAISE xInvalid_GPA;
END;
```

In Listing 1.15, the trigger uses a **WHEN** condition to prevent any update of a student's grade point average from exceeding 4.0. The trigger fires only when the new value of the **overall_gpa** column exceeds 4.0.

The Future Of Database Automation

Is there a logical next step for database automation? The use of Oracle is limited only by the imagination of the system designer. Several distinct patterns have emerged in Oracle systems over the past few years.

- Data warehousing applications store tens of hundreds of gigabytes of data.

- Internet and intranet publishing has taken off through the use of Oracle WebServer, CGI, Java, Oracle's J/SQL, and JDBC.

- Financial and manufacturing systems using Oracle applications are growing both in number and in size.

Combinations of two or more of these patterns is not unusual for any given system.

Many large agencies and corporations throughout the world use Oracle for systems like the ones discussed in this text, including companies such as:

- AT&T

- British Petroleum

- Canada Post

- Conseil Européen pour la Recherche Nucléaire (CERN)

- Cisco Systems

- Hong Kong Public Works Management System

- Kredietbank Belgium

- Wells Fargo Bank

- United States government

With the end of the century and the millenium looming just around the corner, the push to convert legacy systems into more robust systems is continually forcing designers to come up with new and unusual applications for Oracle systems.

The Business Rules Engine

Currently, Oracle requires developers to code the logic to support business rules inside stored PL/SQL objects. While this is a tremendous advantage over the repeating logic inside multiple applications, a change in a business rule still requires the intervention of an application developer to change the code.

It's possible to design an application that stores business rules and code applications that dynamically enforce business rules based on the current state of each rule within the database. While this is certainly not an easy task, the resulting system enables new rules to be implemented quickly and easily (typically through a GUI interface with the database).

In the future, developers can expect the Oracle database to evolve into a system more friendly to this type of application. Perhaps Oracle9 will incorporate a configurable rules engine that dynamically interprets data based on business rules stored in the engine!

Summary

Oracle is a database that is strong on automation features. The use of SQL and PL/SQL allows complex scripts to be developed to accomplish many tasks. The ability to enforce business rules through the use of database triggers and other stored

PL/SQL objects allows systems to be created more quickly, at lower expense, and to be maintained more easily in the future.

Chapter 2 provides an overview of the Oracle7 architecture and introduces some basic concepts in SQL and PL/SQL. If you already have experience with Oracle, SQL, and PL/SQL, you'll probably want to skim Chapter 2 and then move on to Chapter 3 for a detailed discussion of scripting.

The Architecture Of The Oracle Database, SQL, And PL/SQL

The Architecture Of The Oracle Database, SQL, And PL /SQL

The Oracle database is not a simple piece of software. Fortunately, becoming a good PL/SQL developer doesn't require that you know everything about the internal structures of the database. Unfortunately, becoming a good PL/SQL developer requires that you understand a large part of the database architecture. This chapter is intended to provide you with a very high level perspective on what you need to know.

If you are already experienced with Oracle, SQL, and PL/SQL, you'll probably want to browse this chapter and move on to Chapter 3. If you're completely new to Oracle (either with or without previous development experience), make sure that you read this chapter before proceeding.

The Architecture Of The Oracle Database

Your knowledge of the database needs to cover the following basics:

- Constraints
- Indexing
- Locking
- Roles and privileges

- Schemas

- Sequences

- SGA (system global area)

- Snapshots

- Synonyms

- Tables and columns

- Views

This list is by no means comprehensive. Your work as an application developer using Oracle and PL/SQL will continually expose you to new challenges; with hard work and dedication, you'll meet those challenges head on.

Constraints

A *constraint* is a condition placed on a table, typically to satisfy a business rule. When a constraint is placed upon a table, every row in the table must satisfy that constraint. Listing 2.1 provides a definition of the table **STUDENTS**.

Listing 2.1   A sample table creation script using constraints.

```
CREATE TABLE STUDENTS AS
(ssn                 NOT NULL   number(9),
 first_name          NOT NULL   varchar2 (10),
 last_name           NOT NULL   varchar2 (12),
 middle_name                    varchar2 (10),
 street_address      NOT NULL   varchar2 (30),
 apartment_number               varchar2 (4),
 city                NOT NULL   varchar2 (30),
 state_code          NOT NULL   varchar2 (2),
 zip_code            NOT NULL   number (5),
 home_phone          NOT NULL   number (10),
 degree_plan                    varchar2 (20),
 overall_gpa                    number (3, 2),
 most_recent_gpa                number (3, 2));
```

Notice the columns **ssn**, **first_name**, **last_name**, **street_address**, **city**, **state_code**, and **zip_code** have the **NOT NULL** constraint. This constraint requires that each row of data in the **STUDENTS** table has values for these columns.

How Are Constraints Used?

As previously stated, constraints are often used to enforce business rules. A business rule that all students have a home address, name, and social security number is enforced through the use of the **NOT NULL** constraint. Several types of constraints exist, including:

- **NOT NULL**—A **NOT NULL** constraint requires that a column contains a value in all rows of a table. If no value is specified for a column with this constraint and no other database functions or objects affect the data before it is added to the table, an error will occur.

- **default**—Whenever a **NULL** value is inserted for the column, it is replaced with the value of the expression specified in the **default** constraint. For instance, if an hourly salary column is left **NULL**, it would default to the value of the minimum wage.

- **check**—A **check** constraint allows the Database Administrator (DBA) to specify an expression, which the value in the column must satisfy. If the column does not satisfy the expression, an error will occur. The **check** constraint is not extremely powerful, but does provide a handy way to enforce simple conditions without using code.

- **unique**—A **unique** constraint specifies that the value of the particular column is unique to a single row inside the table. For instance, in the **STUDENTS** table, the column **ssn** would be **unique** for every student. If you attempt to add a duplicate social security number to the table, an error will occur.

- **primary key**—A **primary key** constraint specifies that the column is part of the table's primary key. A primary key makes every row within the table unique. A table has only one primary key, which is composed of all the columns that have the **primary key** constraint. To specify that the value for an individual column must be unique in a table with more than one unique column in the primary key, the **unique** constraint must be used. Each element of the table's primary key is, by definition, **NOT NULL**.

- **foreign key**—A **foreign key** constraint specifies that a value for the specified column(s) must exist as **primary key** values in another table. For instance, the column **degree_plan** in the **STUDENTS** table might have a **foreign key** reference to the **DEGREE_PLANS** table's **degree_plan** column (a primary key column for the **DEGREE_PLANS** table). If this is the case, no student can have a degree plan that does not exist in the **DEGREE_PLANS** table.

The use of constraints to enforce business rules does have limitations. Some business rules are simply too complex to enforce with the limited functionality of the **check** constraint; in these situations, the system often has to rely on the use of database triggers (which use PL/SQL and can handle complex logic).

A revised description of the **STUDENTS** table might appear as shown in Listing 2.2.

Listing 2.2   A revised table creation script using constraints.

```
CREATE TABLE STUDENTS AS
(ssn                 NOT NULL   number(9)        primary key,
 first_name          NOT NULL   varchar2 (10),
 last_name           NOT NULL   varchar2 (12),
 middle_name                    varchar2 (10),
 street_address      NOT NULL   varchar2 (30),
 apartment_number               varchar2 (4),
 city                NOT NULL   varchar2 (30),
 state_code          NOT NULL   varchar2 (2),
 zip_code            NOT NULL   number (5),
 home_phone          NOT NULL   number (10),
 degree_plan                    varchar2 (20),
 overall_gpa                    number (3, 2),
 most_recent_gpa                number (3, 2),
 financing_num       NOT NULL   integer (9) unique,
 foreign key (degree_plan) references DEGREE_PLANS.degree_plan);
```

This revised table enforces the following conditions:

- The columns **ssn**, **first_name**, **last_name**, **street_address**, **city**, **state_code**, **zip_code**, **home_phone**, and **financing_num** must all have a value in every row contained in the table.

- The primary key of the table is the **ssn** column. This ensures that each student has a unique social security number. The definition of the **primary key** constraint also creates an index on the table.

- The value of the **degree_plan** column must exist in the **degree_plan** column of the table **DEGREE_PLANS**. A student must be following an existing degree program.

As an application developer with PL/SQL, you will rarely be required to create tables using constraints, but a working knowledge of constraints and their limitations will make you a better developer.

What Is Referential Integrity?

Simply put, *referential integrity* occurs when a value in one table must agree with a value in another table. In our revised **STUDENTS** table, a condition of referential integrity exists between the **STUDENTS** table and the **DEGREE_PLANS** table, because the student's degree plan must correspond to a predefined degree plan.

Referential integrity occurs in three types:

- One-to-one
- One-to-many
- Many-to-many

Understanding each type of referential integrity is crucial to being successful as a PL/SQL application developer.

One-To-One Relationships

A *one-to-one relationship* occurs when a single row in one table corresponds to one (and only one) row in another table. In our revised **STUDENTS** table, notice that each student has been given a unique **financing_num** value; this value will be used to provide a one-to-one relationship with the **STUDENT_FINANCIAL_AID** table. Because this value is unique, a reference to the **STUDENT_FINANCIAL_AID** table can be made once the proper **financing_num** value is queried from the **STU-DENTS** table. Figure 2.1 illustrates this one-to-one relationship.

One-To-Many Relationships

A *one-to-many relationship* occurs when a single row of one table corresponds to multiple rows in another table. In our revised **STUDENTS** table, the column **ssn** will be referenced by the ssn column in the **ENROLLED_CLASSES** table. Each student can be enrolled in one or several classes, so multiple rows in **ENROLLED_CLASSES** will contain the **ssn** for one student. Figure 2.2 illustrates this one-to-many relationship.

Many-To-Many Relationships

A *many-to-many relationship* occurs when one or more rows of a table correspond to one or more rows in another table. For instance, the **CLASSES** table contains a list of classes; each class has a unique **class_number** value. One or more students can

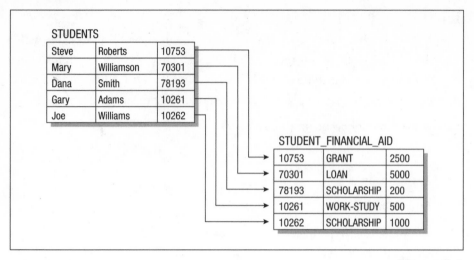

Figure 2.1
A one-to-one relationship.

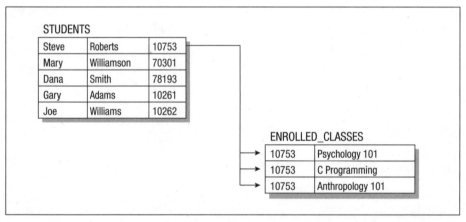

Figure 2.2
A one-to-many relationship.

each take the same class. A student can even take the same class multiple times (consecutively, one would hope). Therefore, the **CLASSES** table and the **STUDENTS** table have a many-to-many relationship (via the **ENROLLED_CLASSES** table). Figure 2.3 illustrates this many-to-many relationship.

Tables with many-to-many relationships usually (but not always) have a table that acts as an intersection for the two tables. In this case, the **ENROLLED_CLASSES**

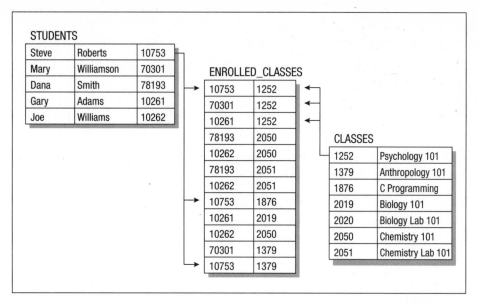

Figure 2.3
A many-to-many relationship.

table fills that role; notice that each of these tables has a one-to-many relationship with the **ENROLLED_CLASSES** table.

Indexing

Think back to the last time you were in a library and needed to find a particular book. While it's certainly feasible to start at the beginning of the shelves and read through each book title to look for that book, it would take hours (or, more likely, days) to find the right book.

Instead of looking through every book, you probably went to a card catalog (or to a computer terminal) and, based on a few keywords, were able to find your book fairly quickly. That card catalog (or the database that you accessed through the terminal) is a perfect example of an index.

When an *index* is created on a table, Oracle creates a data structure very similar to a card catalog. This structure is updated whenever an **UPDATE**, **DELETE**, or **INSERT** is performed on the table. Indexes are created in two ways.

- A **primary key** for a table is associated with a unique index; this index is a composite set of all the columns that have the **primary key** constraint.

- A **CREATE INDEX** statement is run. This is the case with all indexes except for the table's primary key index.

An index provides Oracle with a way to quickly locate and retrieve data from its tables. When tables start to contain thousands of rows, it becomes crucial that indexes be used. In order to achieve high performance, SQL statements then have to be carefully tuned to use (and, in some cases, not to use) one or more indexes for a table.

As an application developer, you should keep an eye out for situations in which none of the indexes on a table is appropriate for the task that your code must accomplish. If this is the case, you should consult your DBA. It might be necessary for the DBA to add an index to a table if your code is to perform as well as possible.

Finding The Indexes For A Table

Before writing code against a table, it's a good idea to get a listing of all the indexes on the table. You can execute this query at the SQL prompt to retrieve a listing of the indexes for a specified table, as shown in Listing 2.3.

Listing 2.3   Finding the indexes for a table.

```
SELECT index_name, column_name
FROM   ALL_IND_COLUMNS
WHERE  table_name = '&1'
ORDER BY index_name, column_name;
```

When prompted for a value for &1, type in the name of the table for which you want to find the indexes. If your database has the same table in multiple schemas, modify this query to include the owner of the table.

Privileges And Roles

The Oracle database incorporates a number of security features, two of which are privileges and roles. Both of these features are explained in some detail in the next few sections of this chapter. The most important thing that you need to know about roles and privileges is that all stored PL/SQL objects execute with the rights of the user who created the object.

For instance, let's say there is a table, **EMPLOYEE_COMPENSATIONS**, which contains the salary and other benefits for each employee. While an individual user should never be able to modify the salaries of employees, occasionally employees get raises and benefits change. If a stored procedure owned by the system references this table, the stored procedure has the same rights as the system, despite the rights of the user who executes the stored procedure.

What Is A Privilege?

Oracle7 has two levels of privileges:

- *System level privileges* give users the ability to create, modify, and drop objects (tables, indexes, views, synonyms, and so on), as well as the ability to execute stored PL/SQL objects.

- *Table level privileges* give users the ability to perform **SELECT**, **INSERT**, **UPDATE**, and **DELETE** operations on tables.

These privileges can be granted to all system users or to individual users as needed. There is no list of privileges included in this book, because that knowledge is rarely needed by application developers.

What Is A Role?

Oracle7 introduced roles as a way to make user maintenance less of a chore for DBAs. Privileges can be granted to roles, and roles can be granted to other roles. Roles are then assigned to system users and application developers, and even to DBAs. Rather than grant privileges on tens or hundreds of tables to each individual user, these privileges can be granted to a role, which is then granted to each user.

Looking Up Existing Roles In Your Database

You can get a listing of all the roles that exist in your system by executing the query shown in Listing 2.4.

Listing 2.4 Finding the existing roles in your database.

```
SELECT AR.role, ARP.granted_role
FROM   ALL_ROLES AR, ALL_ROLE_PRIVS ARP;
```

Understanding which roles exist and what each role does within the system will help you gain a better understanding of system design and, consequently, improve your ability to contribute to the success of your project.

Schemas

A *schema* is a set of objects owned by a particular user's account. For instance, if your login name is *jschmoe*, then *jschmoe* is your schema. If someone wants to reference the table **PHONE_NUMBERS** in your schema, the reference would be as follows:

```
jschmoe.PHONE_NUMBERS
```

Referencing every object with a schema name is not a good idea, because it's quite common for code to be developed in one schema and moved to another, once testing has been completed. Fortunately, objects referenced without a schema are presumed to exist in the schema of the current user.

It is important to remember that a schema is not an object within the database, but a way of referencing objects.

Sequences

Oracle provides *sequences* that allow unique integers to be generated. These integers are typically used as primary key values in tables. Sequence numbers can become quite large and can be configured to roll over once they reach their maximum size (an extremely large number; the actual maximum value for a sequence number depends on your hardware and operating system).

Snapshots

Oracle7 provides the ability to create *snapshots*. A snapshot is a table that contains the result set of a query on one or more tables or views. This is typically used when dealing with remote databases, but can also be used to store the results of complex queries for reporting purposes. A snapshot is automatically refreshed by the database at specified times (which are defined when the snapshot is created).

Using A Snapshot To Simplify Reports

If you need to develop a fairly complex report that must be run several times a day at regular intervals, your best bet is to create a snapshot. Once the snapshot is defined, the database populates the snapshot automatically. The snapshot holds the result set from a query, so your report will be much easier to generate because it must only query and format the data contained in the snapshot.

Another benefit of using snapshots is that the data contained in a snapshot can be presented to users for the development of ad hoc queries, reducing the number of custom reports that have to be developed.

Synonyms

When a typical user references an object without a schema qualifier, it is quite uncommon for the referenced object to exist in that user's schema. You're probably thinking, "Didn't I just read that objects are presumed to exist inside the user's schema?" You did.

The objects being referenced do exist inside the user's schema, but the user is not accessing the *real* objects; instead, that user is referencing a *synonym* that points to the real object (much like your telephone number isn't you, but still allows people to get in touch with you). Because the user accesses a synonym for an object, the user is able to reference objects without using schema qualifiers.

A *public synonym* is a synonym to which all database users have access, unless overridden by a private synonym. A *private synonym* works only for the user who owns the synonym. Public synonyms are created by the DBA to allow all users to reference an object; private synonyms are created by the DBA for specific users as the need arises. If a private and public synonym have the same name, the private synonym takes precedence. Figure 2.4 illustrates this concept.

Tables And Columns

Data in an Oracle database resides in *tables*. A database typically contains many tables, each of which typically has many referential integrity links to other tables. There are two types of elements within tables: columns and rows.

A *column* is a single data element that contributes to the structure of a row. All tables must have at least one column; most have at least four or five columns. The

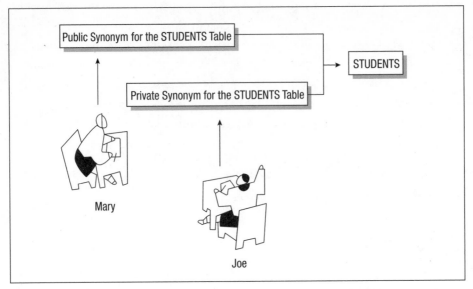

Figure 2.4

The resolution of public and private synonyms.

maximum number of columns that can exist in a table is 255. Each column within the table is given a datatype.

A *row* is a group of related data elements in which each item of the group corresponds to a column. A table typically contains many rows. In large data warehouses, large tables may contain tens of millions of rows.

Views

A structure quite similar to a table is a *view*. Views are essential SQL queries stored in a database as an object. When a reference is made to the object, the query is executed and the result set is returned to the user. Figure 2.5 illustrates the relationship of a view to its base tables.

The use of views has serious performance implications. While the views makes SQL and PL/SQL code easier to develop and maintain, there is significant overhead involved (remember, views are essentially queries that execute when someone references the view).

Views are often used in systems when a certain functionality requires a complex join of tables. This is often the case when several tables must be joined to create the

STUDENTS	STUDENT_FINANCIAL_AID
ssn	financing num
first name	aid type
middle name	aid amount
last name	
street address	**V_STUDENT_AID**
apartment number	ssn
city	first name
state	middle name
zip code	last name
home phone	overall_gpa
degree plan	most_recent_gpa
overall gpa	financing num
most recent gpa	aid type
financing num	aid amount

Figure 2.5
The relationship of a view to its base tables.

structure of the view, since the typical user doesn't have the knowledge needed to join the tables effectively.

The System Global Area

Oracle's *System Global Area* (*SGA*) is essentially short-term memory for the database. As the database references data and stored PL/SQL objects, the database stores information in the SGA on the assumption that you will be referencing this information again.

Figure 2.6 illustrates an SGA composed of these four distinct areas:

- *Shared SQL pool* stores SQL statements. When you execute an SQL statement, it is matched against statements stored in the shared SQL pool.

- *Data block buffers* contain the data being accessed by the users.

- *Dictionary cache* contains information about the structures that hold the data in the data block buffers.

- *Redo log buffers* store information about changes made to the data in the database.

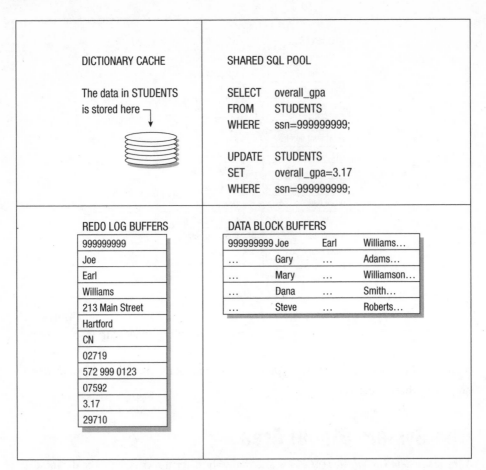

DICTIONARY CACHE

The data in STUDENTS
is stored here

SHARED SQL POOL

SELECT   overall_gpa
FROM   STUDENTS
WHERE   ssn=999999999;

UPDATE STUDENTS
SET   overall_gpa=3.17
WHERE   ssn=999999999;

REDO LOG BUFFERS

999999999
Joe
Earl
Williams
213 Main Street
Hartford
CN
02719
572 999 0123
07592
3.17
29710

DATA BLOCK BUFFERS

999999999 Joe	Earl	Williams...
... Gary	...	Adams...
... Mary	...	Williamson...
... Dana	...	Smith...
... Steve	...	Roberts...

Figure 2.6
The structure of Oracle's system global area.

When the database needs to add more information to the SGA and no more memory is available, the database removes the oldest data and objects from the SGA until there is sufficient free memory to hold the new data and objects.

Oracle also allows you to pin data and stored PL/SQL objects into the SGA. For instance, lookup tables are often very small; the contents of these tables can often be pinned entirely in the SGA to make accesses to the descriptions and codes contained in the table extremely fast. Objects that are pinned in the SGA are not removed from the SGA when Oracle needs to make room for new data and code.

Standardizing SQL And PL/SQL Code

Oracle allows you to pin data and stored PL/SQL objects into the SGA. To take maximum advantage of this ability, you'll need to create some common stored PL/SQL objects for your system that you and other developers can reuse. Have the DBA modify the database startup script so that these common objects get pinned into the SGA when your database is started. By making frequent use of these objects, you can improve the performance of your applications.

In addition, you can improve your system performance by implementing and following a set of coding standards for your system. Appendix D contains a sample SQL and PL/SQL coding standard, which can be modified to suit the needs of your organization.

What Is SQL?

Structured Query Language (SQL) is a relatively young language compared to languages like COBOL and Fortran, and it's quite different from those early ancestors.

SQL is a fourth-generation programming language (4GL), which means that it allows the user to describe the data he or she wants without giving precise instructions to the computer about how to retrieve the data. This was a remarkable idea when SQL was first introduced, and SQL remains the only 4GL in widespread use today. All of the major relational database systems use SQL for accessing data (although all of them, like Oracle's SQL*Plus, include proprietary modifications to the language).

SQL statements come in two varieties: data definition language and data manipulation language.

Data Definition Language

Data definition language (DDL) is language that defines how data is stored within the relational database. A simple example of a DDL statement is shown in Listing 2.5.

Listing 2.5   A simple DDL statement.

```
CREATE TABLE STUDENTS AS
(ssn                  NOT NULL   number(9),
 first_name           NOT NULL   varchar2 (10),
```

```
last_name           NOT NULL    varchar2 (12),
middle_name                     varchar2 (10),
street_address      NOT NULL    varchar2 (30),
apartment_number                varchar2 (4),
city                NOT NULL    varchar2 (30),
state               NOT NULL    varchar2 (2),
zip_code            NOT NULL    number (5),
home_phone          NOT NULL    number (10));
```

This statement creates a table within the Oracle database to hold information about students. Obviously, this is a very simple example. As you become a more advanced developer, you'll learn more about DDL.

Data Manipulation Language

Data manipulation language (DML) is the most common type of SQL that you'll encounter. In case you haven't already figured it out by reading the name, this is the SQL that creates, deletes, reads, and modifies data. Listing 2.6 displays a simple DML statement.

Listing 2.6   A simple DML statement.

```
SELECT last_name || ', ' || first_name || ' ' || middle_name
FROM    STUDENTS
WHERE   ssn = 999999999;
```

This statement returns the name of the student whose social security number is 999-99-9999 from the **STUDENTS** table, in the format "Doe, John Adam". In addition to querying data from tables using the **SELECT** statement, you can add data to tables with the **INSERT** statement, modify the data in tables with the **UPDATE** statement, and remove data from tables with the **DELETE** statement.

COMMIT And ROLLBACK

In order to save changes to the database, you must issue a **COMMIT** statement. This instructs Oracle that your changes are complete and that the database should write the changes to the data and release any locks that you have on database objects.

If you make a mistake and wish to have your changes to the database erased, you must issue a **ROLLBACK** statement. This instructs the database to discard your changes and release any locks that you have on database objects.

Datatypes

Table 2.1 shows a complete list of internal datatypes used by the Oracle7 database.

Table 2.1 Datatypes used by the Oracle7 database.

Datatype	Description
char	A fixed-length datatype, having a maximum width of 255 bytes. A size must be specified. A single character takes one byte in most systems, although some systems use multibyte characters.
varchar	In Oracle7, this is the same as the **varchar2** datatype (below). However, Oracle suggests that the function of this type will change in a future release. Developers and DBAs are advised not to use this datatype; instead, use the **varchar2** datatype.
varchar2	A variable length character string of up to 2,000 bytes. A maximum length for the column must be defined.
rowid	Not a real datatype, **rowid** is a pseudocolumn that is stored for each row of data in the database. A **rowid** is the physical location of a row on disk and allows Oracle to quickly access the data contained in the row.
date	A fixed length field that is seven bytes in length. Time is stored along with the date in this format. The default format for dates is DD-MM-YY HH:MM:SS AM (For example, 01-JAN-98 12:00:01 AM). Any date between 4712 BC and AD 4712 can be stored. The time of day is stored using a seconds-since-midnight algorithm.
number	A variable length column that holds real values as well as integer values. Precision and scale can be specified. Up to 38 significant digits can be stored. The ANSI standard **float** may also be used; this is synonymous with the **number** type.
long	A variable length column that can hold up to 2 GB of data, most commonly used to store character data for which a **varchar2** column is inappropriate.
raw	A variable length column used to store binary data and can be up to 255 bytes in length. A size must be defined.
longraw	A variable length column, similar to the **raw** type, that has a length of up to 2 GB. This type might be used to store music or image files.
mlslabel	This is the binary format of a secure operating system label. It is primarily used with Trusted Oracle, but can be used with standard Oracle as well.

The most common datatypes that you'll encounter are **date**, **varchar2**, and **number** (and their subtypes). Even in databases that use the other datatypes, the majority of the columns tend to be of these three types.

Converting Data Of Different Types

Oracle has two methods of converting data between differing types:

- *Implicit conversion* of a datatype can be performed automatically. Oracle will attempt to convert data from one type to another if types are mixed in an expression.

- *Explicit conversion* of datatypes is provided via SQL functions.

Oracle Corporation recommends that explicit data conversion always be used for a number of reasons, including:

- SQL code is easier to understand.

- Implicit conversions can have a negative performance impact.

- Implicit conversions rely on the context in which the columns are referenced and will not always work consistently.

- Oracle Corporation might choose to change the functionality of implicit conversions in a future release.

Joins

A *join* occurs when a **SELECT** statement references more than one table, view, or snapshot in the **FROM** clause. Joins do take some processing power to handle, but a well-written join typically doesn't drag down the performance of the database. There are three types of joins that can be used: Cartesian products, simple joins, and outer joins.

Cartesian Products

A *Cartesian product* occurs when you fail to specify a join condition for the tables in the **WHERE** clause of your **SELECT** statement. Listing 2.7 displays a query that causes a Cartesian product.

Listing 2.7 A query that causes a Cartesian product.

```
SELECT S.last_name, S.first_name, S.gpa,
       DP.degree_plan_description,
```

```
        SFA.total_financial_aid
FROM    STUDENTS S,
        DEGREE_PLANS DP,
        STUDENT_FINANCIAL_AID SFA;
```

If the **STUDENTS** table contains 10,000 rows, **DEGREE_PLANS** contains 120 rows, and **STUDENT_FINANCIAL_AID** contains 9,000 rows, the Cartesian product generated by the query will contain 10,000 × 9,000 × 120 (10,800,000,000) rows! A result set this large is rarely useful and extremely detrimental to the performance of a database.

Simple Joins

A simple join returns all rows that match one or more specified conditions between tables. The columns compared in the join conditions do not have to have the same name, but should have similar datatypes. Listing 2.8 shows a query using a simple join.

Listing 2.8   A query using a simple join.

```
SELECT  S.last_name, S.first_name, S.gpa,
        DP.degree_plan_description,
        SFA.total_financial_aid
FROM    STUDENTS S,
        DEGREE_PLANS DP,
        STUDENT_FINANCIAL_AID SFA
WHERE   S.financing_num = SFA.financing_num
AND     S.degree_plan = DP.degree_plan
AND     SFA.total_aid >= 1000.00
AND     S.gpa > 3.0;
```

This query will return a result set containing all students who have declared degree plans, have earned at least $1,000 in financial aid, and have a grade point average greater than 3.0. If a student has not declared a degree plan, no row will be returned for that student.

Outer Joins

An outer join instructs the database to return a row from one table, even if no corresponding row is found in another table. Listing 2.9 uses an outer join to get the names and grade point averages of students who have not declared a degree plan.

Listing 2.9 A query using an outer join.

```
SELECT  S.last_name, S.first_name, S.gpa,
        DP.degree_plan_description,
        SFA.total_financial_aid
FROM    STUDENTS S,
        DEGREE_PLANS DP,
        STUDENT_FINANCIAL_AID SFA
WHERE   S.financing_num = SFA.financing_num
AND     S.degree_plan = DP.degree_plan (+)
AND     S.gpa > 3.0;
```

This query will return the names of students who have not declared a degree plan as well as those students who have declared a degree plan.

Table Aliases

When joining two or more tables in a query, columns that exist in both tables must be referenced by the name of the source table for the column. Oracle allows developers to assign an alias to a table to make column name references less of a chore to use. The following example illustrates this type of reference—first using full table names and then using table aliases.

```
SELECT  STUDENTS.ssn, STUDENT_FINANCIAL_AID.total_aid
FROM    STUDENTS, STUDENT_FINANCIAL_AID
WHERE   STUDENTS.financing_num = STUDENT_FINANCIAL_AID.financing_num;

SELECT  S.ssn, SFA.total_aid
FROM    STUDENTS S, STUDENT_FINANCIAL_AID SFA
WHERE   S.financing_num = SFA.financing_num;
```

The second query is functionally identical to the first, but is much less tiresome to write.

Creating Meaningful Table Aliases

A simple method of creating a meaningful alias for a table name is to use the initial of each word in the table name. For instance, in the previous example the STUDENT_FINANCIAL_AID table was given the alias SFA.

Locks

Oracle uses a sophisticated *lock* mechanism to prevent multiple users from altering the same data at the same time. This mechanism is typically invisible to database users. It's not uncommon, especially during system development or after system hang-ups, for a *deadlock* to exist.

Consider this situation: user jallen has the **STUDENTS** table locked and needs to obtain a lock on the **STUDENT_FINANCIAL_AID** table. User msmith has the **STUDENT_FINANCIAL_AID** table locked and needs to obtain a lock on the **STUDENTS** table. This is a deadlock, because each user is preventing the other from completing a transaction.

Locks are cleared when a user issues a **COMMIT** or **ROLLBACK** statement. Locks can also be explicitly obtained, but this is a rare event. It's best to let Oracle determine which objects that you need to lock.

NULL Values

A **NULL** value is a column that does not have a defined value. A **NULL** value is never equal to any other value, including zero and **NULL**. The expression

```
NULL = NULL
```

returns a **FALSE** result. Any column in a table that is not constrained by a **NOT NULL** or **primary key** constraint can contain a **NULL** value.

You can test for **NULL** values in a column using the **IS NULL** operator:

```
WHERE <column> IS NULL
WHERE <column> IS NOT NULL
```

In reality, unexpected **NULL** values can cause all sorts of heartache for developers. The best way to handle this situation is to be aware that columns can contain **NULL** values while you're coding and to be on the lookout for situations in which **NULL** values are likely to be present.

Operators

SQL incorporates operators that are quite similar to the operators in other languages, as shown in Table 2.2.

Table 2.2 SQL operators.

Operator	Usage
**	The exponentiation operator (**2**2 IS 4**)
NOT	Negates a condition (**IS NOT NULL, NOT IN, NOT BETWEEN**)
+	The addition operator (**2 + 2 IS 4**) as well as the unary indicator of a positive number (+2)
-	The subtraction operator (**4 - 2 IS 2**) as well as the unary indicator of a negative number (-2)
*	The multiplication operator (**2 * 2 IS 4**)
/	The division operator (**4 / 2 IS 2**)
||	The concatenation operator (**'A' || 'B' IS 'AB'**)
=	The equation operator (**2 = 2**)
!=	The non-equation operator (**3 != 2**)
<	The less than operator (**2 < 4**)
>	The greater than operator (**4 > 2**)
<=	The less than or equal to operator (**2 <= 4, 2 <= 2**)
>=	The greater than or equal to operator (**4 >= 2, 2 >= 2**)
IS NULL	Tests a variable or condition for a **NULL** value (**first_name IS NULL**)
LIKE	Allows wildcard searches (**last_name LIKE 'SM%'**)
BETWEEN	An inclusive range test (**1, 2, AND 3 ARE BETWEEN 1 AND 3**)
IN	A set operator (**2 IS IN {1, 2, 3}**)
AND	A logical and (**x < y AND y < z**)
OR	A logical or (**x < y OR y < z**)

Any of these operators may be used anywhere in a DML statement with the exception of the **FROM** clause, as shown by these examples:

```
SELECT 2**nRealValue
FROM   CHECK_VALUES
WHERE  nRealValueProcessed = 'F';

DELETE
FROM   STUDENTS
WHERE  overall_gpa < 0.2;
```

```
UPDATE STUDENTS
SET    overall_gpa = 1.02 * most_recent_gpa
WHERE  ssn = 999999999;

INSERT
INTO   CHECK_VALUES
       (nRealValueProcessed,
        nRealValue)
VALUES ('F',
       (2.031 ** 3) / 9);
```

Subqueries

A subquery is a query within the **WHERE** clause of a DML statement, as shown in this example:

```
SELECT ssn
FROM   STUDENTS
WHERE  overall_gpa = (SELECT max (overall_gpa)
                      FROM   STUDENTS);
```

Subqueries can be used in any type of DML statement.

An Overview Of PL/SQL

The Procedural Language extension to SQL (PL/SQL) was first introduced in late 1991 and dramatically reshaped the role of the Oracle developer. PL/SQL literally made the impossible possible for SQL developers; for the first time, they could develop complex applications without using a 3GL program from inside Oracle*Forms.

PL/SQL introduced several abilities to the Oracle developer, including:

- Looping structures

- The ability to embed SQL statements inside PL/SQL code

- **IF-THEN-ELSE** logic

- The ability to deal with multiple rows of data

- A robust method of handling errors

In its first incarnation, PL/SQL was used only inside Oracle*Forms 3.0 (in special blocks called procedures). Triggers inside a form could execute both SQL DML statements and PL/SQL procedures (which in turn could execute SQL DML statements and other PL/SQL procedures). Today, PL/SQL has matured considerably, adding many new features and becoming more tightly integrated with the Oracle database.

PL/SQL code runs in any Oracle database on any hardware platform, making the code highly transportable. Applications developed for your Personal Oracle database can easily be moved up to larger machines and vice versa.

Blocks

PL/SQL is written in sections called blocks. Listing 2.10 shows the structure of a typical PL/SQL block.

Listing 2.10   A sample PL/SQL block.

```
DECLARE
    <variable declarations>

BEGIN
    <statements>
EXCEPTION
    <error condition>
        <code for handling error>
END;
```

Blocks of PL/SQL code may be nested within each other to form sub-blocks, as shown in Listing 2.11.

Listing 2.11   A sample PL/SQL block with a sub-block.

```
DECLARE
    <variable declarations>
BEGIN
    <statements>
    DECLARE
        <variable declarations>
    BEGIN
        <statements>
    EXCEPTION
        <error condition>
            <code for handling error condition>
    END;
```

```
    <statements>
EXCEPTION
    <error condition>
        <code for handling error>
END;
```

In practice, there is no limit to how far PL/SQL blocks may be nested within each other (although too many levels of indentation becomes confusing).

The structure of a PL/SQL block is simple. The **DECLARE** statement is followed by variable, constant, and other definitions. You can then manipulate variables and data following the **BEGIN** statement. The **EXCEPTION** statement (errors in PL/SQL are called *exceptions*; this term originated within Ada, PL/SQL's root language) allows you to define code to handle specific error conditions. The **END** statement signifies the end of the PL/SQL block.

Not every PL/SQL block will have a **DECLARE** statement. This is especially true of sub-blocks, because variables inside a block cease to exist once the block is closed.

Cursors

A *cursor* is a reference to a private SQL area inside Oracle. Figure 2.7 illustrates the functionality of a cursor.

There are two types of cursors: implicit and explicit. PL/SQL also provides a **CURSOR FOR** loop that makes the process of looping through the cursor data simpler.

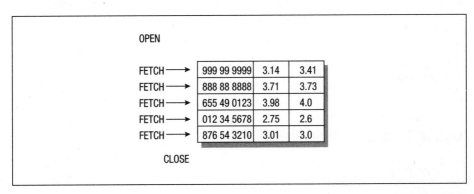

Figure 2.7
The functionality of a cursor.

Explicit Cursors

An *explicit* cursor is defined in the **DECLARE** section of a PL/SQL block, as shown in Listing 2.12.

Listing 2.12   The declaration of an explicit cursor.

```
DECLARE
    CURSOR Students_cur
    IS
    SELECT last_name, first_name, middle_name, gpa
    FROM    STUDENTS
    WHERE   gpa > 3.0;
```

The use of explicit cursors allows PL/SQL programs to handle sets of rows, rather than being forced to query a single row for each operation. Each row that meets the criteria defined by the cursor's **WHERE** clause can be processed individually.

Several PL/SQL statements are used to deal with explicit cursors:

- **OPEN**—Parses a cursor and prepares the result set for retrieval. If the cursor is already open, an error will occur.

- **CLOSE**—Disables the cursor. If the specified cursor hasn't been opened, an error will result.

- **FETCH**—Retrieves the next row of the result set into variables for processing inside the PL/SQL block. If the specified cursor hasn't been opened, an error will occur.

A cursor is not an array; once a row has been bypassed using the **FETCH** statement, it is impossible to go backwards inside the cursor. The only way to get back to a row that has been bypassed is to close and reopen the cursor.

The CURSOR FOR Loop

The **CURSOR FOR** loop allows you to handle cursors without using the **OPEN**, **FETCH**, and **CLOSE** statements. Listing 2.13 shows a **CURSOR FOR** loop.

Listing 2.13   A **CURSOR FOR** loop.

```
DECLARE
    CURSOR Students_cur
    IS
    SELECT last_name, first_name, middle_name, gpa
    FROM    STUDENTS
    WHERE   gpa > 3.0;
```

```
BEGIN
    FOR Students_rec IN Students_cur LOOP
        <statements>
    END LOOP;
END;
```

This type of loop automatically opens the cursor, loops through each row in the result set, and closes the cursor when the last row has been processed. In this example, the loop index variable **Students_rec** is implicitly declared by the cursor for loop as a **%ROWTYPE** variable based on the structure of the cursor (**%ROWTYPE** will be discussed later in this chapter).

Cursors can be used with any type of loop available in PL/SQL; the use of **CURSOR FOR** loops is not required.

Implicit Cursors

An *implicit* cursor is created by Oracle for all SQL statements that manipulate data (even if the query returns only a single row). If a query has a chance of returning multiple rows, it's a good idea to use an explicit cursor to retrieve the rows instead of using a single **SELECT** statement.

Datatypes

Table 2.3 lists a number of datatypes that are usable inside PL/SQL blocks, in addition to the default datatypes supported by the Oracle7 database.

In addition to the datatypes listed in Table 2.3, PL/SQL allows developers to define custom datatypes.

Datatype Conversions

Like Oracle and SQL, PL/SQL supports both implicit and explicit conversions of datatypes. The use of explicit conversions is strongly suggested.

Records

PL/SQL allows developers to create a record containing one or more columns. To use records, the record type must be specified before a variable can be created based on the type; this is shown by Listing 2.14. Figure 2.8 shows the structure of a record.

Table 2.3 PL/SQL supported datatypes.

Datatype	Description
binary_integer	Variables of this type store signed integers, ranging from -2^{31} - 1 through 2^{31} -1 (-2147483647..2147483647). Unlike **number** values, variables of the **binary_integer** type (and its subtypes) can be used in expressions without being converted (theoretically providing a performance boost).
natural	A subtype of the **binary_integer** type that holds only positive integers ranging from 0 through 2^{31} - 1 (0..2147483647).
positive	A subtype of the **binary_integer** type that holds only positive integers ranging from 1 through 2^{31} - 1 (1..2147483647).
dec, decimal, double precision, float, integer, int, numeric, real, smallint	Subtypes of the **number** type that have the same constraints and range of values as the **number** type.
boolean	This type contains the values **TRUE** and **FALSE**. Variables of this type can also contain a **NULL** value. Since this datatype isn't implicitly supported by the database engine, you cannot define a column using this type or select output into a variable of this type.

Listing 2.14 A PL/SQL record declaration.

```
TYPE Student_rectype IS RECORD
    (first_name          varchar2 (12),
     last_name           varchar2 (15),
     gpa                 number (3, 2));

Student_rec     Student_rectype;
```

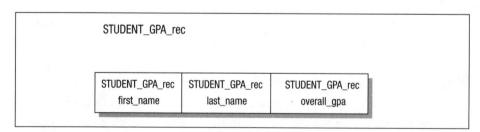

Figure 2.8
The structure of a PL/SQL record.

Individual columns within **Student_rec** are referenced as

```
Student_rec.first_name
```

Records are *composite datatypes*, constructed by the developer to suit a particular set of needs. (*Scalar datatypes* are those datatypes that are automatically supported by the database engine and PL/SQL, like **varchar2**, **integer**, and **date.**) The values returned from cursors are often fetched into record variables, which are then referenced by PL/SQL statements both as whole records and as individual columns.

Tables

A PL/SQL table is very similar to an array in C or Pascal. Like a record, the PL/SQL table must be declared first as a type declaration and then as a variable of the user-defined type, as shown in Listing 2.15.

Listing 2.15   A PL/SQL table declaration.

```
DECLARE
    TYPE Student_SSN_tabtype IS TABLE OF
        integer (9)
        INDEX BY binary_integer;

    Student_SSN_table      Student_SSN_tabtype;
```

Like records, the PL/SQL table is a composite datatype. The number of rows that can be held in a PL/SQL table is limited only by the range of values for the **INDEX** variable. The PL/SQL table is indexed using a signed integer and can be navigated either forward or backward (unlike cursors, which can only be moved forward). Figure 2.9 illustrates the structure of a PL/SQL table.

As can be seen in the following line of code, references to records in a PL/SQL table are very similar to references to an array in C or Pascal.

```
Student_SSN_table (1)
```

The main difference in the reference is the use of parentheses instead of square brackets to reference the index variable.

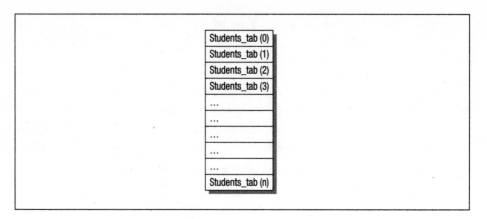

Figure 2.9
The structure of a PL/SQL table.

Referencing Elements In A PL/SQL Table

The elements in a PL/SQL table must be initialized to some value (even NULL) before you can make any other reference to it in your code. If you reference an element that has not been initialized to some value, a NO_DATA_FOUND exception will be raised. Unlike the scalar datatypes, a PL/SQL table element does not automatically contain a NULL value. The safest method for dealing with these elements is to initialize each element to NULL, even before attempting to populate the element with another value.

Prior to version 2.3, PL/SQL tables could only have a scalar datatype column in addition to the index column. PL/SQL version 2.3 allows composite datatypes (records and tables) to be referenced inside a PL/SQL table. This limitation was probably the primary factor limiting the use of PL/SQL tables in applications. PL/SQL tables will become more common now that they are not quite as unwieldy to use.

Variables And Constants

Declaring variables and constants in a PL/SQL block is quite simple, as shown by the following section of code:

```
DECLARE
    vStudentFirstName     varchar2 (12);
    <other variable declarations>

    YES     CONSTANT     char (1) := 'Y';
```

A constant must be initialized when it is declared. Variables may be initialized when they are declared or after the **BEGIN** statement. Once initialized, a PL/SQL variable may be referenced in an embedded SQL statement or an expression.

Initializing Variables

It's a good idea to initialize most variables when they are declared. If you don't initialize a variable in the DECLARE subsection of the block, make sure you initialize it prior to using it in an expression or you'll get stung by a comparison with a NULL value.

%TYPE And %ROWTYPE

PL/SQL allows variables to be declared dynamically, depending on the type of a referenced column or variable. Consider this code:

```
vFirstName      STUDENTS.first_name%TYPE;
Students_rec    Students_cur%ROWTYPE;
```

The **vFirstName** variable will have the same datatype and size as the column **first_name** in the **STUDENTS** table. If the length of the **first_name** column is increased, the length of **vFirstName** will also be increased. The use of **%TYPE** allows you to develop a variable that is dependent on the structure of your data; if the structure of the data changes, your variable will change as well.

Using **%TYPE** references to variables is an excellent idea for making maintenance of your code simpler; however, this is not a complete solution. Imagine that you have a variable referencing a column of type **integer**; if this changes to type **number** or one of the other subtypes of type **number**, **%TYPE** has done its job.

Now imagine that your variable is a **%TYPE** reference to a **number** column, perhaps a unique sequence number for records. If a business rule changes, you may suddenly find yourself with a sequence that includes characters and a block of code that calls a numeric function such as **min()** or **max()**. In this instance, your code will have to change.

Admittedly, this is a fairly radical change in the data model that your code is based upon, but it has been known to occur. Using **%TYPE** is a good idea (fields changing in size is quite common, especially during system development), but don't expect **%TYPE** to solve all your future maintenance woes.

%ROWTYPE is very similar to %TYPE, except the it creates a variable of record type. %ROWTYPE is typically used with cursors, but can duplicate the structure of a table or record as well.

Exceptions And Exception Handling

PL/SQL was originally based on the Ada programming language (once widely used in software written for the Department of Defense). One of the primary reasons that Ada was chosen as the mother language for PL/SQL is the concept of exceptions. Figure 2.10 illustrates how exceptions are raised and handled.

When a PL/SQL block encounters an error condition, an exception is raised. Each PL/SQL block can have an exception handler prior to the **END** statement. In this section of the block, the developer specifies what actions should be taken for specific exceptions. If no exception handler is declared in a block, the exception is raised to the calling PL/SQL block.

Table 2.4 lists the standard exceptions that you will encounter most frequently.

Table 2.4 The five most commonly encountered exceptions.

Exception	Situation
NO_DATA_FOUND	You executed a query for which no rows were found.
TOO_MANY_ROWS	You executed a query for which more than one row was found. Your query was only structured to receive a single row in the result set.
DUP_VAL_ON_INDEX	You attempted to insert a row into a table, but the row violates the table's primary key or unique index.
VALUE_ERROR	You assigned a value to a variable that is too short to hold the value. This occurs most commonly with variables of type **varchar2** or **char**, but this can also happen to variables of other types.
INVALID_NUMBER	You referenced a value containing a character in an expression that attempted to convert the value to a number, either explicitly or implicitly.

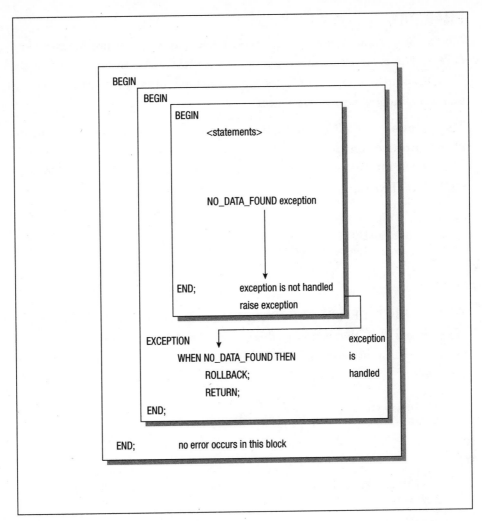

Figure 2.10
How PL/SQL handles exceptions.

If no exception is raised from a PL/SQL block (or stored PL/SQL object), the calling object assumes that the block completed successfully. Unlike a function written in C, there are no status values that are found in the database environment to indicate if a procedure or function call encountered an error.

PRAGMAs

Most of the code that you write will be executable code, with one notable exception. A **PRAGMA** is not executable code; instead, a **PRAGMA** is an instruction to the PL/SQL compiler. PL/SQL provides two distinct uses of the **PRAGMA** statement: **exception_init** and **restrict_references**.

The **exception_init PRAGMA** instructs Oracle to assign a name to a standard Oracle error message that does not have an associated named exception. In this example, the ORA-00942 error is renamed to a user-defined exception **xTABLE-DOESNOTEXIST**:

```
DECLARE
    xTABLEDOESNOTEXIST     EXCEPTION;
    PRAGMA exception_init (xTABLEDOESNOTEXIST -942);
...
END;
```

The **RESTRICT_REFERENCES PRAGMA** instructs Oracle about the purity level of a packaged PL/SQL function. In this example, the **Conversions** package instructs the database that the function **Feet_To_Meters** does not alter any database or package states:

```
PACKAGE Conversions

IS

    FUNCTION Feet_To_Meters (nFeet IN     number) RETURN number;
    RESTRICT_REFERENCES (Feet_To_Meters, WNDS, RNDS, WNPS, RNPS);
END Conversions;
```

Once the function has been declared in this fashion, it can be execute inside a DML statement without receiving an error message, as shown in this example:

```
SELECT Feet_To_Meters (3.45)
FROM    DUAL;
```

There are four purity levels that can be asserted for packaged functions:

- **WNDS**—The function does not write to any tables.

- **RNDS**—The function does not read from any tables.

- **WNPS**—The function does not modify any variables inside the package.

- **RNPS**—The function does not read any variables inside the package.

User-Defined Exceptions

PL/SQL allows developers to define their own exceptions. This is a useful method of returning a specific status to calling procedures and functions. Giving user-defined exceptions meaningful names helps make code easier to understand. User-defined exceptions must be explicitly raised through the use of the **RAISE** statement. Listing 2.16 illustrates how user-defined exceptions are declared and raised.

Listing 2.16   A user-defined exception.

```
DECLARE
    xSTUDENTNOTELIGIBLEFORAID      EXCEPTION;


...
IF <condition> THEN
    RAISE xSTUDENTNOTELIGIBLEFORAID;
END IF;
```

An exception raised using the **RAISE** statement is processed just like any exception raised by Oracle.

The OTHERS Exception Handler

The **OTHERS** exception handler functions as a catch-all exception handler for a PL/SQL block. The **OTHERS** exception handler is used as follows:

```
WHEN OTHERS THEN
    System_Error_Handler (<parameters>);
```

Care must be taken when raising user-defined exceptions in a block that uses the **OTHERS** exception handler. If the user-defined exception is to be raised to a calling procedure, an exception handler for the user-defined exception should be defined that explicitly re-raises the exception, as follows:

```
EXCEPTION
    WHEN StudentNotEligibleForAid THEN
        RAISE;
```

```
WHEN OTHERS THEN
     System_Error_Handler (<parameters>);
```

The **OTHERS** exception handler should follow any other exception handlers. Any exception not handled by another exception handler is handled by the **OTHERS** exception handler.

IF-THEN-ELSE Logic

PL/SQL introduced to Oracle developers the ability to control the flow of code using **IF-THEN-ELSE** logic. This type of logic is very similar to the logic found in other languages, as shown by the following code block:

```
IF <condition> THEN
    <statements>

ELSIF <condition> THEN
    <statements>

ELSE
    <statements>
END IF;
```

The NULL Statement

Not to be confused with a **NULL** value, the **NULL** statement is often placed in code to indicate that the code is to take no action. The **NULL** statement does nothing.

Looping Constructs

In addition to the **CURSOR FOR** loop that was discussed previously, PL/SQL supports **FOR** and **WHILE** loops, as well as allowing developers to use a generic loop structure.

The FOR Loop

As you can see, the **FOR** loop in PL/SQL is quite similar to **FOR** loops in other languages:

```
FOR x IN 1..50 LOOP
    <statements>
END LOOP;
```

The lower and upper bounds of the **FOR** loop must evaluate to integers. If the lower and upper bounds of the loop are equal, the loop will execute only once. If the lower bound is greater than the upper bound, the loop will not execute at all. Variables may be substituted for both the lower and upper bounds of the loop.

To run a loop from a high value to a low value, the syntax is slightly different from other languages, as shown by this example:

```
FOR x IN REVERSE 1..50 LOOP
    <statements>
END LOOP;
```

Just like a **CURSOR FOR** loop, the loop index variable (in this case *x*) never has to be declared.

The number of iterations of a **FOR** loop can be easily calculated before the loop is entered by checking the difference between the upper and lower bounds. A **FOR** loop can execute between zero and **MAXINT** (the largest integer supported by your hardware and operating system) times.

The LOOP Statement

The PL/SQL **LOOP** statement can be used alone to create the precise loop structure you need. For instance, you might create a loop that always executes at least once, as follows:

```
LOOP
    <statements>
   IF <condition> THEN
        EXIT;
    END IF;
END LOOP;
```

The WHILE Loop

As with the **FOR** loop, the **WHILE** Loop is quite similar to a **WHILE** loop in other languages. For example:

```
WHILE MoreRowsToProcess = TRUE LOOP
    <statements>
END LOOP;
```

A **WHILE** loop can execute from zero to an infinite number of times. The number of iterations of a **WHILE** loop can never be known until after the loop has finished executing.

The EXIT Statement

PL/SQL provides the **EXIT** statement to end a loop prematurely. The functionality of the **EXIT** statement will allow you to exit a single loop or all loops currently executing. If you wish to be able to use the statement to accomplish either type of exit, each of your loops must be given a label. Listing 2.17 illustrates the use of the **EXIT** statement with multiple loops.

Listing 2.17   Using an **EXIT** statement with multiple loops.

```
<<outer_loop>>
LOOP
    <<inner_loop>>
    LOOP
        IF <condition> THEN
            EXIT inner_loop;
        END IF;

        IF <condition> THEN
            EXIT outer_loop;
        END IF:
    END LOOP;
END LOOP;
```

In addition to this functionality, the **EXIT** statement can also be followed by a **WHEN** condition, instead of using **IF-THEN** logic to test the condition. For example:

```
EXIT WHEN Students_cur%NOTFOUND;
```

Stored Objects

The release of PL/SQL 2.0 and Oracle7 revolutionized the Oracle world. Previously, all code for enforcing business rules was stored at the application level, often leading to multiple occurrences of the same code in different applications. This was a nightmare when a business rule changed, since it was extremely difficult to track which applications enforced which rules.

Oracle7 allowed developers to store code at the database level, introducing stored procedures, functions, and packages, as well as database triggers. These objects must exist in only one place (inside the database). Not only did this reduce maintenance costs and duration, it also speeded application development time because code only needed to be written once. In many IS departments that use Oracle7, most or all enforcement of business rules is now handled through triggers and stored procedures.

Database Triggers

Database triggers are objects that are closely associated with tables. There are four distinct times at which database triggers fire, twice at the statement level and twice at the row level, as shown in Table 2.5.

Database triggers can fire on **INSERT**, **UPDATE**, and **DELETE** events. Thus, there are 12 possible triggers that can be written for a table. The types of database triggers execute in a specific order, as illustrated in Figure 2.11.

Database triggers are covered in more detail in Chapters 7.

Stored Procedures And Functions

While database triggers allow the enforcement of complex business rules at the database level, they fall short in a number of ways. First, there is no way to explicitly call a database trigger without altering one or more rows in the trigger's associated table.

Table 2.5 When database triggers fire.

Trigger Type	Fires
before	The statement level trigger fires before a statement is executed on the trigger's associated table.
after	The statement level trigger fires after a statement is executed on the trigger's associated table.
before row	The row level trigger fires once for each row affected by a statement executed on the trigger's associated table. The trigger fires prior to the execution of the statement and can alter the contents of the data.
after row	The row level trigger fires once for each row affected by a statement executed on the trigger's associated table. The trigger fires following the execution of the statement.

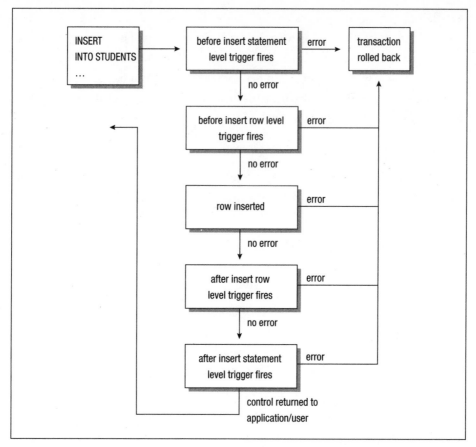

Figure 2.11
The execution order of database triggers.

Second, the code is tightly restricted in its role, because by nature Oracle7's triggers are very specific to data.

Stored procedures and *functions* don't suffer from these shortcomings (nor do they have the value associated with being closely tied to a table). Instead, these objects stand alone in the database and are referenced by triggers and other stored procedures. These objects allow developers to write applications at the database level that are truly modular.

The only real difference between a stored procedure and a stored function is that a function must explicitly return a value using a **RETURN** statement. Listing 2.18 shows a typical stored procedure, and Listing 2.19 shows a typical stored function.

Listing 2.18 A typical stored procedure.

```
CREATE OR REPLACE
PROCEDURE Update_Student_GPA (SSN IN    number)

IS

    <variable declarations>

BEGIN
    <statements>
END Update_Student_GPA;
```

Listing 2.19 A typical stored function.

```
CREATE OR REPLACE
FUNCTION Get_Student_GPA (SSN IN     number) RETURN number

IS
    <variable declarations>

BEGIN
    <statements>
    <RETURN statement>
END Get_Student_GPA;
```

You can execute stored procedures and functions as follows:

Procedure:
```
Update_Student_GPA (SSN => 999999999);
```

Function:
```
nSSN := Get_Student_GPA (SSN => 999999999);
```

Notice the output of the function is assigned to a variable. This is the only way a stored function can be called, other than from inside a DML statement.

Parameters

Stored procedures and functions can accept *parameters* from their calling application. There are three types of parameters: **IN**, **OUT**, and **IN OUT**.

- **IN** parameters—Pass a value into the procedure or function. This value cannot be altered within the procedure.

- **OUT** parameters—Pass a **NULL** value into the procedure or function, but can be altered by the procedure to return a value to the calling application via the **OUT** parameter.

- **IN OUT** parameters—Pass a value into the procedure or function, which can then be modified by the procedure so that a different value is returned to the calling application via the parameter.

There are two methods of referencing parameters in procedure and function calls: positional and named. The *positional* method of calling a procedure takes the following form:

```
Update_Student_GPA (999999999);
```

The *named* method of calling a procedure takes the following form:

```
Update_Student_GPA (ssn => 999999999);
```

Positional notation assumes that the first value passed to the procedure or function corresponds to the first parameter, the second value to the second parameter, and so forth. Named notation allows the parameters to be specified in any order, because the developer must specify which parameter a value is intended to fill.

It is possible to mix both named and positional notation in a procedure or function call, but once named notation is used, all parameters must be specified using named notation.

Any parameter may have a default value. This is accomplished in one of two ways, as shown in this example:

```
PROCEDURE Calculate_Interest (nAccountNumber IN      number,
                              nInterestRate  IN      number DEFAULT 5.35);

PROCEDURE Calculate_Interest (nAccountNumber IN      number,
                              nInterestRate  IN      number := 5.35);
```

Stored procedures and functions will receive much more detailed attention in Chapters 4 and 5.

Packages

PL/SQL allows developers to group stored procedures and functions into *packages*. Ideally, packages are groups of related procedures and functions, each handling a small part of a larger task. Organizing code into packages is quite useful when trying to modularize a system design.

A *package specification* (or spec) specifies the interface for the procedures and functions that will be contained in the package body. It goes almost without saying that the interfaces for procedures and functions defined in the package spec must be mirrored in the package body.

In addition to grouping related procedures and functions into a cohesive unit, packages also enable developers to define variables and data types that are global to all the procedures and functions contained inside a package (a good example of this is the **Build_SUID_Matrix** package contained in Appendix D, which defines a global cursor that is used by multiple procedures within the package body). These variables can then be used and reused to store data for reference between modules, allow all the modules to work with the same data, keep track of errors, and perform a multitude of other functions.

A typical package spec might look like the one shown in Listing 2.20.

Listing 2.20 A sample package spec.

```
CREATE OR REPLACE PACKAGE Update_Student AS
    -- Holds the name of the current object inside the package
    vCurrentContext           varchar2 (61);

    YES                 CONSTANT char(1) := 'Y';
    NO                  CONSTANT char (1) := 'N';

    PROCEDURE Calculate_Semester_GPA (SSN IN     number);
    FUNCTION Get_Student_GPA (SSN IN    number) RETURN number;
END Update_Student;
```

The variable **vCurrentContext** is global within the package and can be referenced by both the procedure and function listed (as well as any other procedures or functions that exist in the package body).

Procedures and functions declared in the package spec are public and can be seen by other procedures and functions. However, the package body can also contain procedures and functions that are not declared as part of the package spec; these procedures and functions are private and can only be referenced by procedures and functions within the package body.

Like stored procedures and functions that stand alone, objects inside packages are executed with the privileges of the user who created the package.

Calling a packaged procedure or function is quite simple, as shown in the following code sample:

Procedure:

```
Update_Student.Calculate_Semester_GPA (ssn => nSSN);
```

Function:

```
nGPA := Update_Student.Get_Student_GPA (ssn => nSSN);
```

The only difference between calling a standalone stored procedure and calling a stored procedure inside a package is that the procedure inside the package must be prefaced with the name of the package.

Packages are covered more thoroughly in Chapter 4.

A PL/SQL Wish List

PL/SQL is not a perfect programming language (someone from Oracle told me in 1992 that it wasn't really a programming language at all). If you have any experience with other programming languages, you'll find that some really useful things are missing from PL/SQL. While these aren't serious deficiencies, their incorporation would make PL/SQL a bit less tedious to use at times.

The continue Statement

The **continue** statement in C is a marvelous tool, allowing you to immediately skip to the next iteration of a loop without executing any steps that occur inside the loop after the **continue** statement. Unfortunately, PL/SQL has only a **GOTO** statement to allow you to accomplish this simple task. The **GOTO** statement is illustrated by this example:

```
LOOP
    <<START_OF_LOOP>>
    ...PL/SQL statements..
    GOTO <<START_OF_LOOP>>
END LOOP;
```

You can also mirror this functionality by putting the contents of your loop inside a stored procedure and using the **RETURN** statement to exit out of the stored procedure if you determine that your data can't or shouldn't be processed any further. This example calls a procedure that holds the internal logic of the loop.

```
LOOP
    MyLoopContents (parameter1 => value);
END LOOP;
```

Listing 2.21 illustrates a loop that simulates the functionality of a **continue** statement by using a stored procedure.

Listing 2.21 Using a stored procedure to simulate a C **continue** statement.

```
PROCEDURE MyLoopContents (parameter1    <datatype>)

IS
    <variable declarations>

BEGIN
    ...PL/SQL statements...
    IF some_condition THEN
        RETURN;
    END IF;
END;
```

The case/switch Statement

While not an essential part of any language, the **case** statement is more elegant than:

```
IF (x < 100) THEN
    <statements>

ELSIF (X <200) THEN
    <statements>

ELSIF (x < 300) THEN
    <statements>

ELSE
    <statements>
END IF;
```

Unfortunately, PL/SQL allows only the clumsy **IF-THEN-ELSE** method of testing multiple conditions.

Incrementing Variables

The ability to increment or decrement a variable in C using the **++**, **--**, **+=**, and **-=** operators is something that I've often wished for while coding a procedure or function. Instead, you'll have to settle for the less elegant method shown here:

```
nSum := nSum + 1;
```

While functionally equivalent, the previous example simply seems less graceful than a similar C statement:

```
nSum++;
```

You can create a stored function that accepts an **integer** value and returns the value incremented by one, although it hardly seems worth the effort.

How Does The Database Parse SQL And PL/SQL?

Sit down in front of a computer and get to an SQL prompt. Get comfortable. Then execute the following commands at the SQL prompt:

```
set serveroutput on
SELECT 23 FROM DUAL;
```

Notice that as soon as you finished typing your command, SQL*Plus sent the command off to the database for a response. Now enter this block of PL/SQL code:

```
DECLARE
    iRowCount       integer;

BEGIN
    SELECT 23
    INTO    iRowCount
    FROM DUAL;
```

```
SELECT 18
INTO    iRowCount
FROM DUAL;

    DBMS_Output.Put_Line ('The value of iRowCount is ' || to_char
(iRowCount));
END;
/
```

You might notice that none of your SQL commands were executed until you finished your PL/SQL block and told SQL to execute the block with the / character.

You may sit in front of SQL every day and not have noticed this difference before, but you should notice it now. The Oracle7 database handles SQL and PL/SQL commands differently. Each SQL statement inside your PL/SQL block was sent to the database only when the PL/SQL block went to the database. Figure 2.12 illustrates this concept.

An SQL statement is immediately matched against existing statements in the SGA. If no matching SQL statement is found, the statement is reparsed and then executed; otherwise, a statement that is already cached in the SGA is executed instead.

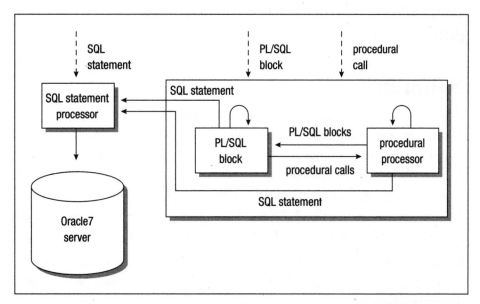

Figure 2.12
How Oracle7 parses SQL and PL/SQL statements.

When the database has retrieved the necessary data or an error occurs, the database returns a response to the user.

A PL/SQL block is sent to the database as a whole concept. Because a PL/SQL block can contain both SQL statements and other PL/SQL blocks, the database will then handle each SQL statement and each PL/SQL block inside the main PL/SQL block. When the procedure has finished executing or an error condition occurs, a response is given to the user who executed the procedure.

This difference may seem to be insignificant, but the nature of PL/SQL makes it much better suited for client/server development than SQL. Each SQL statement travels over the network singly, while PL/SQL sends one block of code to the database, which then handles PL/SQL sub-blocks, embedded SQL statements, and calls to stored PL/SQL objects internally.

Consider 10 SQL statements sent over a network individually versus 1 PL/SQL block that contains 10 embedded SQL statements; 1 call to the network is necessary to send the PL/SQL block, while 10 calls are required for the individual SQL statements. Furthermore, the result sets for the embedded SQL statements are not sent back across the network, further reducing the number of packets required to complete the PL/SQL call.

Summary

Hopefully, this chapter has given you a basic grounding for the coming chapters, which contain some rather detailed examples of SQL and PL/SQL code. I have tried to avoid lapsing into a primer on syntax, but in some cases an adequate explanation demands the most elementary terms. By no means should you consider this chapter to be a complete tutorial or reference on SQL or PL/SQL; for that type of material the best sources are the *Oracle7 Server SQL Language Reference Manual* and the *PL/SQL User's Guide* that you can borrow from your database administrator.

In the coming chapters, you'll cover not only some detailed examples of SQL and PL/SQL code, but you'll also be given insight into the design and testing of these procedures.

SQL And PL /SQL Scripting

CHAPTER

3

SQL And PL/SQL Scripting

The use of scripts and batch processes is the oldest aspect of computing and still plays a very active role in most systems. Most major operating systems support at least one scripting language. Table 3.1 highlights the predominent scripting language for each major operating system.

As you can see, Unix is particularly rich in scripting tools. Unix is also the predominant platform for Oracle databases (Windows NT is gaining strength, while VMS and OpenVMS are gradually disappearing). Consequently, the scripts included in this chapter (where appropriate) contain examples of scripts on a Unix system, but keep in mind that SQL*Plus and PL/SQL can be used with the scripting language of any operating system.

This chapter will introduce you to the basic uses of scripts in an Oracle database and discuss the tools you'll need to script using SQL*Plus and PL/SQL.

The Many Faces Of Scripting

Scripts are used to perform many types of tasks in an Oracle database. The database administrator's duties often involve complex tasks that are automated with scripts,

Table 3.1   The scripting languages supported by major operating systems.

Operating System	Scripting Language
MS-DOS	MS-DOS batch language
OS/2	REXX
VMS and OpenVMS	DCL
Windows 95	Visual Basic, Perl, MS-DOS batch language
Windows NT	Visual Basic, Perl, MS-DOS batch language
Unix	C shell, Bourne shell, Korn shell, Perl, awk, sed

but this isn't the entire world of scripting. Scripts perform many different tasks within a system, including:

- Performing system backups and helping with restoration.

- Administering system security and user creation.

- Dynamically generating code.

- Testing stored PL/SQL objects.

- Any other task that has to be performed regularly.

Backup And Restore

The most well-known scripts in an Oracle database are those that the DBA uses to back up the database. Listing 3.1 is a simple generic script that a DBA could use to perform a cold backup of an Oracle database (you may remember this script from Chapter 1).

Listing 3.1   A generic cold backup script for an Oracle database.

```
#
# Set up the environment variables.
#
ORACLE_SID=registrar_db; export ORACLE_SID
ORACLE_HOME=/dbhost/database/oracle/v722; export ORACLE_HOME

#
# Shut down the database.
#
svrmgrl
connect internal
shutdown immediate

#
# Backup the database control files, redo logs, and dbf files.
#
tar -cvf /dev/backup/tdr $ORACLE_HOME

#
# Restart the database.
#
svrmgrl
connect internal
startup
```

Dynamic Code Generation

One common use of SQL scripts is the generation of other SQL scripts. Consider the script shown in Listing 3.2, which dynamically builds and executes an SQL script containing commands to drop all the objects in the specified user's schema.

Listing 3.2   The **DROP_ALL.SQL** script.

```
set head off
set pages 0
set verify off
set lines 80
set feedback off
set termout off

spool &&1.sql

SELECT 'DROP ' || object_type || ' ' || &&1 || '.' ||
       object_name || ';'
FROM   ALL_OBJECTS
WHERE  owner = upper ('&&1')
ORDER BY object_type desc;

spool off

@&&1.sql

host rm &&1.sql

exit
```

When run for the **jschmoe** schema (assuming that the person running the script has access to the schema), this script would generate and execute an SQL script containing the following SQL commands:

```
DROP TABLE JSCHMOE.STUDENTS;
DROP TABLE JSCHMOE.ENROLLED_COURSES;
DROP TABLE JSCHMOE.STUDENT_FINANCIAL_AID;
DROP PROCEDURE JSCHMOE.CALCULATE_GPA;
DROP PACKAGE BODY JSCHMOE.STUDENT_UPDATES;
DROP PACKAGE JSCHMOE.STUDENT_UPDATES;
DROP FUNCTION JSCHMOE.GRANT_FINANCIAL_AID;
```

Security And User Administration

Even with the advent of roles in Oracle7, the DBA still has to maintain a record of the rights a role has. If a role is a template user, the template must still be configured. The configuration of the roles for a system is often done with a script, like the one shown in Listing 3.3.

Listing 3.3   A script that grants privileges to roles.

```
-- ****************************************************************
-- This role will be granted to accounts that process financial
-- aid applications.
--
CREATE ROLE Financial_Aid_Processor;


--
-- This role must be able to read the student's contact information.
--
GRANT SELECT ON STUDENTS TO Financial_Aid_Processor;


--
-- This role assigns all financial aid application data.
--
GRANT SELECT ON STUDENT_FINANCIAL_AID TO Financial_Aid_Processor;
GRANT INSERT ON STUDENT_FINANCIAL_AID TO Financial_Aid_Processor;


--
-- This role needs read access to students' grades.
--
GRANT SELECT ON ENROLLED_COURSES TO Financial_Aid_Processor;


--
-- This role is granted to management accounts in the financial aid
-- office.
--
CREATE ROLE Financial_Aid_Manager;


-- ****************************************************************
-- The manager will have all the privileges of a processor.
--
GRANT Financial_Aid_Processor TO Financial_Aid_Manager;
```

```
--
-- The manager must also be able to update a student's financial
-- aid records.
--
GRANT UPDATE ON STUDENT_FINANCIAL_AID TO Financial_Aid_Processor;
```

Although the configuration of individual users can be done through roles, a security feature in Oracle requires granted rights to individual tables (including views and snapshots) before a developer can compile objects that reference the table. The DBA must maintain a script to create developer accounts, like the one shown in Listing 3.4.

Listing 3.4   A script to create an application developer's account.

```
GRANT CONNECT, RESOURCE TO &&1 IDENTIFIED BY &&2;


--
-- Allow the developer to create stored procedures, functions,
-- packages, and triggers.
--
GRANT CREATE ANY OBJECT TO &&1;


--
-- The developer must have full access to these tables.
--
GRANT ALL ON STUDENTS TO &&1;
GRANT ALL ON STUDENT_FINANCIAL_AID TO &&1;
GRANT ALL ON ENROLLED_CLASSES TO &&1;

EXIT
```

The scope of the rights and the fact that the rights granted directly to the account makes a developer's account very powerful (as it should be). Most systems find it prudent to not create development accounts on production systems, for reasons that should be obvious.

Reporting

Before reporting tools were available for Oracle, reports were written using SQL*Plus. A simple report could take a full day to write; complex reports could take a week or more. SQL*Plus includes some very robust controls that support the development of reports, even though most reports are now generated using Oracle Reports or other reporting tools. The script shown in Listing 3.5 generates a report about the code stored in an Oracle data dictionary.

Listing 3.5 An SQL report on code stored in the data dictionary.

```
clear computes
clear breaks

compute avg of length on type
break on type report skip page

spool code_rep.txt

SELECT type, name, max (line) "length"
FROM    ALL_SOURCE A
WHERE   A.owner = upper ('&&1')
AND     A.line = (SELECT max (B.line)
                  FROM    ALL_SOURCE B
                  WHERE   A.owner = B.owner
                  AND     A.name  = B.name
                  AND     A.type  = B.type)
GROUP BY type, name;

spool off

EXIT
```

This report computes the average number of lines for each type of stored PL/SQL object. By calculating the average number of lines for each type of object, the report (theoretically) indicates the level of modularity in the code (the lower the average number of lines, the more modular the code). The output of the script is shown in Figure 3.1.

Testing

The most monotonous part of application development is testing, but testing is vital to the success of a project. The use of a testing script provides the following three advantages over typical ad hoc testing:

- *Definition of assumptions*—The script defines its assumptions about the code being tested. The act of writing the test also clarifies the developer's assumptions about the code, which leads to a better piece of code.

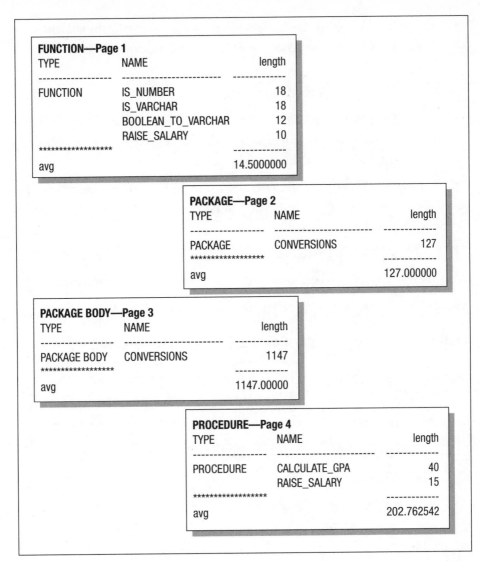

Figure 3.1
Sample output for Listing 3.5.

- *Repeatability*—A test can be repeated multiple times during testing. The script can also be repeated at any point in the future when code is modified. When the code is modified, the script repeats the same steps and creates the same conditions without requiring any additional work on the part of the developer.

- *Reliability*—The test is absolutely reliable. While a script might contain some errors, once a script is debugged, the results are dependent only on the code that the script tests.

A well-written test script performs these four tasks:

- *Setup*—The script creates data that supports a test condition. Often, a script is only one of many testing scripts for a piece of code, with each script validating one of many conditions that must be tested.

- *Prediction*—The script predicts the outputs of the code (or the conditions that will exist after the code is run), based on the data created during the setup portion of the script.

- *Execution*—The script executes the code that it is designed to test.

- *Checks*—The script reports and/or checks the outputs of the procedure.

Listing 3.6 illustrates a test for the procedure **Calculate_GPA()**.

Listing 3.6   A test for the **Calculate_GPA()** procedure.

```
-- ********************************************************************
-- This script is a unit test for the procedure Calculate_GPA. The
-- following conditions are established by the script:
--
--    1) A student is created with a 4.0 GPA.
--
-- The script makes the following assumptions about the data in the
-- system:
--
--    1) The DEGREE_PLANS and STATES tables are fully populated.
--
-- This script is run from the SQL*Plus prompt by executing the
-- command:
--
--    @calculate_gpa.ut
--
-- The script must be run as a user with SELECT and INSERT
-- privileges on the STUDENTS and ENROLLED_COURSES table.
--
-- ********************************************************************

set termout off
set verify off
```

```
set pause off
set feedback off
set lines 80
set pages 0

set serveroutput on
spool calculate_gpa.utr

SELECT 'Creating data in STUDENTS table.'
FROM    DUAL;

INSERT
INTO    STUDENTS
        (ssn,
         first_name,
         last_name,
         middle_name,
         street_address,
         apartment_number,
         city,
         state_code,
         zip_code,
         home_phone,
         degree_plan,
         overall_gpa,
         most_recent_gpa,
         financing_num)
VALUES ('000000000',
         'John',
         'Schmoe',
         'Jacob',
         '613 North Peach Lane',
         NULL,
         'Raymond',
         'MS',
         '39154',
         '6018570900',
         'BA ANTHROPOLOGY',
         NULL,
         NULL,
         FINANCING_SEQ.NEXTVAL);


--
-- Create the grades for the student.
--
```

```
SELECT 'Creating course data.'
FROM   DUAL;


INSERT
INTO   ENROLLED_COURSES
       (course_id,
        ssn,
        course_grade)
VALUES (1934,
        000000000,
        'A');


INSERT
INTO   ENROLLED_COURSES
       (course_id,
        ssn,
        course_grade)
VALUES (2103,
        000000000,
        'A');


--
-- Call the Calculate_GPA procedure.
--
SELECT 'Calling procedure.'
FROM   DUAL;


BEGIN
   Calculate_GPA (nSSN => 000000000);
END;


--
-- Retrieve the newly calculate GPA from the STUDENTS table.
--
SELECT 'Retrieving GPA.'
FROM   DUAL;


DECLARE
   nGPA   number := 0;

BEGIN
   SELECT overall_gpa
   INTO   nGPA
   FROM   STUDENTS
   WHERE  ssn = 000000000;
```

```
    DBMS_Output.Put_Line ('GPA is: ' || to_char (nGPA));

    IF (nGPA != 4.0) THEN
        DBMS_Output.Put_Line ('** ERROR: GPA does not match ' ||
                              'expected results! **');
    END IF;
END;

spool off

EXIT
```

This script sets up a test condition by inserting rows into the **STUDENTS** table and **ENROLLED_COURSES** table. The script then calls the **Calculate_GPA()** procedure to calculate a new GPA for the student. Finally, the script queries the new GPA from the **STUDENTS** table and writes out the GPA using the **DBMS_Output** package; if the GPA doesn't match the expected result, the script also writes out an error message.

Obviously, setting up a script to perform a test can take some time, but the advantages of having a reliable and repeatable test are hard to overlook. If a piece of code is complex, using a script of this type is essential to validating the code.

Other Tasks

Almost any task can be automated. There are several factors that come into play when deciding whether a task should be performed with a script:

- *Complexity*—If a task requires a complex set of conditions to perform, then a script may be required to repeat the steps until the task is completed (even if the task will never be performed again).

- *Repetition*—If the task will need to be repeated regularly, a script might be ideal for the job. This reduces the amount of monotonous work that must be done by the DBA or developers because the script can simply be run as a **cron** job.

- *Interaction*—If a task requires little or no interaction, a script can easily perform the task. If interaction is required, it should be required at the start of the task. (This type of interaction often involves setting up parameters for the script.)

- *Functionality*—If the functionality of the task can be expressed in code, a script can do the job. For instance, a script can double-check account balances with ease, but it would take a bit of work to make a script understand when an account balance that sums properly is still wrong.

Let's consider several tasks and determine whether or not the task should be scripted.

Daily Conversion Of Data From A Legacy System

Every day a set of data must be loaded from the university's mainframe system. Some special applications have been developed on the mainframe, and IS (that's you) hasn't had time to implement those special applications on the new system. Consider these points:

- The data from the mainframe always comes in the same format.

- The data doesn't require complex interpretation.

- The data must be imported every morning before the start of business.

Given these conditions, this task should definitely be scripted.

Preparing Summary Data For Daily Transactions

Every day at 4:30 P.M., IS must prepare a report for the University Accounting Office that summarizes the university's transactions for the day.

- The data must be calculated in a standard format.

- The data comes from many different locations in the database.

- The report has to be generated every day.

Given these conditions, the task should be automated.

Pattern Analysis Of Stock Trends

The Vice President of Finance wants to see a report of trends in the university's investments. The stock prices are keyed into the database by his secretary every morning, but the standard report doesn't help him predict where the investments are going.

- You have all the data needed for the report, but it's not 100 percent reliable. (Remember, the Vice President's secretary keys the data in by hand every morning, and everyone makes mistakes.)

- The code for the report would have to follow some logical method of predicting trends in the stock market, but a large part of predicting trends is intuition.

- The Vice President wants to see this report once.

Unless you've created a reliable method for predicting where stock prices are going and can translate that method into simple logical steps, you're unlikely to have any success using a script to generate a usable report. (And let's face it, if you had created a reliable method of predicting where stock prices are going, you probably wouldn't be working for a living.)

Documenting Scripts

Scripts play a large role in most systems. If a script performs a task within your system, the script should be documented. A script to restore your database isn't any good if no one has any idea how to run it. The best place to document scripts is within the script's header (or prologue), as illustrated in Listing 3.7.

Listing 3.7   A documented header for a script.

```
-- ****************************************************************
-- This script performs an analysis report of trends in student
-- grades, broken down by professor. The report should help indicate
-- if specific professors are showing unusual trends in grades.
--
-- The script accepts the following parameters:
--
--    1) The first parameter specifies a department for which the
--       script should be run.
--    2) The second parameter specifies what level of students should
--       be examined. The values for this parameter are:
--
--           1 -- calculate grades for all undergraduates
--           2 -- calculate grades for all Masters candidates
--           3 -- calculate grades for all doctoral candidates
--
-- The script is run from the Unix prompt by issuing the following
-- command:
--
--    sqlplus @grade_trends.report PSYCHOLOGY 2
--
--
-- The script uses these variables:
```

```
--
--    1) &&MeanGrade -- indicates the mean grade for all students
--       in the program.
--
-- There are no expected errors that occur when running this script.
--
-- The script requires SELECT privileges on the STUDENTS,
-- DEPARTMENTS, and ENROLLED_COURSES tables.
-- *****************************************************************
```

The header shown in Listing 3.7 documents several important aspects of the script:

- *Purpose*—A statement about the general functionality of the script.

- *Parameters*—The parameters expected when the script is called are documented. An explanation is given for the use of each parameter within the script. An example of calling the script from the command line is given.

- *Variables*—Any variables used within the script are documented, and the use of the variables is discussed. While this isn't critical to the person who runs the script, it will be critical to the person who has to update the script down the road.

- *Errors*—Any errors that can occur while running the script are documented. If possible, reasons are given for these errors, and workarounds are documented.

- *Account privileges*—The privileges required to run the script are specified.

- *Leftovers*—Any special information about the script is documented.

Scripts for your system should be in version control with the rest of the code; no one wants to have to re-create the backup script for your database or the report that took a week to write and debug. It's especially critical that test scripts (and their results) be stored in version control, because, at some point, the tests will need to be executed again.

Scripting In SQL*Plus

SQL*Plus contains a number of features that allow developers to write complex scripts to accomplish a variety of tasks. Although many of these features have been supplanted by the evolution of reporting tools for Oracle, the features still exist and can be used to give your scripts some extra oomph.

SQL*Plus Commands

SQL*Plus provides numerous commands that allow you to control almost every aspect of the way data is displayed. Some of these commands are now used infrequently at best, but a general familiarity with them will give you a better understanding of the kinds of tasks that you can accomplish with SQL scripts.

In addition to these commands, SQL*Plus provides a number of functions (such as **min**() and **max**()) that handle common operations. These functions are documented in Appendix A, along with some other useful functions.

The @ Command

The @ (at sign) command is used to open and run a script from the SQL*Plus command prompt, as shown in the following example:

```
@set_grade 999999999 2103 'A'
```

The / Command

The / (forward slash) command instructs SQL*Plus to execute the commands stored in the command buffer.

Commenting

SQL*Plus and PL/SQL support both single and multiple line comments, as shown in the following example:

```
-- This is a single line comment.

/*
 This is a multiline comment, like you might find in a C program.
*/
```

You may use either style of commenting inside your scripts.

The accept Command

You can use the **accept** command to have your script require input from the user. The syntax for the **accept** command is:

```
accept <variable> datatype [prompt <input prompt>}]
```

where **variable** is the name of the variable, **datatype** is **char** or **number**, and **input prompt** is the prompt that should be displayed. You may use the **no prompt** option if you do not want a prompt for input, as shown in the following statement:

```
accept password char no prompt;
```

If for some reason you do not wish for the user's input to be echoed to the screen, you may use the **hide** option, as follows:

```
accept password char no prompt hide;
```

The break Command

The **break** command instructs SQL*Plus to perform certain actions when a specified event occurs while processing the results of a **SELECT** command. There are four types of events that can be specified as part of the **break** command: **expression**, **row**, **page**, and **report**.

- **expression**—The name of a column being queried is used as an event. Every time the value of the specified column changes, SQL*Plus will perform the action defined in the **break** event for the expression. In Listing 3.5, the **type** column is specified as the **break** event. When the value of this column changes, SQL*Plus calculates the average value of the **length** column for every **type** object.

- **row**—Every row retrieved is used as an event.

- **page**—The end of a page is used as an event.

- **report**—The end of the report is used as an event.

Multiple events can be used with the **break** statement. Consider again the script shown in Listing 3.5, and notice that the report calculates the average number of lines for each type of object and for all the objects. This is accomplished with the following **break** command:

```
break on type report skip page
```

There is a distinct set of actions that can be performed with a break: **skip** *n*, **skip page**, **noduplicates**, and **duplicates**.

- **skip** *n*—Instructs SQL*Plus to skip *n* lines when the event occurs.

- **skip page**—Instructs SQL*Plus to skip to the next page when the event occurs.

- **noduplicates**—Instructs SQL*Plus to print blanks for the value of a **break** column when the value hasn't changed. This is usually abbreviated as **nodup**.

- **duplicates**—Instructs SQL*Plus to always print the value of a **break** column.

When used alone, the **break** command will display the break events that are currently in place.

The btitle Command

The **btitle** command instructs SQL*Plus to print a title (or footer) at the bottom of each page of a report. The command allows you to perform the following actions:

- You can use multiple lines in the footer using the **skip** clause, as shown in this example:

```
btitle skip n SYSDATE;
```

In this example, **n** is the number of lines to be skipped and defaults to one line. If **n** is set to **0**, SQL*Plus returns to the beginning of the current line.

- You can align text to the left, right, or center, or to a specified column, as follows:

```
btitle left 'Malden Power' center 'Quality Control' right SYSDATE;
btitle col 50 'Report';
```

- You can specify a number of tabs for alignment of the footer, as shown in this example:

```
btitle tab n 'Malden Power';
```

In this example, **n** is an integer value; a negative value skips backward, and a positive value skips forward.

- You can turn the title off and on without affecting its definition, as shown in this example:

```
btitle off;
btitle on;
```

The clear Command

The **clear** command allows you to erase certain settings from your current SQL*Plus environment using the following conditions:

- **breaks**—Erases all defined break conditions set by the **break** command.

- **buffer**—Erases text from the current buffer.

- **columns**—Erases all options set by the **column** command.

- **computes**—Erases all options set by the **compute** command.

- **sql**—Erases the SQL command buffer.

Before setting up new conditions (especially with the **break** and **compute** commands), it's a good idea to clear these options first.

The column Command

The **column** command is probably the most powerful command in SQL*Plus, allowing you to control almost every aspect of how data is displayed. The **column** command can define these aspects of a column and its values:

- **alias**—Allows you to specify an alias for a column name. This is very useful with columns that are the result of an expression or function call.

- **clear**—Instructs SQL*Plus to remove the column definition.

- **default**—Instructs SQL*Plus to reset a column to its default definition.

- **format**—Allows you to specify the display format of the column. This option is often used to enforce minimum widths on columns to prevent column headers from being truncated.

- **heading**—Allows you to specify the label for the column header on the report. Headings can be forced to wrap with the use of the | (pipe) character.

- **justify**—Instructs SQL*Plus to align the heading at the specified point (left, right, or center). The default alignment is right for numbers and left for all other types.

- **like**—Instructs SQL*Plus to use the specifications for another column.

- **newline**—Instructs SQL*Plus to print a new line before printing the column value.

- **new_value**—Places the value of the column into a variable that can be referenced using the **ttitle** and **btitle** commands.

- **noprint**—Instructs SQL*Plus not to print the column.

- **null**—Instructs SQL*Plus to replace **NULL** values with specific text. By default, this is a string of blanks.

- **off**—Instructs SQL*Plus to turn off the formatting options set with this command. The options are still in operation; SQL*Plus simply ignores them.

- **on**—Instructs SQL*Plus to turn on the formatting options set with this command.

- **old_value**—Instructs SQL*Plus to store the column's value in a variable.

- **print**—Instructs SQL*Plus to print the column. This is the default.

- **trunc**—Instructs SQL*Plus to truncate heading and character values that are too wide for their column definition. This is the default.

- **word_wrapped**—Instructs SQL*Plus to wrap heading and character values that are too wide for their column definition. Words are kept together.

- **wrapped**—Instructs SQL*Plus to wrap heading and character values that are too wide for their column definition. This type of wrap makes no effort to keep words together.

Consider the following example of a **column** command:

```
column overall_gpa alias 'GPA' justify center
column name ALIAS 'NAME' format A20 justify right

SELECT last_name || ', ' || first_name name, overall_gpa
FROM    STUDENTS
WHERE   ssn = 999999999;
```

Without the **column** commands, the query would produce this output:

```
last_name || ', ' || first_ over
--------------------------- ----
Schmoe, John                3.73
```

Because the **column** commands were used, the query produces the following output:

```
                 NAME  GPA
--------------------------- ----
          Schmoe, John 3.73
```

Table 3.2 lists the format model elements for date values.

Table 3.2 Valid date format models.

Element	Explanation
SCC or CC	Century. S prefixes a BC date with a negative sign.
YYYY or SYYYY	Year. S prefixes a BC date with a negative sign.
YYY, YY, or Y	The last 3, 2, or 1 digit(s) of a year.
Y,YYY	Year, with a comma in the specified position.
SYEAR or YEAR	Year, spelled out. S prefixes a BC date with a negative sign.
BC or AD	Indicates that the BC or AD should be included as part of the date.
B.C. or A.D.	Indicates that the B.C. or A.D. should be included as part of the date.
Q	Quarter of the year.
MM	Month.
MONTH	Name of the month. The value is padded with blanks to a length of nine characters.
MON	Three letter abbreviated name of a month.
WW or W	Week of year or month.
DDD, DD, or D	Day of year, month, or week.
DAY	Name of day padded with spaces to a length of nine characters.
DY	Three letter abbreviated name of a day.
J	Julian day (number of days since December 31, 4713 BC).
AM or PM	Meridian indicator.
A.M. or P.M.	Meridian indicator.
HH or HH12	Hour of the day from 1 through 12.
HH24	Military hour of the day.
MI	Minute.
SS	Second.
SSSSS	Seconds past midnight (ranges from 0 through 86399).
Punctuation characters	Specified characters are reproduced in the result.
Quoted string	The string is reproduced in the result.

Table 3.3 Refining the date format.

Prefix/Suffix	Usage
fm	This prefix instructs Oracle not to pad the elements of the column with spaces, which will yield a string of variable length.
TH	This suffix allows the output of an ordinal number, like 4th. The usage to retrieve an ordinal day value is DDTH (giving 4 as an input will return 4th).
SP	This suffix indicates that the number of the date should be spelled out. The usage to retrieve a spelled out day is DDSP (giving 4 as an input will return four).
SPTH or THSP	These suffixes indicate that Oracle should spell out ordinal numbers. The usage to retrieve a spelled out ordinal number is DDSPTH (giving 4 as an input will return fourth).

In addition to these formats, the prefixes and suffixes in Table 3.3 can be used to further define the format of date data:

All of these examples show valid formatting commands for dates.

```
column enrolled_date format MM-DD-YYYY
column class_time format HH:MI
column hastings_date format YYYY
column hastings_date format Y,YYY
column graduation_date format fm ddth "of" Month, YYYY A.D.
```

Table 3.4 lists the format model elements for numerical values. SQL*Plus will always round to the specified number of significant digits. If a column has no format model, the column's width defaults to the value of the **numwidth** SQL setting (**numwidth** is discussed later in this chapter).

All of these examples contain valid formats for numbers:

```
column account_balance format $999,999.99
column account_balance format $000,000.09
column account_balance format $099999.99
column variance format 9.999EEEE
column account_balance format $999999.99MI
```

Table 3.4 Valid number format models.

Element	Explanation
9	Represents a digit. If no digit occupies this space, it will be blank.
0	Represents a digit. If no digit occupies this space, a leading 0 will be used.
$	Prefixes a value with a dollar sign.
B	Displays a value of zero as blank, not 0.
MI	Displays a negative sign (-) after a negative value.
PR	Displays a negative value in angle brackets (<>).
,	Displays a comma in this position.
.	Displays a period in this position.
V	Multiplies the value by n, where *n* is the number of digits following V.
E	Displays the value in scientific notation (the format model must contain four Es).

The compute Command

The **compute** command allows basic mathematical operations to be carried out when a **break** event is reached. This command works only with the **break** command. The following eight types of operations can be performed with the **compute** command:

- **avg**—Calculates the average value for the column. This may only be used for columns of a numerical datatype.

- **count**—Counts all non-**NULL** values in the column. This can be used for columns of any datatype.

- **max**—Determines the highest value of the column. This may only be used for numerical and character datatypes.

- **min**—Determines the lowest value of the column. Like **max**, this may only be used for numerical and character datatypes.

- **number**—Counts all rows. Like **count**, this may be used on columns of any datatype.

- **std**—Determines the standard deviation of the column from the mean. This may only be used on columns of a numerical datatype.

- **sum**—Reports the total of the values in the column. This may only be used on columns of a numerical datatype.

- **variance**—Calculates the variance of the column. This may only be used on columns of a numerical datatype.

More than one operation can be performed on any given column, as shown in this example:

```
compute avg number max of length on type;
```

The values that **compute** generates can be stored in variables, as follows:

```
compute avg of length on type into avglength;
```

When used alone, the **compute** command displays all the **compute** operations that are currently in effect.

The define Command

The **define** command allows you to see the status of variables inside SQL*Plus. This is typically used with variables that have been created using the **accept** command. Typing **define** alone will show the status of the variables that are currently available. You may also type *define <variable>* to see the status of a particular variable.

The host Command

The **host** command allows you to execute a command at the OS level from inside SQL*Plus. When the command has finished executing, control returns to SQL*Plus.

The pause Command

The **pause** command allows you to halt a script and require the user to press a carriage return, typically as acknowledgment of a status or error message that the script has written.

The remark Command

The **remark** command (more commonly known as **rem**) is used at the start of a line and instructs SQL*Plus to proceed to the next line. This command is still used, although it has been supplanted to some extent by the use of single and multiple line comments.

The set Command

The most common command issued inside a script is the **set** command, which allows the user to configure SQL environment settings. A listing of the most commonly used SQL settings is presented in Table 3.5.

Table 3.5 The most commonly used SQL settings.

SQL Setting	Functionality
define	Defines the symbol used to prefix variables in SQL*Plus. This defaults to an ampersand (&).
echo	Instructs SQL*Plus to echo each command to standard output as they are run from a script. This setting defaults to **OFF** and can also be set to **ON**.
editfile	Sets the filename created by the **ed** command in SQL*Plus.
escape	Sets the character that can be used to display the define character as a normal character. The default escape character is a backslash (\). The setting can also be set to **ON** or **OFF**. Turning the setting to **ON** restores the backslash as the escape character.
feedback	Determines when SQL*Plus will display the number of records returned from a query and defaults to **ON**. The setting can also be set to **OFF** or n (an integer value greater than -1). A value of 0 is synonymous to setting the setting to **ON**; a value of n greater than 0 instructs SQL*Plus to display the message if n records are returned.
flush	Turns off standard output from a script file when set to **OFF**. The default value is **ON**.
heading	Instructs SQL*Plus about the display of column headings. The default is **ON**. Turning the setting to **OFF** causes SQL*Plus to not display headers for columns.
linesize	Sets the maximum line width that can be displayed in SQL*Plus. The default value is 80. The value of this setting is used to calculate column values for titles and footers displayed with an alignment of **CENTER** or **RIGHT**. The maximum value is 999.
long	Sets the maximum width for the display of long variables. The default value is 80, but the setting can be set to any value between 1 and 32767 (the value must be less than the **maxdata** setting).

continued

Table 3.5   The most commonly used SQL settings (Continued).

SQL Setting	Functionality
maxdata	Defines the maximum row width that SQL*Plus can handle (including wrapped lines). The default and maximum values for this setting are OS dependent.
newpage	Defines the number of blank lines printed between the bottom of one page and the title at the top of the next page. The default value is 1. A value of 0 sends a form feed character.
null	Sets the value to be displayed when a column is **NULL**. The default is a string of blanks.
numformat	Defines the default number format for numerical data. See Table 3.4 for a listing of valid formats.
numwidth	Defines the default width for numerical columns. The default value is 10.
pagesize	Defines the number of lines per page. The default is 14 lines.
pause	Instructs SQL*Plus to pause while displaying data and require acknowledgement from the user before returning the next page of data returned from a query. The default value is **OFF**. The setting may be set to **ON**. Turning this setting to **ON** requires a carriage return before the first page of data is displayed.
serveroutput	Allows the display of output from the **DBMS_Output** package inside SQL*Plus. The default is **OFF**. The setting may be set to **ON** as well.
showmode	Instructs SQL*Plus to display both the old and new values of an SQL setting when the setting is changed using the **set** command.
sqlprompt	Sets the text to be displayed for the SQL*Plus command prompt.
termout	Determines if output will be spooled to standard output. The default is **ON**. Using **OFF** improves performance.
timing	Instructs SQL*Plus to display the execution time of a command after the command has been completed. On Unix systems, the value is typically displayed in hundredths of a second.
verify	Controls the display of old and new values for variables in SQL statements. The default is **ON**.

The show Command

The **show** command instructs SQL*Plus to display the current settings for a session. The command takes the following arguments:

- **all**—Shows all current settings.
- **btitle**—Shows the current **btitle** definition.
- **lno**—Shows the position on the current page.
- **pno**—Shows the current page number.
- **release**—Shows the release number of the Oracle database.
- **spool**—Shows the current spool status.
- **sqlcode**—Shows the value of the system variable **SQL.SQLCODE** (the most recent operation's return code).
- **sqlerrm**—Shows the value of the system variable **SQL.SQLERRM** (the most recent operation's error).
- **ttitle**—Shows the value of the current **ttitle** definition.
- **user**—Shows your user ID.
- **wrap**—Indicates if data is being wrapped or truncated in output.

You may also specify the name of any SQL setting as the target of the **show** command.

The ttitle Command

The **ttitle** command instructs SQL*Plus to print a title at the top of each page of a report. You can perform a number of actions using the **ttitle** command, such as:

- You can use multiple lines in the title using the **skip** clause, as shown in this example:

```
ttitle skip n SYSDATE;
```

In this example, **n** is the number of lines to be skipped and defaults to one line. If **n** is set to 0, SQL*Plus returns to the beginning of the current line.

- You can align text to the left, right, center, or to a specified column, as shown in the following example:

```
ttitle left 'MaldenPower' center 'Quality Control' right SYSDATE;
ttitle col 50 'Report';
```

- You can specify a number of tabs for alignment of the footer, as shown in this example:

```
ttitle tab n 'Malden Power';
```

In this example, **n** is an integer value; a negative value skips backward and a positive value skips forward.

- You can turn the title off and on without affecting its definition, as shown in this example:

```
ttitle off;
ttitle on;
```

The undefine Command

The **undefine** command is used to dispose of a variable inside an SQL session. The format of the **undefine** command is:

```
undefine <variable>;
```

Once a variable has been undefined, it can no longer be referenced unless it is redefined.

Connecting To SQL*Plus

You'll probably connect to SQL*Plus using a command like:

```
sqlplus username/password
```

SQL*Plus provides some alternative methods of connecting that you should be aware of. For instance:

```
sqlplus [-silent] username/password
```

Logging into SQL*Plus using the **-silent** flag instructs the program not to give any informational messages (not even a prompt). This is particularly useful when your script is dynamically generating code or when executing SQL*Plus from inside another piece of software.

If you login and find that you need to be working under another schema, you can login to a new schema without exiting SQL*Plus and reconnecting by using the following command:

```
connect username/password
```

You can use any of these login commands without typing your username or password as part of the command; SQL*Plus will prompt you for these values if you don't include them in the command. Using your password as part of a command reveals the password to anyone who sees the command, so it's probably better to enter your password when prompted in most situations.

Logging Out Of SQL*Plus

The **exit** and **quit** commands are used to leave SQL*Plus and return to the operating system. You should be aware that using either of these commands implicitly commits changes to the database. If you've made changes that you don't want to save, you'll have to roll back prior to issuing one of these commands.

You can use this command to return a status to an OS-level application that called the script, as shown in the following example:

```
exit success
```

There are five values that can be returned: **success**, **failure**, **warning**, **integer**, and **variable**.

- **success**—The script ended execution normally. The value of this status depends on the host operating system.

- **failure**—The script failed at some point. The value of this status depends on the host operating system.

- **warning**—The script exited in a warning state. The value of this status depends on the host operating system.

- **integer**—You can return specific integer values that suit your needs.

- **variable**—You can return the contents of a variable as the status. This variable does not have to be an **integer** or **number** variable.

Script Parameters

When you call a script, you can pass parameters to the script in the command line, as shown in the following example:

```
sqlplus username/password @set_grade 999999999 2103 'A'
```

This is what the set_grade.sql script looks like:

```
UPDATE ENROLLED_COURSES
SET     course_grade  = upper ('&&3')
WHERE   ssn           = &&1
AND     course_number = &&2;
```

In this example, **999999999** is referenced in the script as **&&1**, and **2103** is referenced in the script as **&&2**. The student's grade for course 2103 is referenced as **&&3**.

Parameters are referenced by integer values in the order in which they are passed (one of the reasons why it's important to document what parameters are used and in what order they should be passed).

References to parameters are typically made using the ampersand (&) character; this character can be altered using the **set define** command. A single ampersand instructs SQL to prompt the user for the value of the parameter. Double ampersands (&&) instruct SQL to prompt the user for a value if there is no value already stored for the parameter; variables defined with a single & are undefined immediately after the variable is used. Consequently, if a script is to run without interaction, you should use double ampersands to reference your parameters.

Spooling Output To Files

The **spool** command is used to control the direction of output to a file. The syntax for the **spool** command is:

```
spool filename[.sql];
```

If no extension is given for the spool file, SQL*Plus assumes that you want the output file to have an extension of .LST.

To stop spooling to a file, use the following command:

```
spool off;
```

Substitution Variables

A *substitution variable* is a variable name preceded by one or two ampersands, like the variable used in the following example:

```
SELECT count (*)
FROM   STUDENTS
WHERE  last_name = upper (&LastName);
```

When this script is run, SQL*Plus will prompt the user for each *undefined* substitution variable it encounters.

PL/SQL In Scripts

The use of **IF-THEN-ELSE** logic, looping structures, and other features can make writing a powerful script much simpler. It's extremely difficult to simulate these logical control structures using only SQL statements.

Anonymous PL/SQL Blocks

Every use of PL/SQL in your script will be done through an *anonymous PL/SQL block.* Even a call to a stored procedure or function must be executed through an anonymous block. An anonymous PL/SQL block is nothing more than a PL/SQL block that isn't already compiled in the data dictionary. This is shown in the following example:

```
DECLARE
   nGPA    number := 0;

BEGIN
   SELECT overall_gpa
   INTO   nGPA
   FROM   STUDENTS
   WHERE  ssn = 999999999;
END;
```

One of the most common uses of anonymous PL/SQL blocks is a call to a stored PL/SQL object, typically for testing purposes.

The **exec** statement is a quick method to create an anonymous PL/SQL block, but it doesn't allow you to define any variables. The use of the **exec** statement is shown in this example, which calls the **Annual_Review**() procedure.

```
exec Annual_Review;
```

If the **Annual_Review**() procedure required parameters, these would have to be passed as literal values to the procedure. Using **exec** simply nests the call to the stored object between a **BEGIN** and an **END**.

Using DBMS_Output And UTL_File

The **DBMS_Output** package is often used within anonymous PL/SQL blocks to display the values returned from queries and calls to stored PL/SQL objects. The results of queries inside PL/SQL blocks contained in a script are not spooled to standard output (the terminal or monitor). This package provides a useful method of generating messages that are spooled to standard output. In order to use the **DBMS_Output** package, you must use the **set serveroutput on** command at the beginning of your script.

The **UTL_File** package (introduced with Oracle 7.3) can be used within scripts instead of spooling output to a file with the spool command. The package writes to and reads from files at the operating system level. This package is especially useful if the output of the script needs to be stored in a file.

More information about these packages is provided in Chapter 9.

Step-By-Step: Building A Report In SQL*Plus

On the CD-ROM you'll find the source code for the **Build_SUID_Matrix** package, which stores dependency information about stored PL/SQL objects based on the type of table references the object makes. This information is stored in the **SUID_MATRIX** table, which has this structure:

```
object_name                 NOT NULL varchar2(30)
object_type                 NOT NULL varchar2(30)
table_name                  NOT NULL varchar2(30)
ins                                  varchar2(1)
upd                                  varchar2(1)
sel                                  varchar2(1)
del                                  varchar2(1)
typ                                  varchar2(1)
```

Requirements

Since each object can reference numerous tables, we want to avoid listing the name of the object on every row of the report. We want to list the name on the first row and leave it blank on each subsequent row for the same object. This is very easy to do using the **break** command in SQL*Plus:

```
break on object_name skip 0 nodup
```

Pseudocode

The report only has to perform these two tasks:

- Setting up the break command
- Retrieving the data

The pseudocode for accomplishing these two tasks is shown in this example:

```
set up the break command to skip duplicate object_name values

query the SUID_MATRIX table to get the data
```

Code

The code for the report looks like this:

```
break on object_name skip 0 nodup

SELECT object_name, table_name, ins, upd, del, sel, typ
FROM   SUID_MATRIX
ORDER BY object_name;
```

Code for a report to list the objects that reference each table is quite similar:

```
break on table_name skip 0 nodup

SELECT table_name, object_name, ins, upd, del, sel, typ
FROM   SUID_MATRIX
ORDER BY table_name;
```

The reports could easily be altered to run for a specific **object_name** or **table_name** as well. The **object_name** report generates output like this:

OBJECT_NAME	TABLE_NAME	I	U	D	S	T
ANNUAL_REVIEW	EMPLOYEES			Y	Y	Y
	PERFORMANCE_RULES				Y	Y
AWARD_BONUSES	EMPLOYEES			N	Y	Y
	EMPLOYEE_BONUSES	Y		Y		Y
	PERFORMANCE_RULES				Y	Y
GRANT_SICK_LEAVE	EMPLOYEES			Y	Y	Y
GRANT_VACATION	EMPLOYEES			Y	Y	Y
RAISE_SALARY	EMPLOYEES				Y	

The **table_name** report generates output like this:

TABLE_NAME	OBJECT_NAME	I	U	D	S	T
EMPLOYEES	ANNUAL_REVIEW			Y	Y	Y
	AWARD_BONUSES				Y	Y
	GRANT_SICK_LEAVE			Y	Y	Y
	GRANT_VACATION			Y	Y	Y
	RAISE_SALARY			Y	Y	Y
EMPLOYEE_BONUSES	AWARD_BONUSES	Y		Y		Y
PERFORMANCE_RULES	ANNUAL_REVIEW				Y	Y
	AWARD_BONUSES				Y	Y

Summary

Chapter 3 has discussed the basic tools you'll need to develop scripts using SQL*Plus and PL/SQL. An excellent place to go for more information is the *Oracle Server SQL Language Reference* and the *PL/SQL User's Guide*, both of which you should be able to borrow from your DBA. By now, you should have a basic understanding of the various roles that scripts play in a system and the considerations that go into script development, as well as a basic understanding of how you can write your own reports using SQL*Plus. Chapter 4 will discuss the PL/SQL commands needed to create a stored procedure and provide some insights on designing and testing stored procedures.

Procedures

CHAPTER 4

HIGH PERFORMANCE

Procedures

A *stored procedure* is a piece of code that performs a specific task. The procedure is compiled by Oracle and stored within the data dictionary.

This chapter discusses the creation of procedures using PL/SQL. I have provided several detailed examples, and will guide you through the entire process of creating a new procedure. By the end of this chapter, you will be familiar with how stored procedures are used and how to design, create, and test your own procedures.

Advantages Of Procedures

By allowing you to store the executable and source code for your application within the data dictionary, Oracle allows you to create applications that reach new heights in performance, modularity, maintainability, and reliability. Code no longer has to be generated within the front end of a system; instead, logic can be centralized and called from every part of a system's interface.

Embedded SQL

Stored procedures can execute any DML statement that can be executed in SQL*Plus, as shown in Listing 4.1.

Listing 4.1 Embedded SQL within a stored procedure.

```
PROCEDURE Annual_Review
.
.
   SELECT base_salary
   INTO   nBaseSalary
   FROM   EMPLOYEES
   WHERE  CURRENT OF Employees_cur;
.
.
END Annual_Review;
```

Maintainability

The logic of a stored procedure is more easily maintained than individual copies of the same piece of code spread throughout a system. If a logic error is discovered or a business rule changes, only the one stored procedure has to be changed and tested.

If the same logic is coded into several different applications, changing the code could easily take several times longer than changing a single piece of code. There are also reliability issues because making several changes increases the likelihood of a defect being introduced into the code.

Modularity

By coding logic for a specific task into a stored procedure, the logic for the task becomes readily available to any code that needs to perform the specific task. The procedure will accept a defined set of input values and will process those values in exactly the same manner every time the procedure executes. Figure 4.1 illustrates the concepts behind modular code.

Performance Improvement

There are several reasons why stored procedures provide some performance improvements over code that is implemented in multiple locations to perform the same task, including:

- On large projects, code to perform a similar task in multiple locations is rarely written by the same developer. Calling a stored procedure to perform a task increases the likelihood that the DML statements inside the stored procedure are already cached in the SGA because those statements are written only once.

- The implementation of a stored procedure does not change depending on which part of the system calls the procedure. The parameter values are the only differences in the procedure's execution.

- Oracle maintains a copy of the executable version of the stored procedure (*p-code*) and executes this copy rather than recompiling the procedure.

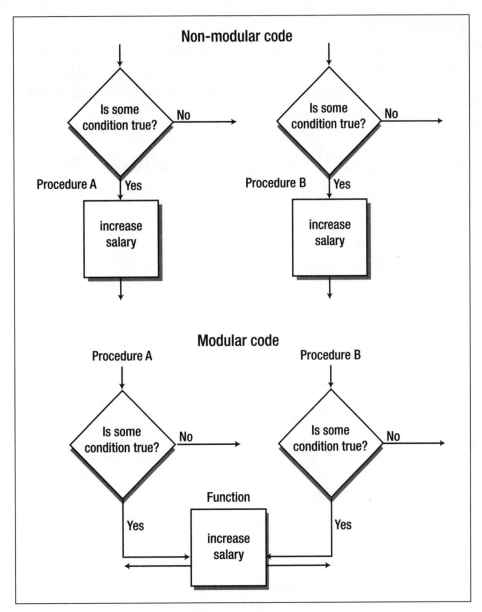

Figure 4.1
Modular versus non-modular code.

Reusability

A stored procedure only has to be written once and can be called from many different parts of a system. Even if a logic error is found or a business rule changes, the change only has to be made once and every part of the system that calls the stored procedure is corrected.

Creating And Dropping Procedures

Procedures are created in SQL*Plus using a command like the one shown in Listing 4.2.

Listing 4.2   Creating a stored procedure.

```
CREATE OR REPLACE
PROCEDURE Annual_Review

IS

    <declarations>

BEGIN
    <statements>;
END Annual_Review;
/
```

Using the **OR REPLACE** clause indicates that Oracle should replace an existing procedure of the same name if it exists. If the object exists and the **OR REPLACE** clause isn't used, an error will occur.

Procedures can be dropped using the **DROP** command inside SQL*Plus, as follows:

```
DROP PROCEDURE Annual_Review;
```

Procedures can also be created and dropped using Oracle's Procedure Builder or one of several available third-party editors. These products have become quite sophisticated.

It's very rare to compile a procedure (or other stored object) successfully on the first time through; very often you will receive compilation errors. Resolving compilation errors is discussed in Chapter 8.

Recompiling Procedures

While procedures (and other objects) can be recompiled by simply reissuing the **CRE-ATE OR REPLACE** command for the object, there's another method of recompiling stored objects without having a copy of the source code in a standalone file.

A stored PL/SQL object can be recompiled by using an **ALTER** command in SQL*Plus, like the commands shown here:

```
ALTER PROCEDURE Annual_Review COMPILE;
ALTER FUNCTION Raise_Salary COMPILE;
ALTER PACKAGE End_Of_Year COMPILE;
ALTER PACKAGE BODY End_Of_Year COMPILE;
```

In order to recompile objects using this method, you must be running under an account with the **ALTER ANY OBJECT** privilege. This method of recompiling stored PL/SQL objects is useful when objects become marked as invalid due to changes to their dependent objects. Dependencies are discussed in detail a bit later in this chapter.

Automatically Recompiling Invalid Stored Objects

When an object that your procedure references is altered in some manner (a column in a table is modified, a new column is added, or a stored PL/SQL object called by your procedure is recompiled), your procedure will be marked as invalid because Oracle is uncertain of its status. The next time your procedure is called, Oracle will generate an error message and remove the p-code for the invalid procedure. When your procedure is called again, Oracle will automatically attempt to recompile the p-code.

A package spec isn't marked as invalid when a package body is altered. However, altering the package spec does invalidate the package body.

There isn't any way that I've found to force Oracle to automatically recompile the p-code for an invalid stored procedure or function without first generating an error. This minor annoyance is a relatively common complaint among PL/SQL developers.

Local Procedures

Procedures can be declared within another block of PL/SQL code. This is very unusual. Most stored objects are written as standalone objects to provide greater modularity. This approach does, however, allow the local procedure to reference variables and constants within the calling PL/SQL block as global values.

To create a local procedure within a PL/SQL block, simply declare the procedure at the end of the variable declarations for the block. Listing 4.3 illustrates the definition of a procedure as part of another procedure's declarations.

Listing 4.3   Declaring a local procedure within a procedure.

```
CREATE OR REPLACE
PROCEDURE Calculate_GPA (nSSN IN OUT number)

IS

    iNumHours            integer;
    iTotalCredits        integer;
    iHoursForClass       integer;
    iCreditsForClass     integer;

    PROCEDURE Course_Credit (nSSN       IN     number,
                             nCourseID IN     number,
                             iCredits       OUT integer,
                             iHours         OUT integer)

    IS

    BEGIN
        SELECT SC.course_credits, C.course_hours
        INTO   iCredits,          iHours
        FROM   SCHEDULED_CLASSES SC,
               CLASSES           C
        WHERE  C.course_number = nCourseID
        AND    SC.course_number = C.course_number
        AND    social_security_number = nSSN
        AND    audit_flag = 'N'
        AND    no_credit_flag = 'N';

    EXCEPTION
        WHEN NO_DATA_FOUND THEN
            iCredits := 0;
            iHours   := 0;
    END;
```

```
BEGIN
   FOR Classes_rec IN Classes_cur LOOP
      Course_Credit (nSSN       => nStudentSSN,
                     iCourseID => Classes_rec.course_number,
                     iCredits  => iCreditsForClass,
                     iHours    => iHoursForClass);

      IF (iHoursForClass > 0) THEN
         iNumHours     := iNumHours     + iHoursForClass;
         iTotalCredits := iTotalCredits + iCreditsForClass;
      END IF;
   END LOOP;

   UPDATE STUDENTS
   SET    overall_gpa = (iTotalCredits / iNumHours)
   WHERE  ssn = nStudentSSN;
END;
/
```

Locally declared functions are somewhat more common than local procedures, but they are still rather uncommon. Multiple local procedures and functions can be used, but all of the local programs must be declared at the end of the variable declarations section of the main block.

Forward Declarations

In the event that you have more than one local declared procedure or function within a block of PL/SQL and the procedures must reference each other, you won't be able to compile your code without getting an error. Each local procedure must be declared before the other.

To get around this problem, you can use a *forward declaration* to specify the interface for the procedures. This will allow your PL/SQL block to compile without errors. Listing 4.4 illustrates the use of a forward declaration.

Listing 4.4   Using a forward declaration for a local procedure.

```
CREATE OR REPLACE
PROCEDURE Calculate_Lot_Size (nWidth    IN    number,
                              nLength   IN    number,
                              nLotSize  OUT number)

IS
```

```
    PROCEDURE Convert_Feet_To_Yards (nFeet  IN      number,
                                     nYards IN OUT number);

  PROCEDURE Convert_Yards_To_Feet (nYards IN      number,
                                   nFeet  IN OUT number)

  IS

    nCheckCalc         number := 0;
    xBAD_CALCULATION   EXCEPTION;

  BEGIN
    nFeet := nYards * 3;

    Convert_Feet_To_Yards (nFeet  => nFeet,
                           nYards => iCheckCalc);

    IF (nCheckCalc != nYards) THEN
       RAISE xBAD_CALCULATION;
    END IF;
  END Convert_Yards_To_Feet;

  PROCEDURE Convert_Feet_To_Yards (nFeet  IN      number,
                                   nYards IN OUT number)

  IS

    nCheckCalc         number := 0;
    xBAD_CALCULATION   EXCEPTION;

  BEGIN
    nYards := nFeet/3;

    Convert_Yards_To_Feet (nYards => nYards,
                           nFeet  => iCheckCalc);

    IF (nCheckCalc != nFeet) THEN
       RAISE xBAD_CALCULATION;
    END IF;
  END Convert_Feet_To_Yards;
BEGIN
   <statements>
END Calculate_Lot_Size;
/
```

In this example, the first highlighted portion of the code is the forward declaration of the **Convert_Feet_To_Yards**() procedure, the second highlighted portion of the code is the call to the procedure, and the last highlighted portion of the code is the definition of the procedure's logic. If the forward declaration of the procedure **Convert_Feet_To_Yards**() were removed from this example, the code would not compile.

Dependencies

A *dependency* is created when one object is referenced by another. The structure of the **ALL_DEPENDENCIES** view is shown in Listing 4.5.

Listing 4.5   The structure of the **ALL_DEPENDENCIES** view.

```
name                varchar2 (30)
type                varchar2 (12)
owner               varchar2 (30)
referenced_name     varchar2 (30)
referenced_type     varchar2 (12)
referenced_owner    varchar2 (30)
```

The **ALL_DEPENDENCIES** view in Oracle's data dictionary has a list of all the dependencies between objects stored in the database.

Determining The Effects Of A Code Change

You can use the following query to determine which objects could be affected by modifications to a stored procedure:

```
SELECT type || ' ' || owner || '.' || name
FROM   ALL_DEPENDENCIES
WHERE  referenced_owner = upper ('&1')
AND    referenced_name  = upper ('&2')
ORDER BY type;
```

In this example, &1 is the schema of the object that you need to modify, and &2 is the name of the object. The query will produce output like this:

```
PROCEDURE ACCOUNTING.CALCULATE_AGENT_COMMISSION
PROCEDURE ACCOUNTING.CALCULATE_AGENT_BONUS
PROCEDURE SALES.FIND_AVAILABLE_LOTS
PROCEDURE SALES.CALCULATE_LOT_SIZE
PACKAGE BODY ACCOUNTING.PERFORMANCE_REVIEWS
```

Parameters

A *parameter* is a value that is passed to and/or returned from a stored procedure or function. Listing 4.6 illustrates how parameters are defined for a stored procedure.

Listing 4.6 Defining parameters for a stored procedure.

```
PROCEDURE Calculate_Lot_Size (nWidth    IN      number,
                             nLength   IN      number,
                             nLotSize     OUT number);
```

Datatypes

Like variables and constants, parameters for procedures must have a datatype specified. The datatype for a parameter can be either a scalar or user-defined datatype. Parameters of a user-defined datatype must make a reference to a type definition, typically inside a package spec.

Constraining Parameters

While parameters must have a datatype specified, it's not possible to constrain the length of a parameter. That is, if you define a parameter of datatype **varchar2**, that parameter can accept between 0 and 2,000 characters via that parameter! Likewise, you cannot require that a parameter be passed to the procedure.

If you must constrain parameters, explicit checks must be made inside your procedure, like the ones shown in Listing 4.7.

Listing 4.7 Checking the values of parameters.

```
PROCEDURE Test_Parameters (vString  IN      varchar2,
                          nBalance IN      number)

IS

   xSTRING_TOO_LONG     EXCEPTION;
   xNEGATIVE_BALANCE    EXCEPTION;

BEGIN
   IF (length (vString) > 20) THEN
      RAISE xSTRING_TOO_LONG;
   END IF;
```

```
    IF (nBalance < 0) THEN
        RAISE xNEGATIVE_BALANCE;
    END IF;
END Test_Parameters;
```

%TYPE Parameters

Parameters can reference the datatype of a column in a table using %TYPE, as shown in Listing 4.8.

Listing 4.8   Defining a parameter using **%TYPE**.

```
PROCEDURE Calculate_GPA (nSSN IN    STUDENTS.ssn%TYPE);
```

If a parameter references the datatype of a column this way and the datatype of the column changes, the datatype of the parameter changes to correspond to the column's datatype.

%ROWTYPE Parameters

Parameters can also reference the structure of a table or record by using %ROWTYPE, as shown in Listing 4.9.

Listing 4.9   Defining a parameter using **%ROWTYPE**.

```
PROCEDURE Print_Diploma (nStudent_rec IN    STUDENTS%ROWTYPE);
```

Parameters defined using **%ROWTYPE** change their definition if the referenced record type or row structure changes.

Parameter Types

There are three types of parameters for stored procedures: **IN**, **OUT**, and **IN OUT**. Each parameter type is described in Table 4.1.

If a type is not specified for a parameter, the parameter defaults to type **IN**.

Default Values

IN parameters (and only **IN** parameters) can be given a default value by using either the assignment operator (:=) or the **DEFAULT** statement, as shown in Listing 4.10.

Table 4.1 The three parameter types.

Type	Description
IN	**IN** parameters are used to pass a value to the procedure. The procedure is not able to alter the value of the parameter in any way. This is the most commonly used type of parameter.
OUT	**OUT** parameters are used to return a value from the procedure. The procedure can assign a value to the parameter but can never read the value contained in the parameter.
IN OUT	**IN OUT** parameters are used to pass a value to the procedure, which the procedure can then alter. The procedure is able to read values from and write values to the parameter.

Listing 4.10 Default values for parameters.

```
PROCEDURE Raise_Salary (nEmployeeID IN      number,
                        nRaiseAmt   IN      number DEFAULT .001);

PROCEDURE Raise_Salary (nEmployeeID IN      number,
                        nRaiseAmt   IN      number := .001);
```

When a **NULL** value is passed for a parameter with a default value, the parameter's value is set to the default value. If a value is passed for the parameter, the default value has no effect.

Calling Procedures

Stored procedures are typically called from a system's GUI front end, but can also be called from other stored PL/SQL objects and from anonymous PL/SQL blocks.

Anonymous PL/SQL Blocks

It's very common to create anonymous blocks of PL/SQL that call a stored procedure, especially when the procedure is being tested. Stored procedures can be called from any PL/SQL block. Consider the block of PL/SQL in Listing 4.11, which is part of a test for the **Annual_Review()** procedure.

Listing 4.11   An anonymous PL/SQL block that calls a procedure.

```
DECLARE
    nNewSalary      number;

BEGIN
    --
    -- Set up a sample employee.
    --
    INSERT
    INTO    EMPLOYEES
            (employee_num,
             employee_ssn,
             first_name,
             middle_name,
             last_name,
             eff_hire_date,
             eff_termination_date,
             base_salary,
             late_days,
             warnings,
             overtime_hours,
             performance_rating)
    VALUES (999,
             999999999,
             'Joe',
             'Grant',
             'Lewis',
             '01/01/80',
             NULL,
             20000,
             0,
             0,
             80,
             10);


    Annual_Review;


    SELECT base_salary
    INTO    nNewSalary
    FROM    EMPLOYEES
    WHERE   employee_num = 999;

    DBMS_Output.Put_Line ('Salary is: ' || to_char (nNewSalary));
END;
```

The highlighted portion of this example is a call to the **Annual_Review**() procedure. This call is the heart and soul of the test—after all, how can code be tested if it's never run?

Stored PL/SQL Objects

In all but the simplest of systems, stored procedures are often called by other stored procedures. Stored procedures can also be called from stored functions and PL/SQL objects inside packages. Listing 4.12 illustrates a call to a stored procedure from inside another stored procedure.

Listing 4.12   Calling a stored procedure from another stored procedure.

```
PROCEDURE Check_Code (vObjectName IN      varchar2,
                      vOwner      IN      varchar2)

IS

    iObjectExists           integer := 0;
    xMISSING_PARAMETER      EXCEPTION;
    xOBJECT_DOES_NOT_EXIST  EXCEPTION;

BEGIN
    IF vObjectName IS NULL THEN
        RAISE xMISSING_PARAMETER;
    END IF;

    IF vOwner IS NULL THEN
        RAISE xMISSING_PARAMETER;
    END IF;

    BEGIN
        SELECT 1
        INTO   iObjectExists
        FROM   ALL_OBJECTS
        WHERE  owner       = vOwner
        AND    object_name = vObjectName
        AND    object_type IN ('PROCEDURE',
                               'FUNCTION',
                               'PACKAGE BODY');
```

```
EXCEPTION
   WHEN NO_DATA_FOUND THEN
         RAISE xOBJECT_DOES_NOT_EXIST;
END;


Check_Source_For_Insert (vOwner  => vOwner,
                         vObject => vObjectName);


EXCEPTION
   WHEN xMISSING_PARAMETER THEN
         DBMS_Output.Put_Line ('Both parameters are required.');

   WHEN xOBJECT_DOES_NOT_EXIST THEN
         DBMS_Output.Put_Line ('The named object does not exist.');
END Check_Code;
```

In this example, the **Check_Source_For_Insert**() procedure is called from inside the **Check_Code**() procedure. This allows the **Check_Code**() procedure to perform the functionality of the **Check_Source_For_Insert**() procedure without including that procedure's logic.

Notation

PL/SQL supports two types of notation when calling procedures with parameters: *named notation* and *positional notation.*

Named Notation

Named notation is calling a stored procedure by specifying both the parameter names and each parameter's value. Listing 4.13 illustrates the use of named notation when calling a stored procedure.

Listing 4.13   Calling a procedure using named notation.

```
Check_Source_For_Insert (vOwner  => 'JSCHMOE',
                         vObject => 'CALCULATE_GPA');
```

When using named notation, the parameters for a procedure can be specified in any order (after all, the developer knows which values are intended for which parameters). Obviously, the use of named notation requires that the developer knows the names of the parameters and specifies the parameter names in procedure calls.

Positional Notation

Positional notation is calling a stored procedure by simply passing parameter values and assuming that the values will be associated with parameters in the order of declaration. The first value passed is associated with the first parameter, the second value with the second parameter, and so forth. Listing 4.14 illustrates a call to a stored procedure using positional notation.

Listing 4.14   Calling a stored procedure using positional notation.

```
Check_Source_For_Insert ('JSCHMOE',
                  'CALCULATE_GPA');
```

When using positional notation, the values must be passed to the stored procedure in the proper order. This requires that developers know the order of the parameters.

Mixing Notations

It's possible to use both named notation and positional notation in a single call to a stored procedure, as shown in Listing 4.15.

Listing 4.15   Mixing named and positional notation.

```
Approve_For_Credit (999999999,
                9032012912,
                'C',
                iBounced_Checks => 0,
                iOverdrafts     => 0);
```

When mixing notation like this, it's important to keep in mind that positional notation can be used only before named notation has been used. If even one parameter is populated by using named notation, all subsequent parameters must also be populated using named notation.

Named Or Positional Notation?

Consider again the code in Listing 4.15. While you may have figured out that the first parameter is a social security number, you probably have no idea what the second and third parameters are supposed to represent. If the code had used named notation (or if variables were being passed instead of literal values), you would be able to see that the second parameter holds an account number and the third pa-rameter indicates whether the account is a checking or savings account.

I prefer the use of named notation when calling procedures and functions. While somewhat more work is involved during development, it's much clearer down the road to see what values are being passed to which parameters. And when combined with meaningfully named variables, named notation contributes a great deal to making the code self-documenting.

Procedure Structure

Stored procedures contain the following five components:

- *Procedure declaration*—Defines the name of the procedure and the parameters the procedure accepts.

- *Variable declarations*—Defines the variables, constants, and user-defined exceptions used by the procedure.

- *Executable declarations*—Defines local procedures and functions that can be executed by the procedure.

- *Body*—Defines the internal logic of the procedure.

- *Exception handling*—Defines logic for handling exceptions that might occur during execution.

The Procedure Declaration

The procedure declaration consists of two portions:

- *Procedure name*—Name of the procedure, which identifies the procedure to other stored objects.

- *Parameter definitions*—Names, parameter types, datatypes, and default values of the procedure's parameters. These specify how the procedure must be called.

The procedure declaration is highlighted in Listing 4.16.

Listing 4.16   The procedure declaration portion of a procedure.

```
PROCEDURE Calculate_GPA (iStudentSSN IN     number)

IS

    CURSOR StudentClasses_cur
    IS
    SELECT SC.course_number, C.course_hours
    FROM   SCHEDULED_CLASSES SC,
           CLASSES           C
    WHERE  ssn = iStudentSSN
    AND    credit_flag = 'Y'
    AND    audit_flag = 'N';

    iTotalCredits    integer := 0;
    iTotalHours      integer := 0;

    FUNCTION Get_Course_Credits (iCourseID IN     integer)
    RETURN integer

    IS

        iCreditsForClass integer := 0;

    BEGIN
        SELECT decode (course_grade, 'A', 4,
                                     'B', 3,
                                     'C', 2,
                                     'D', 1, 0)
        INTO    iCreditsForClass
        FROM    SCHEDULED_CLASSES
        WHERE   course_number = iCourseID
        AND     ssn           = iStudentSSN;

        RETURN iCreditsForClass;
    END Get_Course_Credits;

BEGIN
    FOR StudentClasses_rec IN StudentClasses_cur LOOP
        iCourse     := StudentClasses_rec.course_number;
        iTotalHours := StudentClasses_rec.course_hours;

        iTotalCredits :=   iTotalCredits
                         + Get_Course_Credits (iCourse);
    END LOOP;
```

```
    UPDATE STUDENTS
    SET    overall_gpa = (iTotalCredits / iTotalHours)
    WHERE  ssn = iStudentSSN;

EXCEPTION
   WHEN ZERO_DIVIDE THEN
       System.Log_Error (vObjectName =>'Calculate_GPA',
                         vErrorText  => SQLERRM,
                         vParameters => to_char (iCourseID) ||
                                        '^' ||
                                        to_char (iStudentSSN));
END Calculate_GPA;
```

Variable Declarations

The variable declarations section of a procedure allows you to define variables, constants, and user-defined exceptions that will be used by the procedure. The variable declarations section of a procedure is highlighted in Listing 4.17.

Listing 4.17   The variable declarations portion of a procedure.

```
PROCEDURE Calculate_GPA (iStudentSSN IN     number)

IS

    CURSOR StudentClasses_cur
    IS
    SELECT SC.course_number, C.course_hours
    FROM   SCHEDULED_CLASSES SC,
           CLASSES           C
    WHERE  ssn = iStudentSSN
    AND    credit_flag = 'Y'
    AND    audit_flag  = 'N';

    iTotalCredits    integer := 0;
    iTotalHours      integer := 0;

    FUNCTION Get_Course_Credits (iCourseID IN     integer)
    RETURN integer

    IS

      iCreditsForClass integer := 0;
```

```
    BEGIN
        SELECT decode (course_grade, 'A', 4,
                                     'B', 3,
                                     'C', 2,
                                     'D', 1, 0)
        INTO    iCreditsForClass
        FROM    SCHEDULED_CLASSES
        WHERE   course_number = iCourseID
        AND     ssn           = iStudentSSN;

        RETURN iCreditsForClass;
    END Get_Course_Credits;

BEGIN
    FOR StudentClasses_rec IN StudentClasses_cur LOOP
        iCourse     := StudentClasses_rec.course_number;
        iTotalHours := StudentClasses_rec.course_hours;

        iTotalCredits :=   iTotalCredits
                       + Get_Course_Credits (iCourse);
    END LOOP;

    UPDATE STUDENTS
    SET    overall_gpa = (iTotalCredits / iTotalHours)
    WHERE  ssn = iStudentSSN;

EXCEPTION
    WHEN ZERO_DIVIDE THEN
        System.Log_Error (vObjectName =>'Calculate_GPA',
                          vErrorText  => SQLERRM,
                          vParameters => to_char (iCourseID) ||
                                         '^' ||
                                         to_char (iStudentSSN));
END Calculate_GPA;
```

Executable Declarations

The executable declarations portion of a procedure allows the definition of local procedures and functions that will be used by the procedure. The executable declarations portion of the procedure is highlighted in Listing 4.18.

Listing 4.18 The executable declarations portion of a procedure.

```
PROCEDURE Calculate_GPA (iStudentSSN IN    number)

IS

    CURSOR StudentClasses_cur
    IS
    SELECT SC.course_number, C.course_hours
    FROM   SCHEDULED_CLASSES SC,
           CLASSES           C
    WHERE  ssn = iStudentSSN
    AND    credit_flag = 'Y'
    AND    audit_flag  = 'N';

    iTotalCredits   integer := 0;
    iTotalHours     integer := 0;

    FUNCTION Get_Course_Credits (iCourseID IN    integer)
    RETURN integer

    IS

        iCreditsForClass integer := 0;

    BEGIN
        SELECT decode (course_grade, 'A', 4,
                                     'B', 3,
                                     'C', 2,
                                     'D', 1, 0)
        INTO    iCreditsForClass
        FROM    SCHEDULED_CLASSES
        WHERE   course_number = iCourseID
        AND     ssn           = iStudentSSN;

        RETURN iCreditsForClass;
    END Get_Course_Credits;

BEGIN
    FOR StudentClasses_rec IN StudentClasses_cur LOOP
        iCourse      := StudentClasses_rec.course_number;
        iTotalHours  := StudentClasses_rec.course_hours;
```

```
    iTotalCredits :=   iTotalCredits
                    + Get_Course_Credits (iCourse);
END LOOP;

UPDATE STUDENTS
SET    overall_gpa = (iTotalCredits / iTotalHours)
WHERE  ssn = iStudentSSN;

EXCEPTION
   WHEN ZERO_DIVIDE THEN
       System.Log_Error (vObjectName =>'Calculate_GPA',
                         vErrorText  => SQLERRM,
                         vParameters => to_char (iCourseID) ||
                                        '^' ||
                                        to_char (iStudentSSN));
END Calculate_GPA;
```

The Procedure Body

The SQL and PL/SQL statements that follow the **BEGIN** statement and precede
the **EXCEPTION** and/or **END** statements is the body of the procedure. The highlighted portion of Listing 4.19 is the procedure's body.

Listing 4.19   The body of a procedure.

```
PROCEDURE Calculate_GPA (iStudentSSN IN     number)

IS

   CURSOR StudentClasses_cur
   IS
   SELECT SC.course_number, C.course_hours
   FROM   SCHEDULED_CLASSES SC,
          CLASSES           C
   WHERE  ssn = iStudentSSN
   AND    credit_flag = 'Y'
   AND    audit_flag  = 'N';

   iTotalCredits     integer := 0;
   iTotalHours       integer := 0;

   FUNCTION Get_Course_Credits (iCourseID IN     integer)
   RETURN integer
```

```
    IS

        iCreditsForClass integer := 0;

    BEGIN
        SELECT decode (course_grade, 'A', 4,
                                     'B', 3,
                                     'C', 2,
                                     'D', 1, 0)
        INTO    iCreditsForClass
        FROM    SCHEDULED_CLASSES
        WHERE   course_number = iCourseID
        AND     ssn           = iStudentSSN;

        RETURN iCreditsForClass;
    END Get_Course_Credits;

BEGIN
    FOR StudentClasses_rec IN StudentClasses_cur LOOP
        iCourse     := StudentClasses_rec.course_number;
        iTotalHours := StudentClasses_rec.course_hours;


        iTotalCredits :=    iTotalCredits
                          + Get_Course_Credits (iCourse);
    END LOOP;


    UPDATE STUDENTS
    SET    overall_gpa = (iTotalCredits / iTotalHours)
    WHERE  ssn = iStudentSSN;

EXCEPTION
    WHEN ZERO_DIVIDE THEN
        System.Log_Error (vObjectName =>'Calculate_GPA',
                          vErrorText  => SQLERRM,
                          vParameters => to_char (iCourseID) ||
                                         '^' ||
                                         to_char (iStudentSSN));
END Calculate_GPA;
```

Exception Handlers

Exception handlers are defined within the procedure to handle error conditions that could reasonably be expected to occur while the procedure is executing. In

Listing 4.20, the developer feels that the **ZERO_DIVIDE** exception (one of the standard PL/SQL exceptions) could reasonably be expected to occur while calculating the student's new GPA.

Listing 4.20   The exception handler of a procedure.

```
PROCEDURE Calculate_GPA (iStudentSSN IN    number)

IS

    CURSOR StudentClasses_cur
    IS
    SELECT SC.course_number, C.course_hours
    FROM   SCHEDULED_CLASSES SC,
           CLASSES            C
    WHERE  ssn = iStudentSSN
    AND    credit_flag = 'Y'
    AND    audit_flag  = 'N';

    iTotalCredits    integer := 0;
    iTotalHours      integer := 0;

    FUNCTION Get_Course_Credits (iCourseID IN    integer)
    RETURN integer

    IS

        iCreditsForClass integer := 0;

    BEGIN
        SELECT decode (course_grade, 'A', 4,
                                     'B', 3,
                                     'C', 2,
                                     'D', 1, 0)
        INTO   iCreditsForClass
        FROM   SCHEDULED_CLASSES
        WHERE  course_number = iCourseID
        AND    ssn           = iStudentSSN;

        RETURN iCreditsForClass;
    END Get_Course_Credits;

BEGIN
    FOR StudentClasses_rec IN StudentClasses_cur LOOP
        iCourse     := StudentClasses_rec.course_number;
        iTotalHours := StudentClasses_rec.course_hours;
```

```
        iTotalCredits :=    iTotalCredits
                      + Get_Course_Credits (iCourse);
    END LOOP;

    UPDATE STUDENTS
    SET    overall_gpa = (iTotalCredits / iTotalHours)
    WHERE  ssn = iStudentSSN;

EXCEPTION
    WHEN ZERO_DIVIDE THEN
        System.Log_Error (vObjectName =>'Calculate_GPA',
                          vErrorText  => SQLERRM,
                          vParameters => to_char (iCourseID) ||
                                         '^' ||
                                         to_char (iStudentSSN));
END Calculate_GPA;
```

Exceptions occur for one of three reasons:

- Oracle detects an unexpected error while the object is executing.

- An exception is explicitly raised using the **RAISE** statement.

- An exception is raised using the **Raise_Application_Error**() procedure.

Unexpected Errors

If an error occurs during the execution of an object, Oracle raises an exception and generates the most appropriate error text.

If the error message corresponds to one of the predefined exceptions that PL/SQL uses, the error can be handled using an exception handler for the predefined exception. Table 4.2 lists these predefined exceptions and their associated Oracle error message numbers.

You can redeclare these predefined exceptions and create custom handlers for your new exceptions, but Oracle will not recognize your new exception when it attempts to raise one of the predefined exceptions. Your best bet is to leave the predefined exceptions alone and create your own user-defined exceptions.

While the predefined exceptions are quite useful and deal with the most commonly encountered error conditions quite well, it's not uncommon for other errors to be encountered as well. To allow you to handle specified errors that don't have a predefined exception, Oracle has provided the **OTHERS** exception handler.

Table 4.2   Predefined exceptions in PL/SQL.

Exception	Associated Oracle Error
CURSOR_ALREADY_OPEN	ORA-06511
DUP_VAL_ON_INDEX	ORA-00001
INVALID_CURSOR	ORA-01001
INVALID_NUMBER	ORA-01722
LOGIN_DENIED	ORA-01017
NO_DATA_FOUND	ORA-01403
NOT_LOGGED_ON	ORA-01012
PROGRAM_ERROR	ORA-06501
STORAGE_ERROR	ORA-06500
TIMEOUT_ON_RESOURCE	ORA-00051
TOO_MANY_ROWS	ORA-01422
TRANSACTION_BACKED_OUT	ORA-00061
VALUE_ERROR	ORA-06502
ZERO_DIVIDE	ORA-01476

Listing 4.21 illustrates the use of an **OTHERS** exception handler.

Listing 4.21   Using the **OTHERS** exception handler.

```
BEGIN
   <statements>

EXCEPTION
   WHEN OTHERS THEN
      <error handling code>
END;
```

The code that follows the **OTHERS** exception handler is written to handle errors that you don't expect. Often, this code is a call to another procedure that logs a message to a table containing specific information about the error (the text of the Oracle error, the parameters of the procedure or function in which the error occurred, and any other relevant information).

You can also use the **OTHERS** exception handler in conjunction with the **SQLERRM()** and **SQLCODE()** functions that PL/SQL provides, as shown in Listing 4.22.

Listing 4.22   Using **SQLCODE()** and **SQLERRM()** in an **OTHERS** exception handler.

```
BEGIN
   <statements>

EXCEPTION
   WHEN OTHERS THEN
      IF (SQLCODE = -942) THEN
         DBMS_Output.Put_Line (SQLERRM);

      ELSE
         RAISE;
      END IF;
END;
```

This example calls the **SQLCODE()** function to determine what error is occurring and **SQLERRM()** to record the text of the error message.

Using RAISE

You can cause exceptions to be raised in your code by using the **RAISE** statement. Listing 4.23 illustrates the use of the statement.

Listing 4.23   Using the **RAISE** statement in your code.

```
BEGIN
   IF <some condition> THEN
      RAISE xABORT_PROCEDURE;
   END IF;

EXCEPTION
   WHEN xABORT_PROCEDURE THEN
      ROLLBACK;
END;
```

Using User-Defined Exceptions

It's a good idea not to explicitly raise the predefined Oracle exceptions. Doing so confuses the debugging process. Consider the following example:

```
FOR StudentClasses_rec IN StudentClasses_cur LOOP
   SELECT course_hours
   INTO   iCourseHours
```

```
    FROM    CLASSES
    WHERE   course_number = iCourseID;

    iTotalClasses := iTotalClasses + 1;
END LOOP;

IF (iTotalClasses = 0) THEN
    RAISE NO_DATA_FOUND;
END IF;
```

If your code looks like this example and you're receiving a NO_DATA_FOUND exception, you can't be certain where the exception is originating without doing some extra debugging work. It would be much better to define an appropriately named user-defined exception, say xSTUDENT_HAS_NO_CLASSES, and explicitly raise that exception instead.

If you must raise an exception under a certain condition, take advantage of the power and flexibility of user-defined exceptions.

Using Raise_Application_Error()

Oracle provides the **Raise_Application_Error()** procedure to allow you to raise custom error numbers within your applications. You can generate errors and their associated text starting with -20000 and proceeding through -20999 (a grand total of 1,000 error numbers that you can use). Listing 4.24 illustrates the use of the **Raise_Application_Error()** procedure.

Listing 4.24 Using the **Raise_Application_Error()** procedure.

```
DECLARE
    Balance    integer := 24;

BEGIN
    IF (nBalance <= 100) THEN
        Raise_Application_Error (-20343, 'The balance is too low.');
    END IF;
END;
```

In this example, error number -20343 is raised if the value of **nBalance** isn't greater than 100, yielding a message that looks like this:

```
ORA-20343: The balance is too low.
```

Documenting Procedures

The essential elements of documentation are the same for both procedures and functions. Your documentation must cover the following three basic aspects of the procedure:

- *Purpose*—What business rules does the procedure enforce? Are there any special situations that the procedure has to handle?

- *Parameters*—What are the parameters, and how are they used? Are any of the parameters restricted with regard to size or values?

- *Error conditions*—What exceptions can the procedure propagate to the calling module?

The most common and useful place to document a procedure is within the procedure's source code. This is accomplished through the use of header text, meaningfully named identifiers, and thorough commenting. It's also useful to write pseudocode for the procedure before the code is written. This pseudocode can often be turned into a template for the comments that need to be placed in the code.

The Header

The *header* (or prologue) is intended to handle documentation within the procedure itself. While creating and maintaining a header requires some extra work, the trade-off for this work is easier maintenance in the future. Listing 4.25 contains a sample header for the **Calculate_GPA()** procedure.

Listing 4.25   The **Calculate_GPA()** procedure with a header.

```
PROCEDURE Calculate_GPA (iStudentSSN IN    number)

-- ***********************************************************
-- Description: The procedure Calculate_GPA accepts a student's
-- social security number as a parameter, loops through all the
-- classes for the students that are not being audited and are
-- taken for credit, and sums the credit points earned and hours
-- for the class.
--
-- The procedure then updates the overall_gpa column in the
-- STUDENTS table to the value of the total credit points earned
-- divided by the total hours for all classes taken.
--
```

```
--  REVISION HISTORY
--  Date        Author        Reason for Change
--  -------------------------------------------------------------
--  02/28/1997 J. Schmoe    Procedure created.
--  ********************************************************************;

IS

    CURSOR StudentClasses_cur
    IS
    SELECT  SC.course_number, C.course_hours
    FROM    SCHEDULED_CLASSES SC,
            CLASSES           C
    WHERE   SC.ssn        = iStudentSSN
    AND     C.credit_flag = 'Y'
    AND     C.audit_flag  = 'N';

    iTotalCredits    integer := 0;
    iTotalHours      integer := 0;

    FUNCTION Get_Course_Credits (iCourseID IN      integer)
    RETURN integer

    IS

        iCreditsForClass integer := 0;

    BEGIN
        SELECT decode (course_grade, 'A', 4,
                                     'B', 3,
                                     'C', 2,
                                     'D', 1, 0)
        INTO    iCreditsForClass
        FROM    SCHEDULED_CLASSES
        WHERE   course_number = iCourseID
        AND     ssn           = iStudentSSN;

        RETURN iCreditsForClass;
    END Get_Course_Credits;

BEGIN
    FOR StudentClasses_rec IN StudentClasses_cur LOOP
        iCourse     := StudentClasses_rec.course_number;
        iTotalHours := StudentClasses_rec.course_hours;
```

```
        iTotalCredits :=   iTotalCredits
                        + Get_Course_Credits (iCourse);
    END LOOP;

    UPDATE STUDENTS
    SET    overall_gpa = (iTotalCredits / iTotalHours)
    WHERE  ssn = iStudentSSN;

EXCEPTION
    WHEN ZERO_DIVIDE THEN
        System.Log_Error (vObjectName =>'Calculate_GPA',
                          vErrorText  => SQLERRM,
                          vParameters => to_char (iCourseID) ||
                                         '^' ||
                                         to_char (iStudentSSN));
END Calculate_GPA;
```

Pseudocode

It's often useful to write pseudocode when designing a new procedure. Pseudocode should outline the logical steps of a procedure. Listing 4.26 contains pseudocode for the **Calculate_GPA()** procedure.

Listing 4.26   Pseudocode for the **Calculate_GPA()** procedure.

```
for each class taken by the student loop
    if the class is not being audited and earns credit then
        get the credit points earned for the class;
        get the total hours for the class;

        determine the number of credit points earned for the class;

        add hours for the class to credited hours taken total;
        add credit points to a running total;
end loop;

update the STUDENTS table, setting the overall_gpa column
    to the value of the total credit points earned divided by
    the total number of credited hours taken;
```

Creating this type of logical map for a procedure shortens the time required to write the procedure and also allows nondevelopers (perhaps those who are more familiar with the business rules but are not developers) to look at the logic of the procedure and spot errors.

Pseudocode for procedures often serves as a map for commenting the procedure, as well.

Comments

A good comment in source code can describe the functionality of code as effectively as pages and pages of written documentation outside the code. Good comments describe why the code does what it does, often explaining how the code enforces business rules. Consider the following two sample comments:

Comment A:

```
--
-- If the account balance isn't at least $100, we can't upgrade the
-- account to Gold level.
--
IF (nBalance < 100) THEN
    Raise_Application_Error (-20343, 'The balance is too low.');
END IF;
```

Comment B:

```
--
-- If nBalance < 100, raise an error.
--
IF (nBalance < 100) THEN
    Raise_Application_Error (-20343, 'The balance is too low.');
END IF;
```

Comment A explains why the code is written this way. Comment B paraphrases the code but doesn't explain the business rules behind the code. There is very little in Comment B that will help you understand the purpose of the code.

Single-Line Versus Multi-Line Comments

Although PL/SQL supports both single-line and multi-line comments, it's a good idea to only use single-line comments in your code, because, at some point, you might need to comment out a large block of code. PL/SQL doesn't support nested C-style comments.

The exception to this rule is when you're working in a 3GL language using one of Oracle's precompilers. In this situation, you should use the commenting style that is specified by your coding standards for the 3GL, because the Oracle precompilers often don't recognize the single-line style of commenting.

Identifiers

Take a look at this block of code and see if you can recognize the purpose of the variables:

```
IF (x < 100) THEN
   Raise_Application_Error (-20343, 'The balance is too low.');;
END IF;
```

You might recognize this code as the same code described just a few lines ago, sans comments and with different variable names. Keeping track of x in three lines of code is easy, but keeping track of x in a 200-line procedure is another story entirely.

Using meaningful identifier names is the best way to document code, as well as one of the easiest. Six months down the road, you might have to debug your 200-line procedure that uses x, y, and z for variable names.

Step-By-Step: Design A Procedure

Now, it's time dive into building a procedure from scratch. We'll start with a problem and discuss the relevant data structures, then we'll design and write the procedure.

Procedure Requirements

Your assignment is to automate the year-end raise calculations for employees. After some quick thoughts of the wonderful raise you could give yourself, you start taking a look at the following rules that determine eligibility and amounts for the raises:

- If an employee has been on time more than 98 percent of the time, the employee earns a .5 percent raise.

- If an employee is always on time, an extra .1 percent.

- The amount of an employee's raise is the sum of the percentages earned from individual qualifying factors.

- If an employee has received four or more warnings, no raise can be given to the employee.

- A performance rating higher than 8 earns an employee a .5 percent raise.

All the information needed for the procedure is stored in the **EMPLOYEES** table, as follows:

```
employee_num          NOT NULL    number (6)
first_name            NOT NULL    varchar2 (12)
last_name             NOT NULL    varchar2 (12)
ssn                   NOT NULL    number (9)
home_phone            NOT NULL    number (10)
eff_hire_date         NOT NULL    date
base_salary           NOT NULL    number (8,2)
eff_termination_date              date
middle_name                       varchar2 (12)
late_days                         number
warnings                          number
overtime_hours                    number (5,2)
performance_rating                number (2)
```

The procedure won't take any parameters because it has to run for all employees. We'll call the procedure **Annual_Review**(), because it's going to be run once a year and gives raises based on some gauges of employee performance.

Design

The first step to designing the procedure is to determine how each individual requirement can be met.

- We can determine the percentage of the employee's on-time days by subtracting the number of **late_days** from the total working days for a year and then calculating a percentage value. If the percentage value is greater than 98 percent, add to the raise amount.

- It is pretty straightforward if an employee is always on time. No late days, an extra something in the raise. If the total number of **late_days** for the employee equals zero, the employee earns an extra .1 percent on the raise.

- The procedure has to keep a running total of the percentages added and then update the salary once.

- If four or more warnings are received, no raise. This can be determined by checking the **warnings** column in the **EMPLOYEES** table.

- The **EMPLOYEES** table contains a **performance_rating** column, which accepts integer values from 1 through 10. If this value is higher than 8, add .5 percent to the total raise.

Pseudocode

After determining how each individual requirement can be met, we can write some pseudocode that puts the logic for the procedure together. This allows us to clarify our thoughts about the procedure and to put those same thoughts into a form that can be looked over by someone who is more familiar with the business rules.

Listing 4.27 shows the pseudocode for the **Annual_Review**() procedure.

Listing 4.27   Pseudocode for the **Annual_Review()** procedure.

```
open a cursor of all employees;

for each employee loop
    determine how often the employee has been on time;

    if the employee is on time more than 98% then
        grant a .5% raise;

        if the employee has no late days then
            grant another .1% raise;
        end if;
    end if;

    if the employee has four or more warnings then
        skip this employee -- no raise;
    end if;

    if performance rating is higher than 8 then
        grant a .5% raise;
    end if;

    calculate the new salary;

    update the base_salary column in the EMPLOYEES table;
end loop;
```

```
commit changes;

if any errors occur then
    rollback;
end if;
```

This pseudocode seems like it will do the trick, but looking at it a little more closely, we notice that we're checking the warnings after doing some other things. Because warnings can disqualify the employee from getting a raise, the procedure will work a bit more quickly if no work is done until after the warnings are checked. Figure 4.2 illustrates the logical execution of the procedure.

Code

Now that the pseudocode for the procedure has been written and looked over for logic errors, the code can be written using the pseudocode as a base. The final draft of the **Annual_Review()** procedure is shown in Listing 4.28.

Listing 4.28   The code for the **Annual_Review()** procedure.

```
PROCEDURE Annual_Review

IS

    xCONTINUE_LOOP        EXCEPTION;
    iLateDays             integer;
    iPerforanceRating     integer;
    iWarningsIssued       integer;
    nBaseSalary           number;
    nOntimeRating         number;
    nTotalRaisePercent    number;


    --
    -- The total number of working days in the year. This is
    -- calculated as follows:
    --
    --      104 weekend days
    --       10 paid holidays (11 in leap year)
    --       10 sick days
    --
    TOTAL_WORKING_DAYS  CONSTANT integer := 241;


    --
    -- Any employee working for the company for over one year.
```

```
      --
      CURSOR All_Employees_cur
      IS
      SELECT employee_num, eff_hire_date, base_salary,
             late_days, warnings, performance_rating
      FROM    EMPLOYEES
      WHERE    (to_char (SYSDATE, 'YYYY')
               - to_char (eff_hire_date, 'YYYY')) > 1;


      FUNCTION Raise_Salary (nBaseSalary  IN      number,
                             nRaiseAmount IN      number)


      RETURN number

      IS

      BEGIN
         RETURN ( nBaseSalary
               + (nBaseSalary * nRaiseAmount));
      END;

 BEGIN
      FOR All_Employees_rec IN All_Employees_cur LOOP
         BEGIN
             iLateDays          := All_Employees_rec.late_days;
             iPerformanceRating := All_Employees_rec.performance_rating;
             iWarningsIssued    := All_Employees_rec.warnings;
             nBaseSalary        := All_Employees_rec.base_salary;
             nOntimeRating      := 0;
             nTotalRaisePercent := 0.0;
             nIncreasedSalary   := 0.0;


             --
             -- If the employee has 4 or more warnings issued, go to
             -- the next employee.
             --
             IF (iWarningsIssued > 3) THEN
                RAISE xCONTINUE_LOOP;
             END IF;

             nOntimeRating := ( TOTAL_WORKING_DAYS
                             - iLateDays);

             nOntimeRating := (nOntimeRating / TOTAL_WORKING_DAYS) * 100;
```

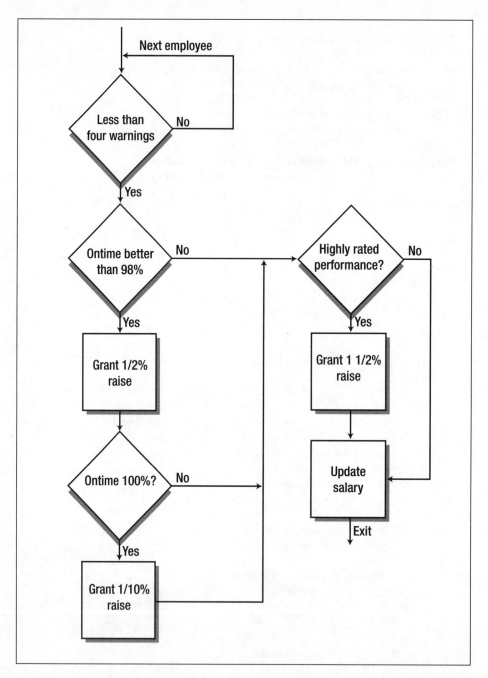

Figure 4.2
The logical execution of the **Annual_Review()** procedure.

```
    IF (nOntimeRating > 98) THEN
        nTotalRaisePercent := nTotalRaisePercent + 0.005;

        IF (iLateDays = 0) THEN
            nTotalRaisePercent := nTotalRaisePercent + 0.001;
        END IF;
    END IF;

    IF (iPerformanceRating > 8) THEN
        nTotalRaisePercent := nTotalRaisePercent + .005;
    END IF;

    nIncreasedSalary := Raise_Salary
                        (nBaseSalary  => nBaseSalary,
                         nRaiseAmount => nTotalRaisePercent);

    UPDATE EMPLOYEES
    SET     base_salary = nIncreasedSalary
    WHERE   CURRENT OF All_Employees_cur;

    EXCEPTION
        WHEN xCONTINUE_LOOP THEN
            NULL;
    END;
END LOOP;

COMMIT;

EXCEPTION
    WHEN OTHERS THEN
        ROLLBACK;
END;
```

The **xCONTINUE_LOOP** user-defined exception is raised when the employee has four or more warnings. Using this exception allows us to avoid using a **GOTO** statement inside the loop to skip to the next iteration.

Testing The Procedure

Our code looks like it will do the trick, and it compiles cleanly, but we're not done yet. The procedure can't go into production until it has been tested thoroughly. After all, these are real dollars we're playing with here!

The unit test script for the procedure can be outlined by breaking the requirements down into both positive and negative tests, as follows:

- Create an employee with only one late day and a base salary of $20,000. Because no other factors will come into play, the employee's new salary should be $20,100 after calling **Annual_Review**().

- Create an employee with five late days (just under 98 percent) and a base salary of $20,000. Because no other factors will come into play, the employee's salary should remain at $20,000 after calling **Annual_Review**().

- Create an employee with no late days and a base salary of $20,000. Because no other factors will come into play, the employee's new salary should be $20,120.

- Create an employee with four warnings and a base salary of $20,000. Because the employee has four warnings, the employee's base salary should remain at $20,000.

- Create an employee with a performance rating of 7 and a base salary of $20,000. Because the employee's performance did not rate above 8, there should be no change in the base salary.

- Create an employee with a performance rating of 9 and a base salary of $20,000. Because the employee has a performance rating higher than 8, the new base salary should be $20,100.

We'll assume that the procedure won't be tested in a real data environment. This will allow us to set up each test condition by creating the appropriate test data in an empty **EMPLOYEES** table. Once we have a proper data set, each requirement can be tested. The logic for each test looks something like this:

```
clean out the EMPLOYEES table;

add test data to the table;

predict the results;

call the procedure;

check the results by querying the table;
```

Now that we've isolated the tests that have to be performed, it's a simple matter to write a script that handles each condition. The first of these scripts is shown in Listing 4.29.

Listing 4.29   Part of the unit testing scripts for the **Annual_Review()** procedure.

```
DECLARE
    nSalary     number;

BEGIN
    --
    -- Create an employee with only 1 late day and no other raise
    -- earning conditions. Base salary will be 20000, the expected
    -- raise will be .5% (100 dollars).
    --
    INSERT
    INTO    EMPLOYEES
            (employee_num,
             first_name,
             last_name,
             ssn,
             home_phone,
             eff_hire_date,
             base_salary,
             eff_termination_date,
             middle_name,
             late_days,
             warnings,
             overtime_hours,
             performance_rating)
    VALUES (999999,
            'Joe',
            'Schmoe',
            999999999,
            2065550123,
            to_date ('02/02/1982'),
            20000,
            NULL,
            NULL,
            1,
            0,
            0,
            8);
```

```
   Annual_Review;

   SELECT base_salary
   INTO   nSalary
   FROM   EMPLOYEES
   WHERE  employee_num = 999999;

   DBMS_Output.Put_Line ('Base salary is now: ' ||
                         to_char (nSalary));

   IF (nSalary != 20100) THEN
      DBMS_Output.Put_Line ('ERROR: Incorrect result!');
   END IF;
END;
```

Summary

Chapter 4 covers the fundamentals of creating stored procedures within the Oracle database. At this point, you should be familiar with the PL/SQL needed to create a stored procedure and have some insights into designing and testing stored procedures. Now, let's take a look at functions in Chapter 5.

Functions

CHAPTER

5

Functions

A *function* is a simple procedure that accomplishes a very specific task and returns a value to the calling procedure. In C, every subprogram is a function and has a return value. PL/SQL supports both functions and procedures (discussed in Chapter 4).

This chapter will discuss the uses and creation of functions using PL/SQL. Several detailed examples are provided, and you are guided through the process of creating a new function, from design to testing. By the end of this chapter, you will be prepared to design, create, and test your own functions.

Advantages Of Functions

The ability to store functions within the Oracle database allows you to reach great heights in modularity, maintainability, and performance improvement. Using functions to accomplish specific tasks improves the reliability of other modules and reduces development time.

Embedded SQL

PL/SQL functions can execute any DML statement that can be executed in SQL*Plus, as shown in Listing 5.1.

Listing 5.1 A PL/SQL function that utilizes a DML statement.

```
FUNCTION Grant_Vacation (nAddDays       IN     number,
                         nFacultyMember IN     number)

    RETURN number

IS

BEGIN
    SELECT base_vacation
    INTO   nVacationDays
```

```
   FROM    FACULTY
   WHERE   faculty_id = nFacultyMember;

   RETURN (nVacationDays + nAddDays);
END;
```

Maintainability

Because functions are ideally small blocks of code, they are easier to code, test, and correct. Assuming that the parameters and return value of a function aren't changed, modifications to the code inside the function will not affect modules that call the function. Consider the example in Listing 5.2.

Listing 5.2   A procedure calling the **Raise_Salary()** function.

```
PROCEDURE Annual_Review (nEmployee IN      number)

IS

   nReviewScore    number;

BEGIN
   SELECT review_score
   INTO   nReviewScore
   FROM   PERFORMANCE_REVIEWS
   WHERE  employee_num = nEmployee;

   IF (nReviewScore > 90) THEN
      SELECT base_salary
      INTO   nEmployeeSalary
      FROM   EMPLOYEES
      WHERE  employee_num = nEmployee;

      UPDATE EMPLOYEES
      SET    base_salary = Raise_Salary
                (nBaseSalary    => nEmployeeSalary,
                 nRaisePercent => 1);
   END IF;
END;
```

Altering the internal logic of the **Raise_Salary**() function will not affect the internal logic of the **Annual_Review**() procedure. If a parameter is altered, added to, or removed from the function, or the datatype of the function's return value is altered, the procedure must also be changed to accommodate the changes to the function.

Modularity

Creating functions to perform specific tasks is an inherently modular approach. Consider again the **Raise_Salary()** function. If more than one procedure needs to be able to give an employee a raise, each of these procedures can call the function.

Performance Improvement

A stored PL/SQL object helps improve performance because the object has already been compiled into *p-code* (the machine executable version of the code) when the function is called. The database does not have to compile the object again before executing it.

If the stored objects contain DML statements, another level of potential performance improvement is gained. This is because the DML statements are more likely to be cached in the SGA when the function is executed, eliminating Oracle's need to re-parse the DML statement if a match is found.

Reliability

Testing a function like **Raise_Salary()** is accomplished easily with a testing script, like the one shown in Listing 5.3.

Listing 5.3 A testing script for the **Raise_Salary()** function.

```
DECLARE
   nResult  number;

BEGIN
   DBMS_Output.Put_Line ('Calling Raise_Salary for 3.5 % ' ||
                         'of $20,000. The result should be ' ||
                         '$20,700.');

   nResult := Raise_Salary (nBaseSalary   => 20000,
                            nRaisePercent => 3.5);

   DBMS_Output.Put_Line (to_char (nResult));

   IF (nResult <> 20700) THEN
      DBMS_Output.Put_Line ('ERROR: Function returned wrong value!');
   END IF;
END;
```

Once the test has been successfully run on the function, any procedure or function can call the **Raise_Salary**() function with the knowledge that the function has already been tested.

Creating And Dropping Functions

Functions are created using a command like the one shown in Listing 5.4.

Listing 5.4   Creating a function.

```
CREATE OR REPLACE
FUNCTION Raise_Salary (nBaseSalary   IN      number,
                       nRaisePercent IN      number)

   RETURN number;

IS

BEGIN
   RETURN (nBaseSalary * nRaisePercent);
END;
/
```

Using the **OR REPLACE** clause indicates that Oracle should replace an existing function of the same name if it exists. If the object exists and the **OR REPLACE** clause isn't used, an error will occur. The **/** instructs SQL*Plus to execute the **CREATE** command.

Functions are dropped from inside SQL*Plus using the **DROP** command:

```
DROP FUNCTION Raise_Salary;
```

Local Functions

Functions may also be declared within another block of stored PL/SQL code. This is somewhat unusual. Most functions are created as standalone objects to provide greater modularity. Listing 5.5 illustrates the definition of a function as part of a procedure's declarations.

Listing 5.5 Declaring a local function within a procedure.

```
PROCEDURE Annual_Review

IS

    iPerformanceRating  integer;
    iWarningsIssued     integer;
    nBaseSalary         number;
    nOntimeRating       number;
    nTotalRaisePercent  number;
    nTotalBonus         number;

    --
    -- The total number of working days in the year. This is
    -- calculated as follows:
    --
    --      104 weekend days
    --       10 paid holidays (11 in leap year)
    --       10 sick days
    --
    TOTAL_WORKING_DAYS  CONSTANT integer := 241;

    --
    -- Any employee working for the company for over one year.
    --
    CURSOR All_Employees_cur
    IS
    SELECT employee_num, eff_hire_date, base_salary,
           late_days, warnings, performance_rating
    FROM   EMPLOYEES
    WHERE   (to_date (SYSDATE, 'YYYY')
            - to_date (eff_hire_date, 'YYYY')) > 1;

    FUNCTION Raise_Salary (nBaseSalary  IN     number,
                           nRaiseAmount IN     number)

    RETURN number

    IS

    BEGIN
        RETURN (nBaseSalary * nRaiseAmount);
    END;

BEGIN
```

```
FOR All_Employees_rec IN All_Employees_cur LOOP
    --
    -- Initialize the variables each time through the
    -- loop (once for each employee).
    --
    iPerformanceRating := All_Employees_rec.performance_rating;
    iWarningsIssued    := All_Employees_rec.warnings;
    nBaseSalary        := All_Employees_rec.base_salary;
    nOntimeRating      := 0;
    nTotalRaisePercent := 0.0;
    nIncreasedSalary   := 0.0;
    nTotalBonus        := 0.0;


    --
    -- Calculate the number of days that the employee was on time
    -- for work. If this percentage is above 98%, the employee
    -- earns a .5% pay raise.
    --
    nOntimeRating := ( TOTAL_WORKING_DAYS
                       - All_Employees_rec.late_days);
    nOntimeRating := (nOntimeRating / TOTAL_WORKING_DAYS) * 100;

    IF (nOntimeRating > 98) THEN
        nTotalRaisePercent := nTotalRaisePercent + 0.005;


        --
        -- Perfect attendance gets a higher bonus percentage too!
        --
        IF (nOntimeRating = 100) THEN
            nTotalRaisePercent := nTotalRaisePercent + 0.001;
        END IF;
    END IF;



        .
        .
        .



    --
    -- Store the outcome of the analysis in the EMPLOYEES table.
    --
    UPDATE EMPLOYEES
    SET    base_salary = nIncreasedSalary,
           xmas_bonus  = nTotalBonus
    WHERE  CURRENT OF All_Employees_cur;
END LOOP;
END;
```

Local functions are accessible only to the procedure or function that declares the local object. Local functions can also reference constants, variables, datatypes, and user-defined exceptions defined within the containing procedure or function. In Listing 5.5, the **Raise_Salary**() function is accessible only to the procedure **Annual_Review**() and can access all the variables and constants defined within the procedure.

If a function needs to be referenced from more than one stored object, local definitions aren't appropriate. For maintenance and testing purposes, it's probably better to define most (if not all) objects as standalone objects.

Dependencies

When an object makes a reference to another object, a *dependency* is created. The **ALL_DEPENDENCIES** view in Oracle's data dictionary contains a complete listing of the dependencies among objects stored in the database. The structure of the **ALL_DEPENDENCIES** view is shown in Listing 5.6.

Listing 5.6   The structure of the **ALL_DEPENDENCIES** view.

```
name               varchar2 (30)
type               varchar2 (12)
owner              varchar2 (30)
referenced_name    varchar2 (30)
referenced_type    varchar2 (12)
referenced_owner   varchar2 (30)
```

Determining The Effects Of A Code Change

You can use the following query to find objects that have a dependency to a block of code that you need to modify.

```
SELECT type || ' ' || owner || '.' || name
FROM   ALL_DEPENDENCIES
WHERE  referenced_owner = upper ('&1')
AND    referenced_name  = upper ('&2')
ORDER BY type;
```

In this example, &1 is the schema of the object that you need to modify, and &2 is the name of the object. The query might produce an output as follows:

```
FUNCTION HR.RAISE_SALARY
FUNCTION HR.ADD_VACATION
FUNCTION HR.ADD_BONUS
FUNCTION HR.VEST_401K
FUNCTION ENGINEERING.ADD_TARDY
FUNCTION ENGINEERING.REMOVE_TARDY
PROCEDURE HR.ANNUAL_REVIEW
PACKAGE BODY HR.PERFORMANCE_LIBRARY
```

Parameters

Parameters for functions are handled in the same way as parameters for procedures. Function parameters may be **IN** parameters, **OUT** parameters, or **IN OUT** parameters. Functions may accept no parameters, one parameter, or many parameters—this is decided by you, the application developer.

Datatypes

Functions are very much like procedures, and the parameters for functions follow the same rules as the parameters for procedures.

Using OUT And IN OUT Parameters

By definition, a PL/SQL function should return a value only through the use of the **RETURN** statement. However, Oracle allows you to define parameters for functions using the **OUT** and **IN OUT** definitions.

Using this approach allows you to have a function return more than one value; however, this is poor programming style and is not recommended. Also, consider that, at some point in the future, Oracle may not allow **OUT** and **IN OUT** parameters to be defined for functions. To be safe, it's better to only return values from functions using the **RETURN** statement.

Return Values

By definition, a PL/SQL function must return a value to any block of code that calls the procedure. If the function doesn't return a value, an exception will be raised. Functions return a value through the use of the **RETURN** statement, as shown in Listing 5.7.

Listing 5.7   Use of the **RETURN** statement in a function.

```
FUNCTION Raise_Salary (nBaseSalary    IN      number,
                       nRaisePercent IN      number)

    RETURN number;

IS

BEGIN
    RETURN (nBaseSalary * nRaisePercent);
END;
```

Datatypes

A function's return value may be of any datatype; however, user-defined datatypes must exist in a referenced package specification or globally (if the function is created within another code module). Consider the function in Listing 5.8, which returns a PL/SQL table.

Listing 5.8   A return value of a user-defined datatype.

```
FUNCTION Parse_String (vStringToParse IN     varchar2)

    RETURN Global_Types.VARCHAR2_TABTYPE

IS

    iStringPos      integer;
    biIndex         binary_integer := 0;
    vString         varchar2 (2000);
    Return_tab      VARCHAR2_TABTYPE;

BEGIN
    vString := vStringToParse;

    LOOP
       --
       -- Get the position of the next delimiter.
       --
       iStringPos := instr (vString, '^');


       --
       -- If there are no more elements in the string, return
       -- the table.
       --
```

```
      IF (iStringPos = 0) THEN
          RETURN Return_tab;
      END IF;

      Return_tab (biIndex) := substr (vString, 1, (iStringPos - 1));

      biIndex := biIndex + 1;

      --
      -- Chop off the first portion of the string.
      --
      vString := substr (vString, (iStringPos + 1));
   END LOOP;

EXCEPTION
   WHEN VALUE_ERROR THEN
       Log_System_Error (vErrorLocation => 'Parse_String',
                         vErrorText     => SQLERRM);
END;
```

In this example, the **VARCHAR2_TABTYPE** is a type declaration in the package spec for the package **Global_Types**. Packages will be discussed in Chapter 6.

Using %TYPE References

Functions can have parameters defined as **%TYPE** references to columns and can also have the datatype of their return value defined as a **%TYPE** reference, as shown in Listing 5.9.

Listing 5.9   Using **%TYPE** definitions for parameters and return values.

```
FUNCTION Raise_Salary (nBaseSalary    IN     EMPLOYEES.base_salary%TYPE,
                       nRaisePercent  IN     number)

   RETURN EMPLOYEES.base_salary%TYPE;

IS

BEGIN
   RETURN (nBaseSalary * nRaisePercent);
END;
```

Using %ROWTYPE References

Functions can also have parameters and return values that are defined using %ROWTYPE, as shown in Listing 5.10.

Listing 5.10 Using **%ROWTYPE** definition of parameters and return values.

```
FUNCTION Raise_Salary (Employee_rec  IN      EMPLOYEES%ROWTYPE,
                        nRaisePercent IN      number)

   RETURN number;

IS

BEGIN
   RETURN (Employee_rec.base_salary * nRaisePercent);
END;
```

Calling Functions

In addition to calls that are made from the system's front end, functions can be called in three ways:

- DML statements
- Anonymous PL/SQL blocks
- Stored PL/SQL objects

Each method of calling a function is quite similar despite the varied origins of the calls.

DML Statements

Stored functions can be executed as part of a DML statement. An example of calling a function this way is shown in Listing 5.11.

Listing 5.11 Calling a function within a DML statement.

```
UPDATE FACULTY
SET    base_salary = Raise_Salary (nRaisePercent => 3.5,
                                    nBaseSalary   => base_salary)
WHERE  faculty_id  = 6572;
```

In this example, the value of the **base_salary** column is passed to the **Raise_Salary()** function. The value returned from the function is stored in the **base_salary** column. The function **Raise_Salary()** might look like the function shown in Listing 5.12.

Listing 5.12   The **Raise_Salary()** function called in Listing 5.11.

```
FUNCTION Raise_Salary (nBaseSalary    IN      number,
                       nRaisePercent  IN      number)

IS

BEGIN
   RETURN (nBaseSalary * nRaisePercent);
END;
```

When packaged functions are used in this way, a purity level for the function must be defined within the package spec. Purity levels for functions are discussed in Chapter 6.

Anonymous PL/SQL Blocks

Functions can be called from any PL/SQL block, including an anonymous block created during an SQL*Plus session or as part of a script. Consider the PL/SQL block in Listing 5.13, which is part of a unit test for the **Raise_Salary()** function.

Listing 5.13   An anonymous PL/SQL block that calls a function.

```
DECLARE
   nResult   number;

BEGIN
   DBMS_Output.Put_Line ('Calling Raise_Salary for 3.5 % ' ||
                         'of $20,000. The result should be ' ||
                         '$20,700.');

   nResult := Raise_Salary (nBaseSalary   => 20000,
                            nRaisePercent => 3.5);

   DBMS_Output.Put_Line (to_char (nResult));

   IF (nResult <> 20700) THEN
      DBMS_Output.Put_Line ('ERROR: Function returned wrong value!');
   END IF;
END;
```

Stored PL/SQL Objects

Functions can be called from other stored functions and procedures, as shown in Listing 5.14.

Listing 5.14 A stored function calling another stored function.

```
FUNCTION Calculate_Bonus (nEmployee IN      number)

    RETURN number;

IS

    nSalary    EMPLOYEES.base_salary%TYPE;

BEGIN
    IF Check_Bonus_Eligibility (nEmployee => nEmployee) THEN
        SELECT base_salary
        INTO   nSalary
        FROM   EMPLOYEES
        WHERE  employee_num = nEmployee;

        RETURN (nSalary * 0.01);
    END IF;
END;
```

In this example, the function **Check_Bonus_Eligibility**() is a boolean function, returning **TRUE** if the employee is eligible for a bonus and **FALSE** if the employee isn't eligible for a bonus. If the response is **FALSE**, the **THEN** clause will not be executed.

The Structure Of A Function

The structure of a stored function consists of the following five sections:

- *Function declaration*—Function name, parameters, and return datatype.

- *Variable declarations*—Variables, constants, and user-defined exceptions.

- *Executable declarations*—Local procedures and functions.

- *Body*—The internal logic of the function.

- *Exception handling*—Handlers for exceptions likely to occur while the function is executing.

Each section of a function has specific components, which are discussed in the following sections.

The Function Declaration

The function declaration consists of three distinct portions: function name, parameter definitions, and return datatypes.

- *Function name*—The name of the function, which identifies the function to other stored objects.

- *Parameter definitions*—The names, parameter types, datatypes, and default values of the function's parameters, which specify how the function must be called.

- *Return datatype*—The datatype that the function returns, which specifies what type of input the calling code should expect as a result.

The function declaration is highlighted in Listing 5.15.

Listing 5.15   The function declaration.

```
FUNCTION Parse_String (vStringToParse IN     varchar2)

    RETURN Global_Types.VARCHAR2_TABTYPE

IS

    iStringPos              integer;
    biIndex                 binary_integer := 0;
    DELIMITER      CONSTANT char (1) := '^';
    vString                 varchar2 (2000);
    Return_tab              VARCHAR2_TABTYPE;

    FUNCTION DelimiterPosition (vString IN      varchar2)
        RETURN integer;

    FUNCTION NextWord (vCheckString IN      varchar2)

        RETURN varchar2

    IS

    BEGIN
        iStringPos := DelimiterPosition (vString => vCheckString));
```

```
        IF (iStringPos > 0) THEN
            RETURN (substr (vCheckString, 1, iStringPos);
        END IF;

        RETURN NULL;
    END NextWord;

    FUNCTION DelimiterPosition (vString IN      varchar2)

        RETURN integer

    IS

    BEGIN
        RETURN (instr (vString, DELIMITER));
    END DelimiterPosition;

BEGIN
    vString := vStringToParse;

    LOOP
        Return_tab (biIndex) := NextWord;
        --
        -- If there are no more elements in the string, return
        -- the table.
        --
        IF (iStringPos = 0) THEN
            RETURN Return_tab;
        END IF;

        Return_tab (biIndex) := substr (vString, 1, (iStringPos - 1));

        biIndex := biIndex + 1;


        --
        -- Chop off the first portion of the string.
        --
        vString := substr (vString, (iStringPos + 1));
    END LOOP;

EXCEPTION
    WHEN VALUE_ERROR THEN
        Log_System_Error (vErrorLocation => 'Parse_String',
                          vErrorText     => SQLERRM);
END;
```

Variable Declarations

The declarations section of a function allows you to define local variables, constants, and user-defined exceptions used by the function. These definitions are highlighted in Listing 5.16.

Listing 5.16   The variable declaration section of a function.

```
FUNCTION Parse_String (vStringToParse IN    varchar2)

    RETURN Global_Types.VARCHAR2_TABTYPE

IS

    iStringPos              integer;
    biIndex                 binary_integer := 0;
    DELIMITER       CONSTANT char (1) := '^';
    vString                 varchar2 (2000);
    Return_tab              VARCHAR2_TABTYPE;

    FUNCTION DelimiterPosition (vString IN    varchar2)
        RETURN integer;

    FUNCTION NextWord (vCheckString IN    varchar2)

        RETURN varchar2

    IS

    BEGIN
        iStringPos := DelimiterPosition (vString => vCheckString));
        IF (iStringPos > 0) THEN
            RETURN (substr (vCheckString, 1, iStringPos));
        END IF;

        RETURN NULL;
    END NextWord;

    FUNCTION DelimiterPosition (vString IN    varchar2)

        RETURN integer

    IS

    BEGIN
```

```
      RETURN (instr (vString, DELIMITER));
   END DelimiterPosition;

BEGIN
   vString := vStringToParse;

   LOOP
      Return_tab (biIndex) := NextWord;
      --
      -- If there are no more elements in the string, return
      -- the table.
      --
      IF (iStringPos = 0) THEN
         RETURN Return_tab;
      END IF;

      Return_tab (biIndex) := substr (vString, 1, (iStringPos - 1));

      biIndex := biIndex + 1;

      --
      -- Chop off the first portion of the string.
      --
      vString := substr (vString, (iStringPos + 1));
   END LOOP;

EXCEPTION
   WHEN VALUE_ERROR THEN
      Log_System_Error (vErrorLocation => 'Parse_String',
                        vErrorText     => SQLERRM);
END;
```

Executable Declarations

The declarations of local procedures and functions are made in the executable declarations section of a function. These definitions are highlighted in Listing 5.17.

Listing 5.17 The executable declarations of a function.

```
FUNCTION Parse_String (vStringToParse IN    varchar2)

   RETURN Global_Types.VARCHAR2_TABTYPE

IS
```

```
iStringPos              integer;
biIndex                 binary_integer := 0;
DELIMITER      CONSTANT char (1) := '^';
vString                 varchar2 (2000);
Return_tab              VARCHAR2_TABTYPE;

FUNCTION DelimiterPosition (vString IN      varchar2)
    RETURN integer;

FUNCTION NextWord (vCheckString IN      varchar2)

    RETURN varchar2

IS

BEGIN
    iStringPos := DelimiterPosition (vString => vCheckString);
    IF (iStringPos > 0) THEN
        RETURN (substr (vCheckString, 1, iStringPos));
    END IF;

    RETURN NULL;
END NextWord;

FUNCTION DelimiterPosition (vString IN      varchar2)

    RETURN integer

IS

BEGIN
    RETURN (instr (vString, DELIMITER));
END DelimiterPosition;

BEGIN
    vString := vStringToParse;

    LOOP
        Return_tab (biIndex) := NextWord;
        --
        -- If there are no more elements in the string, return
        -- the table.
        --
```

```
        IF (iStringPos = 0) THEN
           RETURN Return_tab;
        END IF;

        Return_tab (biIndex) := substr (vString, 1, (iStringPos - 1));

        biIndex := biIndex + 1;

        --
        -- Chop off the first portion of the string.
        --
        vString := substr (vString, (iStringPos + 1));
     END LOOP;

EXCEPTION
   WHEN VALUE_ERROR THEN
        Log_System_Error (vErrorLocation => 'Parse_String',
                          vErrorText     => SQLERRM);
END;
```

The Function Body

The PL/SQL statements that follow the **BEGIN** statement and precede the **EXCEPTION** and/or **END** statement make up the body of a function. The highlighted portion of Listing 5.18 is the function's body.

Listing 5.18   The body of a function.

```
FUNCTION Parse_String (vStringToParse IN    varchar2)

    RETURN Global_Types.VARCHAR2_TABTYPE

IS

    iStringPos              integer;
    biIndex                 binary_integer := 0;
    DELIMITER      CONSTANT char (1) := '^';
    vString                 varchar2 (2000);
    Return_tab              VARCHAR2_TABTYPE;

    FUNCTION DelimiterPosition (vString IN    varchar2)
       RETURN integer;

    FUNCTION NextWord (vCheckString IN    varchar2)

       RETURN varchar2
```

```
   IS

   BEGIN
      iStringPos := DelimiterPosition (vString => vCheckString);
      IF (iStringPos > 0) THEN
         RETURN (substr (vCheckString, 1, iStringPos));
      END IF;

      RETURN NULL;
   END NextWord;

   FUNCTION DelimiterPosition (vString IN     varchar2)

      RETURN integer

   IS

   BEGIN
      RETURN (instr (vString, DELIMITER));
   END DelimiterPosition;

BEGIN
   vString := vStringToParse;

   LOOP
      Return_tab (biIndex) := NextWord;
      --
      -- If there are no more elements in the string, return
      -- the table.
      --
      IF (iStringPos = 0) THEN
         RETURN Return_tab;
      END IF;

      Return_tab (biIndex) := substr (vString, 1, (iStringPos - 1));

      biIndex := biIndex + 1;


      --
      -- Chop off the first portion of the string.
      --
      vString := substr (vString, (iStringPos + 1));
   END LOOP;
```

```
EXCEPTION
   WHEN VALUE_ERROR THEN
       Log_System_Error (vErrorLocation => 'Parse_String',
                         vErrorText     => SQLERRM);
END;
```

Exception Handling

Exception handlers are defined within the function to handle error conditions that could reasonably be expected to occur while the function is executing. In Listing 5.19, the developer feels that the **VALUE_ERROR** exception might be encountered while processing the string if a delimited portion of the string exceeds the defined length of the PL/SQL table row.

Listing 5.19   The exception handling portion of a function.

```
FUNCTION Parse_String (vStringToParse IN    varchar2)

   RETURN Global_Types.VARCHAR2_TABTYPE

IS

   iStringPos            integer;
   biIndex               binary_integer := 0;
   DELIMITER     CONSTANT char (1) := '^';
   vString               varchar2 (2000);
   Return_tab            VARCHAR2_TABTYPE;

   FUNCTION DelimiterPosition (vString IN    varchar2)
      RETURN integer;

   FUNCTION NextWord (vCheckString IN    varchar2)

      RETURN varchar2

   IS

   BEGIN
      iStringPos := DelimiterPosition (vString => vCheckString);
      IF (iStringPos > 0) THEN
         RETURN (substr (vCheckString, 1, iStringPos));
      END IF;

      RETURN NULL;
   END NextWord;
```

```
FUNCTION DelimiterPosition (vString IN      varchar2)

    RETURN integer

IS

BEGIN
    RETURN (instr (vString, DELIMITER));
END DelimiterPosition;

BEGIN
    vString := vStringToParse;

    LOOP
        Return_tab (biIndex) := NextWord;
        --
        -- If there are no more elements in the string, return
        -- the table.
        --
        IF (iStringPos = 0) THEN
            RETURN Return_tab;
        END IF;

        Return_tab (biIndex) := substr (vString, 1, (iStringPos - 1));

        biIndex := biIndex + 1;


        --
        -- Chop off the first portion of the string.
        --
        vString := substr (vString, (iStringPos + 1));
    END LOOP;

EXCEPTION
    WHEN VALUE_ERROR THEN
        Log_System_Error (vErrorLocation => 'Parse_String',
                          vErrorText      => SQLERRM);
END;
```

Documenting Functions

The essential elements of documentation are the same for both functions and procedures. Your documentation must cover the following four basic aspects of the function:

- Purpose

- Parameters

- Return value

- Error conditions

Headers, pseudocode, comments, and identifier names all contribute to creating a well-documented piece of code.

The Header

Listing 5.20 contains a header for the **Parse_String**() function that we've been discussing.

Listing 5.20   The **Parse_String()** function with a header.

```
FUNCTION Parse_String (vStringToParse IN    varchar2)

    RETURN Global_Types.VARCHAR2_TABTYPE

-- *****************************************************************
-- Description: The Parse_String function accepts a single parameter
-- of type varchar2. This parameter is expected to be a series of
-- varchar2 strings delimited by a caret (^) symbol. If any section
-- of the parameter is longer than 10 characters, a VALUE_ERROR
-- exception will be raised when the section is stored in the
-- PL/SQL table.
--
-- The function returns a PL/SQL table, with each element of the
-- table containing a single section of the string.
--
-- REVISON HISTORY
-- Date        Author      Reason For Change
-- ---------------------------------------------------------------
-- 19 FEB 1997 J. Schmoe  Function created.
-- *****************************************************************

IS

    iStringPos      integer;
    biIndex         binary_integer := 0;
    DELIMITER       CONSTANT  char (1) := '^';
    vString         varchar2 (2000);
    Return_tab      VARCHAR2_TABTYPE;
```

```
BEGIN
   vString := vStringToParse;

   LOOP
      --
      -- Get the position of the next delimiter.
      --
      iStringPos := instr (vString, DELIMITER);


      --
      -- If there are no more elements in the string, return
      -- the table.
      --
      IF (iStringPos = 0) THEN
         RETURN Return_tab;
      END IF;

      Return_tab (biIndex) := substr (vString, 1, (iStringPos - 1));

      biIndex := biIndex + 1;


      --
      -- Chop off the first portion of the string so that the
      -- next iteration of the loop will get the next section.
      --
      vString := substr (vString, (iStringPos + 1));
   END LOOP;

EXCEPTION
   WHEN VALUE_ERROR THEN
      Log_System_Error (vErrorLocation => 'Parse_String',
                        vErrorText      => SQLERRM);
END;
```

Pseudocode

It's often useful when designing a module to generate pseudocode that outlines the logical steps that the module must take. Listing 5.21 shows a very simple bit of pseudocode for the **Parse_String()** function.

Listing 5.21 Pseudocode for the **Parse_String()** function.

```
store the string to be parsed in a local variable;

enter a loop
```

```
get the location of the caret inside the string;
if there is no delimiter in the string then
    return the array to the calling procedure;

store the first section of the string in the array;

chop off the first section of the string;
increment the index variable for the array;

if the VALUE_ERROR exception occurs then
    log an error using the system log function;
```

This approach is especially useful with procedures, but functions often handle some very tough problems, too. Breaking the functionality of the module down into steps is the real work when writing code. Once the logic for the function has been thoroughly defined, the code can be written without too many problems.

Comments

Used thoughtfully, comments are an excellent tool for documenting code. The best comments describe *why* code works the way it does instead of describing *how* it works. Consider the following two sample comments:

Comment A:

```
--
-- If the employee has been late for work less than 1% of the time,
-- grant the employee a 0.5% raise.
--
IF (nOntimePercent > 99.0) THEN
    nRaiseAmount := nRaiseAmount + 0.005;
END IF;
```

Comment B:

```
--
-- If nOntimePercent > 99 add .005 to nRaiseAmount.
--
IF (nOntimePercent > 99.0) THEN
    nRaiseAmount := nRaiseAmount + 0.005;
END IF;
```

Comment A explains why the code is written in a particular way. Comment B paraphrases the code but doesn't explain the business rules behind the code. There is nothing in comment B that will help you understand what business rules the code satisfies. The sample PL/SQL coding standard in Appendix D includes some guidelines about the content and location of comments.

Identifiers

Consider this example:

```
IF (x > 99.0) THEN
   y := y + 0.05;
END IF;
```

It might take you a moment to recognize this block of code as the code from the previous example, only with different variable names. While it's relatively easy to keep track of **x** and **y** in this example, when repeated several times in 200 lines of code, **x** and **y** will become painfully and hair-wrenchingly obscure.

The only time variable names like x and y are potentially meaningful is when referencing a loop control variable or the index of a PL/SQL table. Even then, it's better to give variables names related to their functions. Using meaningful identifiers is one of the easiest ways to document code.

Step-By-Step: Creating A Function

Let's get our feet wet by creating a function from scratch. We'll start with a problem and discuss the relevant data, then we'll design, write, and test our new function.

Function Requirements

Your assignment is to create a function that will find a professor who can teach a class. The ID number of the class will be provided as a parameter:. The business rules that the function must enforce are:

- A full professor is not allowed to teach more than four classes.

- A graduate student may not teach more than two classes.

- An instructor may not teach a class with a number above his or her approved level.

- An instructor with a minimum course level may not be assigned to teach a course below that level.

- Obviously, no one can teach two courses at the same time.

The next step is to establish which tables and views hold data that is relevant to the problem.

A record of information about professors is kept in the **INSTRUCTORS** table, which has this structure:

```
instructor_number    NOT NULL number   (5)
last_name                     varchar2 (15)
first_name                    varchar2 (15)
faculty_member_flag           char     (1)
approved_class_level          number   (3)
min_class_level               number   (3)
approved_field                varchar2 (3)
maximum_classes               char     (1)
```

Information about classes is kept in the **SCHEDULED_CLASSES** table, which has this structure:

```
course_number       NOT NULL number   (5)
course_field        NOT NULL char     (3)
instructor_number            number   (5)
semester_id         NOT NULL number   (3)
class_time                   number   (2)
field_level         NOT NULL number   (3)
```

The **class_time** column is a lookup code that points to a more detailed description of the class's day and time in the **CLASS_TIMES** table, which has this structure:

```
class_time          NOT NULL varchar2 (2)
description         NOT NULL varchar2 (9)
```

Now that you understand the relationships between the various pieces of data that the function must consider, it's time to start designing the function.

Designing The Function

To design the function, we first need to examine how each business rule can be satisfied by the function.

1. We can query a count of the classes taught by a particular instructor from the **SCHEDULED_CLASSES** table using the following code:

```
SELECT count (*)
FROM   SCHEDULED_CLASSES
WHERE  instructor_number = <the professor's ID number>;
```

If the result is four or more, the professor can't teach any more classes.

Because there are several hundred professors and several hundred graduate students who will be teaching courses, we can save ourselves some work if a professor is marked off our list once he or she is teaching the maximum number of courses. After some discussions with our DBA, the **maximum_classes** column is added to the **INSTRUCTORS** table. Our function will set this flag to **Y** if the professor can't teach any more classes.

2. If the previous rule is sufficiently handled, then this one is easy. The only difference is that graduate students are only allowed to teach two courses, not four.

3. We can compare the **approved_class_level** from the **INSTRUCTORS** table against the **field_level** from the **SCHEDULED_CLASSES** table. If **field_level** is greater than **approved_class_level**, the instructor can't teach the class.

4. We can compare the **min_class_level** from the **INSTRUCTORS** table against the **field_level** from the **SCHEDULED_CLASSES** table. If **field_level** is less than **approved_class_level**, the instructor can't teach the class.

5. We can get a count of the number of classes to which the instructor is assigned that have the same **class_time** as the course being scheduled. If the count isn't zero, the instructor can't be scheduled for the class.

Pseudocode

After determining how we can meet each individual requirement, we can write the pseudocode in Listing 5.22 for the function.

Listing 5.22   Pseudocode for the **Assign_Instructor()** function.

```
get the information about the specified course;

open a cursor of all instructors still able to teach courses;

for each instructor in the list loop
   determine how many classes the instructor is teaching;
   determine how many classes the instructor can teach;
```

```
    if the instructor can't teach any more classes then
        update the maximum_classes field in the INSTRUCTORS table;
        goto the next professor;
    end if;

    if the instructor's approved level is too low for the course then
        goto the next professor;
    end if;

    if the instructor's min level > the course level then
        goto the next professor;
    end if;

    open a cursor of other classes taught by the instructor;

    for each course taught by the instructor loop
        compare the course time and day against the specified course;

        if there is a conflict then
            goto the next professor;
        end if;

        return the professor's ID to the calling procedure;
    end loop;

end loop;

if the function has come this far then
    raise exception NO_INSTRUCTORS_AVAILABLE;
end if;
```

Once pseudocode is written it's very easy to write the code for the function, because the essential part of the work, deciding the flow of the function's logic, has already been accomplished. Figure 5.1 illustrates the logic for the **Assign_Instructor**() function.

Code

Now that we have the logic of the function outlined, we're ready to write the code. Our largest obstacle is the lack of a **continue** statement in PL/SQL. While our pseudocode can say "skip to the next instructor" or "goto the next instructor," PL/ SQL doesn't provide us with an easy way to do this. We could use the **GOTO** statement to handle this situation, but most people consider that to be bad coding style.

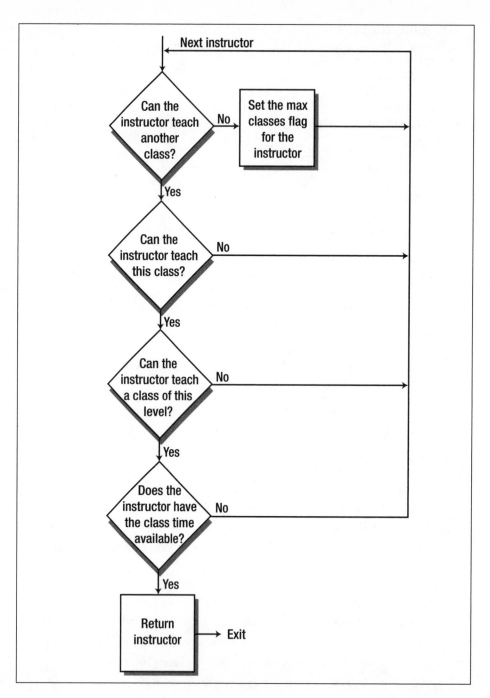

Figure 5.1

The logic flow of the **Assign_Instructor()** function.

To resolve this dilemma, we'll create a boolean variable called **bInstructorValid** that we'll use to keep track of the status. If a condition occurs that forces us to discard an instructor, all subsequent tests inside the loop will be skipped, because the first condition of each test will be that **bInstructorValid** returns **TRUE**. Listing 5.23 is the code for our new function.

Listing 5.23   The code for the new **Assign_Instructor()** function.

```
FUNCTION Assign_Instructor
    (nClassNumber IN      SCHEDULED_CLASSES.course_number%TYPE)

    RETURN INSTRUCTORS.instructor_number%TYPE

IS

    --
    -- Full professors can teach 4 courses. Graduate students
    -- can teach two.
    --
    FULL_COURSES  CONSTANT integer := 4;
    GRAD_COURSES  CONSTANT integer := 2;

    bInstructorValid Boolean := TRUE;
    iCoursesCarried  integer;
    nDummyVariable    number;
    nTeacherID        INSTRUCTORS.instructor_number%TYPE;
    nTeachLevel       INSTRUCTORS.approved_class_level%TYPE;
    nTeachMinLev      INSTRUCTORS.min_class_level%TYPE;
    nTime             SCHEDULED_CLASSES.class_time%TYPE;
    nClassLevel       SCHEDULED_CLASSES.field_level%TYPE;
    rClassROWID       ROWID;
    vCourseField      SCHEDULED_CLASSES.course_field%TYPE;

    xNO_INSTRUCTOR_AVAILABLE    EXCEPTION;

    CURSOR Instructors_cur
       (vCourseField    SCHEDULED_COURSES.course_field%TYPE)
    IS
    SELECT instructor_number,
           --
           -- Course levels are stored as 100, 200, 300,...800. In
           -- order to properly check the course level for an
           -- instructor, the approved number is raised by 100 for the
           -- comparison against the course's level.
           --
```

```
              approved_class_level + 100 approved_class_level,
              min_class_level
    FROM      INSTRUCTORS
    WHERE     maximum_courses = 'N'
    AND       approved_field = vCourseField;

BEGIN
    SELECT class_time, field_level,  course_field, ROWID
    INTO   nTime,      nClass_Level, vCourseField, rClassROWID
    FROM   SCHEDULED_CLASSES
    WHERE  course_number  = nClassNumber;

    FOR Instructors_rec IN Instructors_cur (vCourseField) LOOP
        nTeacherID     := Instructors_rec.instructor_number;
        nTeacherLevel  := Instructors_rec.approved_class_level;
        nTeacherMinLev := Instructors_rec.min_class_level;

        SELECT count (*)
        INTO   iCoursesCarried
        FROM   SCHEDULED_COURSES
        WHERE  instructor_number = nTeacherID;

        bInstructorValid := TRUE;


        --
        -- If the instructor is already teaching the maximum number
        -- of courses allowed, make sure that future executions of
        -- this function don't retrieve the professor.
        --
        IF (iCoursesCarried = decode (vFullProf,
                                        'Y', FULL_COURSES,
                                        'N', GRAD_COURSES)) THEN
            UPDATE INSTRUCTORS
            SET    maximum_courses = 'Y'
            WHERE CURRENT OF Instructors_cur;

            bInstructorValid := FALSE;
        END IF;


        IF bInstructorValid THEN
            --
            -- The course level cannot exceed the instructor's approved
            -- level.
            --
            IF (nClassLevel < nTeacherLevel) THEN
                bInstructorValid := FALSE;
```

```
            END IF;
        END IF;

    IF bInstructorValid THEN
        --
        -- If the instructor has a minimum class level defined, the
        -- course must meet or exceed that minimum level.
        --
        IF (nClassLevel < nTeacherMinLev) THEN
            bInstructorValid := FALSE;
        END IF;
    END IF;

    IF bInstructorValid THEN
        --
        -- If this query returns a row, the instructor already has
        -- a class scheduled for this time.
        --
        BEGIN
            SELECT 1
            INTO   nDummyVariable
            FROM   SCHEDULED_CLASSES
            WHERE  instructor_number = nTeacherID
            AND    class_time        = nTime;

            bInstructorValid := FALSE;

        EXCEPTION
            WHEN NO_DATA_FOUND THEN
                    NULL;
        END;
    END IF;

    --
    -- Everything is OK. Use this instructor.
    --
    IF bInstructorValid THEN
        RETURN nTeacherID;
    END IF;
END LOOP;

RAISE xNO_INSTRUCTOR_AVAILABLE;
END Assign_Instructor;
```

Testing

Now, it's time to write a unit test script for the function. By breaking the requirements down, we find that there are nine tests that must be performed.

- Attempt to assign five classes to a faculty member instructor. This can be accomplished by creating four classes with the professor already assigned to teach them, then creating another class appropriate to the professor. The function should not return a value.

- Attempt to assign three classes to a graduate student instructor. This test is similar to the previous test. Set up two classes with the graduate student as the assigned instructor, then create a third class appropriate to the graduate student. The function should not return a value.

- Attempt to assign four classes to a faculty member instructor. This is similar to the first test, but instead of creating four classes, create three classes that the instructor is already teaching. The function should return the ID number of the instructor.

- Attempt to assign two classes to a graduate student instructor. This test is similar to the previous test: Set up one existing class that the graduate student is teaching and set up the data so that the graduate student should be assigned to teach one more course. The function should return the ID number of the instructor.

- Attempt to assign a class with a **course_level** greater than the instructor's **approved_class_level** by creating a class appropriate to the instructor with the exception of the class level and running the function. The function should return without value.

- Attempt to assign a class with a **course_level** less than the instructor's **approved_class_level** by creating a class appropriate to the instructor. The function should return the instructor's ID number.

- Attempt to assign a course with a **course_level** less than the instructor's **min_class_level** by creating a class appropriate to the instructor and setting the instructor's **min_class_level** to the level above the course. The function should return without a value.

- Attempt to assign two classes at different times to one instructor by creating one class assigned to the instructor and another class at a different class period. The function should return the instructor's ID number.

- Attempt to assign two classes at the same time to one instructor by creating one class assigned to the instructor and another class in the same class period. The function should return without a value.

We'll assume that testing the function will be done in a schema other than the schema that owns the final product. Making this assumption allows us to set up each of our test conditions by completely emptying the tables of data and then populating the tables with the data to support each test (which makes predicting the results of the function much easier).

The logic for each test is fairly close to the following:

- Clean out the tables.

- Add needed test data to tables.

- Predict the results.

- Call the function.

- Check the results by querying the tables.

Now that these test steps have been established, we can set up a test of the function using a script to handle each condition that needs to be tested. The first of these conditions is tested using a script like the one in Listing 5.24.

Listing 5.24   A test script for the **Assign_Instructor()** function.

```
DECLARE

BEGIN
    --
    -- Clean out the local tables before creating baseline data.
    -- The CLASS_TIMES table is a lookup table, so no work needs
    -- to be done there.
    --
    TRUNCATE TABLE INSTRUCTORS;
    TRUNCATE TABLE SCHEDULED_CLASSES;


    --
    -- Create a faculty member psychology instructor qualified
    -- to teach courses at the 800 level, with no minimum level.
    --
    INSERT
    INTO    INSTRUCTORS
```

```
              (instructor_number,
               last_name,
               first_name,
               faculty_member_flag,
             ' approved_class_level,
               min_class_level,
               approved_field,
               maximum_classes)
       VALUES (1000,
               'Williams',
               'Bill',
               'Y',
               800,
               NULL,
               'PSY',
               'Y');


       --
       -- Create four courses with our instructor.
       --
       INSERT
       INTO    SCHEDULED_CLASSES
               (course_number,
               course_field,
               instructor_number,
               semester_id,
               class_time,
               field_level)
       VALUES (2000,
               'PSY',
               1000,
               197,
               'A',
               100);


       INSERT
       INTO    SCHEDULED_CLASSES
               (course_number,
               course_field,
               instructor_number,
               semester_id,
               class_time,
               field_level)
       VALUES (2001,
               'PSY',
               1000,
```

```
        197,
        'B',
        232);

INSERT
INTO    SCHEDULED_CLASSES
        (course_number,
         course_field,
         instructor_number,
         semester_id,
         class_time,
         field_level)
VALUES (2010,
        'PSY',
        1000,
        197,
        'C',
        321);

INSERT
INTO    SCHEDULED_CLASSES
        (course_number,
         course_field,
         instructor_number,
         semester_id,
         class_time,
         field_level)
VALUES (2302,
        'PSY',
        1000,
        197,
        'G',
        810);

--
-- Create a class that this professor could teach.
--
INSERT
INTO    SCHEDULED_CLASSES
        (course_number,
         course_field,
         instructor_number,
         semester_id,
         class_time,
         field_level)
```

```
VALUES (2100,
        'PSY',
        1000,
        197,
        'E',
        201);

    --
    -- Now call the Assign_Instructor function. Since there is only
    -- one professor who can teach psychology courses and that
    -- professor is already teaching four courses, the function
    -- will return without a value (an exception will be raised when
    -- calling the function).
    --
    nTeacherID := Assign_Instructor (nClassNumber => 2100);

    --
    -- If execution reaches this point, the function did return
    -- a value. This should not have happened.
    --
    DBMS_Output.Put_Line ('ERROR: Function executed normally!');
    DBMS_Output.Put_line ('Instructor ID: ' || nTeacherID);

EXCEPTION
    WHEN OTHERS THEN
        DBMS_Output.Put_Line (SQLERRM);
END;
```

As you can see, creating the test is quite simple. The tests for the other conditions are quite similar in content.

Creating Test Scripts

Although creating tests like this takes some time, once the test is set up it can be repeated whenever the function is modified in the future. (Who says the university won't someday change the way it assigns professors to classes?) Creating test scripts that handle the condition allows the modified function to be tested against the same criteria and baseline data as the original function. In programming (as in science), this is a highly desirable goal.

Summary

Chapter 5 has discussed the fundamentals of creating stored functions within the Oracle database. At this point you should have an understanding of the PL/SQL needed to create a function and should also have some insight on how to design and test your functions. Chapter 6 will discuss some specifics of using functions within packages.

HIGH PERFORMANCE

Packages

CHAPTER

6

Packages

A *package* is a group of procedures, functions, and variables, often grouped together because they accomplish related tasks. In PL/SQL, packages consist of two parts: the package specification, or package spec, and the package body.

The Package Spec

The package spec can be clearly illustrated by using a form-based analogy. When a form displays on your terminal, certain buttons are displayed as well. The code behind each button is a call to a procedure or function. Figure 6.1 illustrates this model within the context of a package.

Simply put, a package spec defines how other objects within an Oracle database interact with the package. The package spec contains the following types of definitions:

- Global variables, constants, user-defined datatypes, and user-defined exceptions
- Procedure declarations (interface only)
- Function declarations (interface only)

Every construct and object defined within a package spec is public and can be referenced by any block of PL/SQL code. Objects within a package body that are not defined within the package spec are private objects and can be referenced only by objects within the package.

Global Variables

The package spec can contain definitions for variables, constants, datatypes, and user-defined exceptions that can be referenced by the package spec and body, as well as by outside objects. Listing 6.1 illustrates the definition of these constructs.

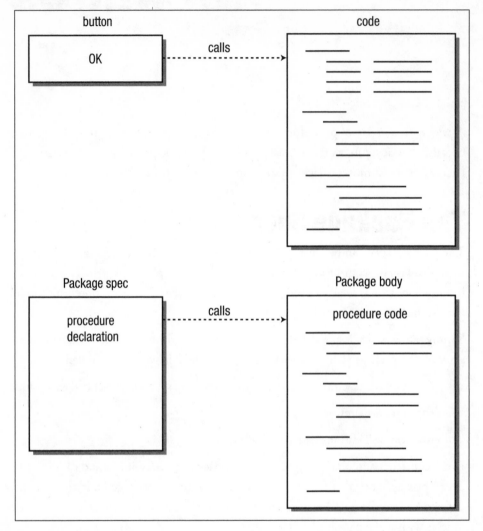

Figure 6.1
The package model.

Listing 6.1 The definition of global constructs in a package spec.

```
PACKAGE System_Errors

IS

   TYPE MessageParts_type IS TABLE OF varchar2 (20)
      INDEX BY binary_integer;
```

```
vLastError                      varchar2 (100);
THIS_PACKAGE      CONSTANT      varchar2 (13) := 'System_Errors';

xUNHANDLED_ERROR                EXCEPTION;

FUNCTION Build_Message (vObjectName  IN      varchar2,
                        iErrorCode   IN      integer,
                        vErrorString IN      varchar2);

PROCEDURE Log_Error (vObjectName   IN      varchar2,
                     vErrorString  IN      varchar2,
                     vErrorData    IN      varchar2,
                     iErrorCode    IN      integer);
```

```
END System_Errors;
```

Each of the highlighted constructs can be referenced by all the procedures and functions contained within the package body. Objects outside the package can also reference the constructs by prefacing the name of the construct with the name of the package, as shown in Listing 6.2.

Listing 6.2   Referencing an object within a package.

```
PROCEDURE Local_Error_Log (vObjectName  IN      varchar2,
                           iErrorCode   IN      integer,
                           vErrorString IN      varchar2)

IS

vMessageParts      System_Errors.MessageParts_type;

BEGIN
   System_Errors.Build_Message (vObjectName  => vObjectName,
                                iErrorCode   => iErrorCode,
                                vErrorString => vErrorString);
END Local_Error_Log;
```

Each construct is specific to the user who references it. For example, user A initializes **vLastError** to 'Student does not exist' and user B initializes **vLastError** to 'Attempted division by zero'. Neither user is overwriting the value of the other user's variable.

The Bodyless Package

Large systems often have a number of definitions that need to be standardized throughout the system. You can define a package spec that contains these definitions and reference the package spec from any object. Although packages are usually defined using both a spec and a body, Oracle doesn't require every package spec to have an associated package body. Consider this package spec:

```
PACKAGE Globals

IS

    FIELD_DELIMITER    CONSTANT varchar2 (1) := chr (29);
    ROW_DELIMITER      CONSTANT varchar2 (1) := chr (30);
    MAX_LENGTH         CONSTANT integer := 255;

    TYPE Student_rec_TYPE
    IS
    RECORD (first_name      varchar2 (20),
            last_name       varchar2 (20),
            middle_initial  varchar2 (1),
            ssn             varchar2 (9));

    TYPE SubStrings_tab_TYPE IS TABLE OF varchar2 (20)
    INDEX BY binary_integer;

END Globals;
```

*Any stored PL/SQL object can reference any of the constants or datatypes defined in the **Globals** package spec. Since the package doesn't contain any actual procedures or functions, there's no need to define a package body that corresponds to the spec.*

Procedures

The most commonly defined object within a package is a procedure. Listing 6.3 shows how a procedure is defined within a package spec.

Listing 6.3   Defining a procedure within a package spec.

```
PACKAGE System_Errors

IS

    TYPE MessageParts_type IS TABLE OF varchar2 (20)
        INDEX BY binary_integer;

    vLastError                   varchar2 (100);
    THIS_PACKAGE     CONSTANT    varchar2 (13) := 'System_Errors';

    xUNHANDLED_ERROR             EXCEPTION;

    FUNCTION Build_Message (vObjectName   IN      varchar2,
                            iErrorCode    IN      integer,
                            vErrorString  IN      varchar2);

    PROCEDURE Log_Error (vObjectName    IN      varchar2,
                         vErrorString   IN      varchar2,
                         vErrorData     IN      varchar2,
                         iErrorCode     IN      integer);

END System_Errors;
```

Chapter 4 provides a detailed discussion of procedures. There are only four differences between a package procedure and a standalone procedure:

- *Creation*—A standalone procedure is created using the **CREATE PROCEDURE** statement. A packaged procedure is created as part of the package body's definition.

- *Memory*—Oracle caches standalone procedures in memory by themselves, but packaged procedures must be stored and cleared from memory with the rest of the package.

- *Execution*—Packaged procedures must be qualified by the package name to be executed by objects that aren't contained within the package, as shown in the following example:

```
System_Log.Log_Error (vObjectName   => 'Conversions.Feet_To_Meters',
                      iErrorCode    => NULL_PARAMETER,
                      vErrorString  => SQLERRM,
                      vErrorData    => nFeet);
```

- *Scope*—Packaged procedures can reference other constructs and objects within the same package without qualifying the reference with a package name.

Procedures aren't created within a package spec, but the interface for a procedure is defined within the spec. Once a procedure has been defined in a package spec, the procedure must be created within the package body before the package body will compile.

Functions

Functions are also commonly defined within a package spec. Listing 6.4 shows how a function is defined within a package spec.

Listing 6.4 Defining a function within a package spec.

```
PACKAGE System_Errors

IS

    TYPE MessageParts_type IS TABLE OF varchar2 (20)
        INDEX BY binary_integer;

    vLastError                  varchar2 (100);
    THIS_PACKAGE        CONSTANT    varchar2 (13) := 'System_Errors';

    xUNHANDLED_ERROR              EXCEPTION;

    FUNCTION Build_Message (vObjectName   IN      varchar2,
                            iErrorCode    IN      integer,
                            vErrorString  IN      varchar2);

    PROCEDURE Log_Error (vObjectName   IN      varchar2,
                         vErrorString  IN      varchar2,
                         vErrorData    IN      varchar2,
                         iErrorCode    IN      integer);

END System_Errors;
```

Chapter 5 provides a detailed discussion of functions. There are five important differences between standalone functions and packaged functions:

- *Creation*—A standalone function is created using the **CREATE FUNCTION** statement. A packaged function is created as part of a package body's definition.

- *Memory*—Oracle caches standalone functions in memory by themselves, but packaged functions must be cached and cleared from memory with the rest of the package.

- *Execution*—Packaged functions must be qualified by a package name to be executed by objects that aren't contained within the package, as shown in the following example:

```
vErrorMsg := Build_Message (vObjectName   => vObjectName,
                            iErrorCode    => iErrorCode,
                            vErrorString => SQLERRM);
```

- *Scope*—Packaged functions can reference other constructs and objects within the same package without qualifying the reference with a package name.

- *Purity Levels*—Functions defined within packages can't be executed successfully inside DML statements, unless a *purity level* for the function is defined within the package spec. Purity levels are discussed in detail in the next section of this chapter.

Like procedures, functions aren't created within a package spec, but the interface for ad the function is defined within a spec. Once a function has been defined in a package spec, the function must be created within the package body before the package body will compile.

Purity Levels

An Oracle database cannot determine the work done by a packaged function when the function is executed from inside a DML statement. Therefore, if packaged functions are to be executed from within a DML statement, developers must use a **PRAGMA** to define a purity level for functions defined as part of the package spec. A **PRAGMA** is a compiler directive that instructs the compiler to handle code in a specific manner. To define a purity level for a packaged function, the **PRAGMA RESTRICT_REFERENCES** is used.

A purity level defined within a package spec instructs Oracle about the kinds of operations that the function performs. Table 6.1 lists the four purity levels that can be defined for a function.

Listing 6.5 illustrates how the purity level of a function is defined within a package spec.

Table 6.1 Purity levels for packaged functions.

Purity Level	Meaning
WNDS	The function doesn't alter the contents of any database table.
RNDS	The function doesn't read the contents of any database table.
WNPS	The function doesn't alter any variables within another package.
RNPS	The function doesn't read any variables within another package.

Listing 6.5 Defining the purity level of a packaged function.

```
PACKAGE System_Errors

IS

   TYPE MessageParts_type IS TABLE OF varchar2 (20)
      INDEX BY binary_integer;

   vLastError              varchar2 (100);
   THIS_PACKAGE    CONSTANT   varchar2 (13) := 'System_Errors';

   xUNHANDLED_ERROR           EXCEPTION;

   FUNCTION Build_Message (vObjectName  IN     varchar2,
                           iErrorCode   IN     integer,
                           vErrorString IN     varchar2)
      RETURN varchar2;

   PRAGMA RESTRICT_REFERENCES (Build_Message,
                           WNDS, RNDS, WNPS, RNPS);

   PROCEDURE Log_Error (vObjectName  IN     varchar2,
                        vErrorString IN     varchar2,
                        vErrorData   IN     varchar2,
                        iErrorCode   IN     integer);

END System_Errors;
```

Notice the **PRAGMA RESTRICT_REFERENCES** call in the highlighted portion of code. This defines the purity level for the **Build_Message** function.

While the **Build_Error**() function in this example is marked with all four purity levels, any number of levels can be defined for a function. As a general rule, it's best to make your functions as "pure" as possible.

Overloading Procedures And Functions

Oracle allows developers to overload procedures and functions that are created within packages. An *overloaded object* is actually several objects that all have the same name, but each object differs from the others in type and/or number of parameters. Listing 6.6 illustrates a package spec that contains the definition for an overloaded function.

Listing 6.6 A package spec containing an overloaded function.

```
PACKAGE Parse_Strings

IS

iLastDelimiter    integer;

--
-- Get the first word from the string using the
-- standard delimiter.
--
FUNCTION NextWord (vStringToParse IN    varchar2) RETURN varchar2;


--
-- Specify what delimiter will be used to signify the
-- end of the word.
--
FUNCTION NextWord (vStringToParse IN    varchar2,
                   vDelimiter     IN    varchar2);


--
-- Get the nth word from the string.
--
FUNCTION NextWord (vStringToParse IN    varchar2,
                   iWordNumber    IN    integer);


--
-- Get the nth word from the string and specify what
-- delimiter signifies the end of the word.
--
FUNCTION NextWord (vStringToParse IN    varchar2,
                   iWordNumber    IN    integer,
                   vDelimiter     IN    varchar2);

END Parse_Strings;
```

In this example, the function **NextWord**() is defined four times, and each definition of the function accomplishes a specific purpose. When a PL/SQL block calls **NextWord**(), Oracle examines the **Parse_Strings** package spec and executes the function that corresponds with the type and number of parameters specified in the call. The calling code doesn't know that there are actually four functions with the same name.

The Package Body

The package body includes the definition of procedures and functions declared in the package spec and, like the package spec, can also include variables, constants, user-defined exceptions, and user-defined datatypes.

Unlike objects declared in a package spec, variables and other constructs defined within a package body are private to the package body. These constructs can only be referenced by procedures and functions within the package body.

Figure 6.2 illustrates the relationship of objects defined within a package body to a package spec.

Package Spec	Package Body
Public function and procedure declarations	Public function and procedure code
Function purity levels	Private function and procedure code
Public global variables, constants, and user-defined exceptions	Private global variables, constants, and user-defined exceptions

Figure 6.2
Relating a package body to a package spec.

Procedures

Procedures are created inside a package without using the **CREATE PROCEDURE** command. Instead, a procedure's definition is defined as part of the **CREATE PACKAGE BODY** command, as shown in Listing 6.7.

Listing 6.7 Creating a procedure inside a package body.

```
CREATE OR REPLACE
PACKAGE BODY GPA_Calculations

AS

FUNCTION Overall_GPA (iStudentSSN IN      integer)

RETURN number

IS

    iTotalCredits    integer := 0;
    iTotalHours      integer := 0;
    nGPA             number  := 0;

    CURSOR StudentClasses_cur
    IS
    SELECT course_credits, course_grade
    FROM   SCHEDULED_CLASSES
    WHERE  ssn             = iStudentSSN
    AND    audit_flag      = 'N'
    AND    no_credit_flag  = 'N';

BEGIN
    FOR StudentClasses_rec IN StudentClasses_cur (iStudentSSN) LOOP
        iTotalCredits :=   iTotalCredits
                        + StudentClasses_rec.course_credits;
        iTotalHours   :=   iTotalHours
                        + StudentClasses_rec.course_hours;
    END LOOP;

    nGPA := (iTotalCredits / iTotalHours);

    RETURN nGPA;
END Overall_GPA;

PROCEDURE Calculate_GPA (iStudentSSN IN      integer)
```

```
IS

    CURSOR Students_cur
    IS
    SELECT ssn
    FROM    STUDENTS;

BEGIN
    FOR Students_rec IN Students_cur LOOP
        UPDATE STUDENTS
        SET    overall_gpa = Overall_GPA (iStudentSSN => iStudentSSN)
        WHERE CURRENT OF Students_cur;
    END LOOP;
END Calculate_GPA;

END GPA_Calculations;
```

Functions

Like procedures, functions are created within a package body as part of the **CRE-ATE PACKAGE BODY** command, as shown in Listing 6.8.

Listing 6.8   Creating a function inside a package body.

```
FUNCTION Overall_GPA (iStudentSSN IN        integer)

RETURN number

IS

    iTotalCredits    integer := 0;
    iTotalHours      integer := 0;
    nGPA             number  := 0;

    CURSOR StudentClasses_cur
    IS
    SELECT course_credits, course_grade
    FROM    SCHEDULED_CLASSES
    WHERE   ssn          = iStudentSSN
    AND     audit_flag      = 'N'
    AND     no_credit_flag = 'N';
```

```
BEGIN
   FOR StudentClasses_rec IN StudentClasses_cur (iStudentSSN) LOOP
      iTotalCredits :=   iTotalCredits
                        + StudentClasses_rec.course_credits;
      iTotalHours   :=   iTotalHours
                        + StudentClasses_rec.course_hours;
   END LOOP;

   nGPA := (iTotalCredits / iTotalHours);

   RETURN nGPA;
END Overall_GPA;

PROCEDURE Calculate_GPA (iStudentSSN IN       integer)

IS

   CURSOR Students_cur
   IS
   SELECT ssn
   FROM   STUDENTS;

BEGIN
   FOR Students_rec IN Students_cur LOOP
      UPDATE STUDENTS
      SET    overall_gpa = Overall_GPA (iStudentSSN => iStudentSSN)
      WHERE CURRENT OF Students_cur;
   END LOOP;
END Calculate_GPA;

END GPA_Calculations;
```

Initializing A Package

It's not unusual for a package to contain one or more variables that must be initialized when the package is first loaded into memory. Consider the package in Listing 6.9.

Listing 6.9   Initializing packaged variables.

```
PACKAGE BODY System_Errors
   .
   .
   .
```

```
BEGIN
    vLastError := 'No error condition exists';
END;
```

```
END System_Errors;
```

The highlighted code in this example is executed the first time the package is loaded into memory. Thus, **vLastError** will always contain the string **'No error condition exists'** when the package is first executed by a user. The initialization code for the package must follow the declaration of all procedures and functions within the package.

Step-By-Step: Building A Package

The primary purpose of a package is to group related procedures and functions into a single object. With this in mind, let's build a package based on a common need for every system—error handling and message generation.

Requirements

Our package needs to provide other stored PL/SQL objects with a way to generate an error message that contains excerpts from the data being processed. While we could certainly format the error messages individually as problems arise, it would be easier on developers if common code handled this process.

Error messages that are generated will be stored in the **SYSTEM_ERRORS** table, as follows:

```
error_number    NOT NULL    number
error_time      NOT NULL    date
error_text                  varchar2 (200)
displayed                   char (1)
```

Our package must satisfy the following conditions:

- The code that generates error messages must be able to insert specific pieces of data into the error message.

- The error messages that are generated will be stored in the **SYSTEM_ERRORS** table and will often be displayed to the system users. However, we also want to be able to specify whether or not the error is displayed to the user.

- Each message should have a severity level defined so that the proper type of message box can be displayed to the user.

- If the problem is an Oracle error, we want to store the data that was being processed at the time (or at least the parameter values of the procedure or function).

- Every piece of code can potentially have several error messages.

Based on these conditions, it seems reasonable that we'll want to store the error messages for each procedure and function in an **ERROR_MESSAGES** table that looks something like this:

```
module_name      NOT NULL   varchar2 (30)
error_number     NOT NULL   number
error_part       NOT NULL   number
error_text       NOT NULL   varchar2 (30)
```

This table makes it possible to store a single error message in several different pieces. Doing so will allow the code to simply pull the pieces of the message from the table and stick a piece of data between each portion of the message.

Severity information for messages will be stored in the **ERROR_SEVERITIES** table, as follows:

```
module_name      NOT NULL   varchar2 (30)
error_number     NOT NULL   number
severity_level   NOT NULL   number
```

At this point, we can be certain that we'll need at least one procedure to be called to build a message. Let's call this procedure *Build_Error()*.

If we put all our logic inside the **Build_Error**() procedure, we won't need a package. However, it sounds like there will be some fairly complex code in this procedure, so it would be better to break the procedure down into some smaller components. We can determine what these components are by specifying parameters for the procedure.

The **Build_Error**() procedure needs to accept the following parameters:

- *The name of the module that owns the calling procedure or function.* This is simply a string, although for the sake of simplicity, we're going to require that it be one of a small set of module names for the system.

- *The name of the calling procedure or function.* This parameter needs to be accepted just in case there is a problem and we need to debug the interface to the error-generating code.

- *The error number for the message that should be generated.* This is an integer value.

- *The data that should be included in the message.* This can be handled either by passing a delimited string to the procedure or by passing a PL/SQL table to the procedure. Either approach will work, so we'll use the delimited string. Using a PL/SQL table would require passing the number of elements in the table as a parameter to several different subroutines in the package.

- *A flag indicating whether the message is being generated for display to the user.* This will be either a **Y** or an **N**.

Because we're using a delimited string to store the data that should be contained in the message, it would be a good idea to have a routine within the package that gets the next portion of data from the string. Let's call this routine *Next_Word()*.

We'll decide on other subroutines as we go along. A lot of this will be decided once we've drafted some pseudocode for the procedure.

Pseudocode

So far, we've identified two subroutines to be included in the package: the function **Next_Word**() and the procedure **Build_Error**(). We also know that the **Build_Error**() procedure must be public and therefore must be declared within the package spec.

Listing 6.10 shows the logic for the **Next_Word**() function.

Listing 6.10   Logic for the function **Next_Word()**.

```
find the location of the specified delimiter in the string;

if the specified delimiter isn't the first delimiter then
   find the previous delimiter's position
end if;

return the portion of the string between the two delimiters;
```

This pseudocode looks a little odd and will look complicated when translated into PL/SQL. It would be better if **Next_Word**() were a procedure and used **OUT** and

IN OUT parameters to return multiple values. Let's rewrite the pseudocode to accommodate this change. The revised logic is shown in Listing 6.11.

Listing 6.11 Revised pseudocode for the **Next_Word()** function.

```
find the first delimiter in the data string;

extract the portion of the data string prior to the delimiter;

shorten the data string;

return the modified data string and the next data portion to
    the calling routine;
```

Listing 6.12 shows the logic for the **Build_Error()** procedure.

Listing 6.12 Logic for the **Build_Error()** procedure.

```
if the specified module or error number doesn't exist then
    write an "unknown module" error message;
    exit the procedure normally;
end if;

get the first portion of the error message for the module;

while there is more data to be included in the message loop
    stick the next piece of data onto the string;
    stick the next portion of the message onto the string;
end loop;

write the message to the system errors table;

if any unhandled errors occur during processing then
    place a recursive call to this procedure to log an "unhandled
      error" error message (watch for infinite loops!);
end if;
```

Looking at the highlighted lines of this pseudocode, we can identify at least one other module that might be usable within the package—a function that retrieves the next portion of the error message, as needed. Let's call this function **Next_String()**. The pseudocode for the **Next_String()** function is shown in Listing 6.13.

Listing 6.13 Logic for the **Next_String()** function.

```
query the next part of the error message from the ERROR_MESSAGES
   table;

increment the message part counter;

return the next part of the error message;
```

This seems pretty straightforward. We're now ready to code.

Code

Translating the pseudocode for the package into code is fairly straightforward. Listing 6.14 contains the package spec and the package body for the **System_Errors** package.

Listing 6.14 The package spec for the **System_Errors** package.

```
PACKAGE System_Errors

IS

    DELIMITER   CONSTANT char (1) := '^';

    PROCEDURE Build_Error (vModule      IN     varchar2,
                           vProcName    IN     varchar2,
                           iErrorNum    IN     integer,
                           vDataString  IN     varchar2,
                           vDisplayFlag IN     varchar2);

    PROCEDURE Next_Word (vDataString IN OUT varchar2,
                         vWord          OUT varchar2);

END System_Errors;


PACKAGE BODY System_Errors

--  ****************************************************************

    iNextPart    integer := 1;

--  ****************************************************************
```

```
FUNCTION Next_String (vModule    IN     varchar2,
                      iErrorNum IN     integer)

   RETURN varchar2

IS

   vNextStringPart    ERROR_MESSAGES.error_text%TYPE;

BEGIN
   SELECT error_text
   INTO   vNextStringPart
   FROM   ERROR_MESSAGES
   WHERE  module_name  = vModule
   AND    error_number = iErrorNum
   AND    error_part   = iNextPart;

   iNextPart := iNextPart + 1;

   RETURN vNextStringPart;
END Next_String;

-- ****************************************************************


PROCEDCURE Build_Error (vModule       IN     varchar2,
                        vProcName     IN     varchar2,
                        iErrorNum     IN     integer,
                        vDataString   IN     varchar2,
                        vDisplayFlag IN     varchar2)

   IS

      MODULE          CONSTANT varchar2 (6)  := 'ERRORS';
      PROCEDURE       CONSTANT varchar2 (30) := 'Build_Error';
      UNKNOWN_ERROR   CONSTANT integer       := 1;

      bRecursion      boolean := FALSE;
      iSeverity       integer;
      vDataString     varchar2 (200);
      vNewMessage     varchar2 (200);
      vNextPart       ERROR_MESSAGES.error_text%TYPE;
      vNextWord       varchar2 (30);

      xRECURSION_ERROR EXCEPTION;
```

```
BEGIN
   IF NOT bRecursion THEN
      bRecursion := FALSE;
   END IF;

   vDataWords  := vDataString;
   vNewMessage := NULL;
   iNextPart   := 1;


   --
   -- If the module that was specified doesn't exist or the error for
   -- the module can't be found, write an "UNKNOWN ERROR" message
   -- here. This is combined with the retrieval of the severity_level
   -- for the message.
   --
   BEGIN
      SELECT severity_level
      INTO   iSeverity
      FROM   ERROR_SEVERITIES
      WHERE  module_name  = vModule
      AND    error_number = iErrorNum;

   EXCEPTION
      WHEN NO_DATA_FOUND THEN
           IF NOT bRecursion THEN
              bRecursion := TRUE;
              Build_Error (vModule      => MODULE,
                           vProcName    => PROCEDURE,
                           iErrorNum    => UNKNOWN_ERROR,
                           vDataString  => vModule   || DELIMITER ||
                                           iErrorNum || DELIMITER ||
                                           vProcName || DELIMITER,
                           vDisplayFlag => 'Y');

           ELSE
              RAISE xRECURSION_ERROR;
           END IF;
   END;


   --
   -- Get the first part of the error message from the ERROR_MESSAGES
   -- table.
   --
   vNextPart := Next_String (vModule   => vModule,
                             iErrorNum => iErrorNum);
```

```
        vNewMessage := vNewMessage || vNextPart;

    WHILE (instr (vDataString, DELIMITER) > 0) LOOP
        --
        -- Get the next piece of data from the string.
        --
        Next_Word (vDataString => vDataWords,
                   vWord       => vNextWord);


        --
        -- Put the next piece of the error message onto the
        -- new message.
        --
        vNextPart := Next_String (vModule   => vModule,
                                  iErrorNum => iErrorNum);


        vNewMessage := vNewMessage || vNextWord || vNextPart;
    END LOOP;

    INSERT
    INTO    SYSTEM_ERRORS
            (error_number,
             error_time,
             error_text,
             displayed)
    VALUES (ERROR_SEQ.nextval,
            SYSDATE,
            vNewMessage,
            vDisplayFlag);
END Build_Error;


-- ****************************************************************


PROCEDURE Next_Word (vDataString IN OUT varchar2,
                     vWord          OUT varchar2)

IS

BEGIN
    iDelimiterPos := instr (vDataString, DELIMITER);
    vWord         := substr (vDataString, 1, iDelimiterPos);
    vDataString   := substr (vDataString, (iDelimiterPos + 1));
END Next_Word;

END System_Errors;
```

Testing

In reality, packages are not tested; procedures and functions within the package are tested individually from the lowest point on the food chain to the highest. Testing a package requires every subroutine inside the package to be tested thoroughly. References to global variables, constants, and other constructs should be closely examined during the test.

Testing private procedures and functions is somewhat difficult. It's often easier to test procedures and functions by making them public for testing purposes, then removing the public definition of the object from the package spec and then testing the security of the private object.

Summary

Chapter 6 has discussed the fundamentals of grouping procedures and functions using packages. At this point, you should be familiar with the creation of packages and have some insights into designing your own packages and testing the routines inside a package.

Database Triggers

CHAPTER

7

Database Triggers

A *database trigger* is a block of stored PL/SQL that is associated with a table and is executed by Oracle whenever certain events are performed on that table. Like other stored PL/SQL objects, a database trigger is compiled and stored within the data dictionary.

Database triggers can be configured to run at four distinct times for each of three different events that can modify data. This chapter discusses the creation of database triggers for several permutations of these events and also provides an example of designing and creating a trigger. By the end of the chapter, you will understand the nature of each type of trigger and the process involved in creating a trigger.

Features Of Database Triggers

The implementation of database triggers in Oracle7 was a major step forward in application development. Developers could write code to enforce complex business rules and be assured that any modification of data would cause the trigger to fire. By using database triggers, you can take advantage of several extremely powerful features.

Embedded DML Statements

Database triggers are blocks of PL/SQL code. Like any other block of PL/SQL code, a database trigger can include embedded SQL statements. Consider the trigger shown in Listing 7.1.

Listing 7.1 Using a DML statement inside a database trigger.

```
CREATE OR REPLACE
TRIGGER STUDENTS_ARIU
AFTER INSERT OR UPDATE OF overall_gpa
ON STUDENTS
FOR EACH ROW
```

```
BEGIN
   IF (:new.overall_gpa = 3.5) THEN
      INSERT
      INTO    DEANS_LIST_STUDENTS
              (ssn)
      VALUES (:new.ssn);
   END IF;
END STUDENTS_ARIU;
/
```

This simple trigger checks the value of the **overall_gpa** column in the **STUDENTS** table. If an **overall_gpa** value is equal to 3.5, the student's social security number is added to the table **DEANS_LIST_STUDENTS**.

Restricted SQL Commands

There are some restrictions on SQL commands that can be used inside a trigger. None of the following statements can be used:

- COMMIT
- POST
- ROLLBACK
- SAVEPOINT

These statements cannot be used because they force a database to perform actions that can only be performed after a statement has finished executing. If a trigger is executing, the statement that fired the trigger has not finished.

This commonly leads to a problem when database triggers call stored procedures that issue **COMMIT** or **ROLLBACK** statements. A runtime error will occur when attempting to execute a trigger that uses one of these statements, either directly or indirectly.

Restricted Datatypes

A database trigger cannot declare any variables of the **long** or **long raw** datatypes. Attempting to do so will cause compilation errors. Additionally, the **:new** and **:old** specifications cannot reference columns of these datatypes (these specifications are discussed later in the chapter).

Event-Driven Processing

Database triggers are, by definition, event-driven and fire when the following DML statements are executed:

- DELETE
- INSERT
- UPDATE

A trigger can be further defined to fire before or after any or all of these DML statements, and can also be defined to fire at the statement level or the row level. By combining these factors, Table 7.1 can be generated to show the 12 types of database triggers.

Table 7.1   The 12 types of database triggers.

Trigger Type	Fires
Before **DELETE** statement level	Before each **DELETE** statement affects the trigger's associated table, no matter how many rows are deleted from the table.
Before **DELETE** row level	For each row affected by a **DELETE** statement, before each row is deleted.
After **DELETE** row level	For each row affected by a **DELETE** statement, after each row is deleted.
After **DELETE** statement level	After each **DELETE** statement that affects the trigger's associated table, no matter how many rows are deleted from the table.
Before **INSERT** statement level	Before each **INSERT** statement affects the trigger's associated table, no matter how many rows are inserted into the table.
Before **INSERT** row level	For each row inserted into the table, before each row is inserted.
After **INSERT** row level	For each row inserted into the table, after each row is inserted.
After **INSERT** statement level	After each **INSERT** statement affects the trigger's associated table, no matter how many rows are inserted into the table.

continued

Table 7.1 The 12 types of database triggers (Continued).

Trigger Type	Fires
Before **UPDATE** statement level	Before each **UPDATE** statement affects the trigger's associated table, no matter how many rows in the table are updated.
Before **UPDATE** row level	For each row updated in the table, before each row is updated.
After **UPDATE** row level	For each row updated in the table, after each row is updated.
After **UPDATE** statement level	After each **UPDATE** statement that affects the trigger's associated table, no matter how many rows in the table are updated.

When database triggers were first introduced in Oracle7, no table could have more than one trigger of any given type. If no triggers combined types, a table could have a dozen different associated triggers.

When PL/SQL 2.1 was implemented in Oracle 7.1, this 12-trigger limitation was removed. It's now possible to have several triggers of the same type on a table, but Oracle cannot be forced to execute the individual triggers in any particular order. If your business rules must be enforced in a particular order, you must enforce the dependent rules using a single trigger.

While Oracle doesn't execute triggers of the same type in the same order each time, Oracle does fire triggers of different levels in a specific order. This order is illustrated in Figure 7.1.

Each row-level trigger can also have a **WHEN** clause defined, which is often used to replace **IF-THEN** processing. In Listing 7.2, the **IF** statement from the trigger in Listing 7.1 has been replaced with a **WHEN** clause.

Listing 7.2 Using a **WHEN** clause.

```
CREATE OR REPLACE
TRIGGER STUDENTS_ARIU
AFTER INSERT OR UPDATE OF overall_gpa
ON STUDENTS
FOR EACH ROW
WHEN new.overall_gpa > 3.5
```

```
BEGIN
   INSERT
   INTO    DEANS_LIST_STUDENTS
           (ssn)
   VALUES (:new.ssn);
END STUDENTS_ARIU;
/
```

The **WHEN** clause is used to specify an expression or condition that must evaluate to **TRUE** before the trigger will be executed.

The **WHEN** clause is normally used to test a column value. Any column referenced in the **WHEN** clause must be preceded by either the **new** or **old** keyword.

Maintainability

Like other stored PL/SQL objects, database triggers provide a single block of code that enforces a business rule when called from any other block of code. Because the business rule is enforced only in the trigger, the amount of code that has to be modified if the rule changes is drastically reduced.

Triggers provide one level of maintainability that is not provided by other stored PL/SQL objects. Because triggers are not called explicitly from code, the trigger can be redefined without affecting the functionality of code that writes to the trigger's associated table. Because there are no calls to change when a trigger is modified, maintenance becomes even simpler.

Performance Improvement

Starting with PL/SQL version 2.3, database triggers were compiled into *p-code* for quicker execution. This p-code is of the same type as the p-code generated when a procedure or function is compiled and allows Oracle to directly call the executable version of the trigger.

If you're working with an earlier version of PL/SQL, your triggers should be bare-bones calls to other stored PL/SQL objects. Complex **IF-THEN** logic (or other types of procedural logic) will slow the execution of your trigger because this logic must be compiled each time the trigger is executed. In this situation, it's advisable to move trigger logic into stored procedures to improve performance.

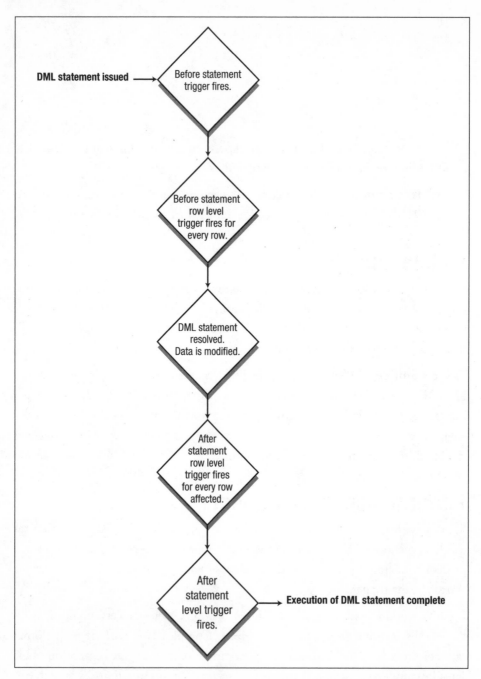

Figure 7.1
The execution order of database triggers.

Referencing Column Values

Row-level database triggers can reference both old and new column values using the **:old** and **:new** specifications. This allows a trigger to determine the change made to a row and then take the appropriate action. These specifications will be discussed in detail later in this chapter.

Reusability

A database trigger is the most inherently reusable stored PL/SQL object. Any code that modifies data in the trigger's associated table will fire the trigger (assuming, of course, that the statement meets the execution criteria for the trigger). This is accomplished without any calls to the trigger from other blocks of code.

The :old And :new Specifications

In row-level triggers, SQL*Plus and PL/SQL statements can reference both the previous and new values of individual columns (other than columns of type **long** and **long raw**) by using the **:old** and **:new** specifications. The **:old** specification refers to the previous value of a column, and the **:new** specification refers to the new value of a column. These specifications allow application developers to test column changes using more complex conditions than can be satisfied by using the **WHEN** clause.

The use of the **:old** and **:new** specifications varies depending on the type of statement that causes the trigger to execute. Figure 7.2 illustrates how these specifications are used in each type of trigger.

Row-level database triggers that fire before a table is modified can also alter data within a new row by assigning a value to a column using the **:new** specification.

Boolean Functions

Database triggers that fire for more than one type of DML statement can use several boolean functions for logical control. These boolean functions are listed in Table 7.2.

Triggering Statement	:old values	:new values
DELETE	Column values for the row being deleted.	All values are NULL.
INSERT	All values are NULL.	Column values for the row being created.
UPDATE	New values for all columns.	Old values for all columns.

Figure 7.2

Using the **:old** and **:new** specifications in a row-level trigger.

Table 7.2   The boolean functions used in database triggers.

Boolean Function	Return Value
DELETING	Returns **TRUE** if the trigger was fired because of a **DELETE** statement; otherwise returns **FALSE**.
INSERTING	Returns **TRUE** if the trigger was fired because of an **INSERT** statement; otherwise returns **FALSE**.
UPDATING	Returns **TRUE** if the trigger was fired because of an **UPDATE** statement; otherwise returns **FALSE**.

The use of these boolean functions is illustrated in Listing 7.3.

Listing 7.3   Using boolean functions in a database trigger.

```
CREATE OR REPLACE
TRIGGER STUDENTS_ARIU
AFTER INSERT OR UPDATE OF overall_gpa
ON STUDENTS
FOR EACH ROW

DECLARE
   xGPA_TOO_HIGH   EXCEPTION;
```

```
BEGIN
   IF UPDATING THEN
      IF (:new.overall_gpa > 4.0) THEN
         RAISE xGPA_TOO_HIGH;
      END IF;

      IF (:new.overall_gpa > 3.5) THEN
         INSERT
         INTO    DEANS_LIST_STUDENTS
                 (ssn)
         VALUES (:new.ssn);

      ELSIF (:new.overall_gpa < 1.5) THEN
         INSERT
         INTO    STUDENTS_NEEDING_ASSISTANCE
                 (ssn)
         VALUES (:new.ssn);
      END IF;

   ELSIF INSERTING THEN
      :new.overall_gpa := NULL;
   END IF;
END STUDENTS_ARIU;
/
```

In Listing 7.3, the trigger **STUDENTS_ARIU** uses the **UPDATING** boolean function to determine if a student's record is being updated, and the **INSERTING** boolean function to determine if the row is for a new student.

Creating And Dropping Triggers

A database trigger is created in SQL*Plus using a **CREATE TRIGGER** command, like the one shown in Listing 7.4.

Listing 7.4   A sample **CREATE TRIGGER** command.

```
CREATE OR REPLACE
TRIGGER STUDENTS_ARIU
AFTER INSERT OR UPDATE OF overall_gpa
ON STUDENTS
FOR EACH ROW

DECLARE
   xGPA_TOO_HIGH    EXCEPTION;
```

```
BEGIN
   IF (:new.overall_gpa > 4.0) THEN
      RAISE xGPA_TOO_HIGH;
   END IF;

   IF (:new.overall_gpa > 3.5) THEN
      INSERT
      INTO    DEANS_LIST_STUDENTS
              (ssn)
      VALUES (:new.ssn);

   ELSIF (:new.overall_gpa < 1.5) THEN
      INSERT
      INTO    STUDENTS_NEEDING_ASSISTANCE
              (ssn)
      VALUES (:new.ssn);

   END IF;
END STUDENTS_ARIU;
/
```

Using **OR REPLACE** in the command instructs Oracle to discard an existing trigger of the same name if it exists. If a trigger of the same name already exists and **OR REPLACE** isn't specified, a compile error will occur.

It's unusual for stored PL/SQL objects, including triggers, to be compiled successfully on the first attempt. For information about resolving compilation errors, refer to Chapter 8.

Triggers can be dropped inside SQL*Plus by using a command such as:

```
DROP TRIGGER STUDENTS_ARIU;
```

Database triggers can also be created or dropped using Oracle's Procedure Builder or one of several third-party editors.

Recompiling Database Triggers

Database triggers can be recompiled (even if you don't have a handy copy of the trigger's source code) using a command like this one:

```
ALTER TRIGGER STUDENTS_ARIU COMPILE;
```

In order to recompile a trigger using this command, you must either have the **ALTER TRIGGER** or **ALTER ANY OBJECT** privilege.

Disabling And Enabling Triggers

Sometimes, you'll want to turn off a trigger so data can be loaded more quickly. This can be done by using the **ALTER TRIGGER** command in SQL*Plus, as illustrated here:

```
ALTER TRIGGER STUDENTS_ARIU DISABLE;
```

If there is more than one trigger on a table and you want to disable all the triggers in one fell swoop, you can use the **ALTER TABLE** command shown here instead:

```
ALTER TABLE STUDENTS DISABLE ALL TRIGGERS;
```

Remember that when a trigger is disabled, data that is loaded into the table isn't processed by the trigger at all. The trigger doesn't even fire. Consequently, if your triggers are validating data or enforcing complex business rules, you run some risks by disabling triggers. Re-enabling a trigger does not cause it to fire retroactively.

Database triggers can be turned on again by using the same commands with **ENABLE** substituted for **DISABLE**, as shown in the following:

```
ALTER TRIGGER STUDENTS_ARIU ENABLE;
ALTER TABLE STUDENTS ENABLE ALL TRIGGERS;
```

Naturally, executing these commands requires that you have the proper privileges (**ALTER TRIGGER, ALTER TABLE,** or **ALTER ANY OBJECT**).

Mutating Table Errors

A *mutating table error* is the most common runtime error for database triggers. This type of error occurs when a row-level database trigger (or an object called from within the trigger) violates one of the following several rules for SQL statements:

- The trigger's associated table can't be queried or modified from the trigger.

- Primary key, unique, and foreign key columns in other tables may not be modified or queried. Columns that are not within one of these indexes may be altered or queried.

- Data in any other tables affected by the triggering DML statement, specifically tables altered because of an **ON DELETE CASCADE** constraint, cannot be read or altered. (This rule applies to statement-level triggers as well.)

Following, you'll find an example of triggers that attempt to violate these rules. You'll also find a way to write triggers that don't break these rules.

Referencing A Trigger's Associated Table

In its simplest incarnation, this error is a reference to the trigger's associated table by the trigger itself. The table is in a state of flux because an operation is in progress, so the trigger can't read from the table. Consider the trigger in Listing 7.5, which attempts to read from the **SCHEDULED_CLASSES** table when a row is created or modified.

Listing 7.5   A trigger that causes a mutating table error.

```
CREATE OR REPLACE
TRIGGER SCHEDULED_CLASSES_ARU
AFTER UPDATE OF course_time, course_location
ON SCHEDULED CLASSES
FOR EACH ROW

DECLARE
   xLOCATION_CONFLICT   EXCEPTION;

BEGIN
   SELECT 1
   INTO   nClassConflicts
   FROM   SCHEDULED_CLASSES
   WHERE  course_number   = :new.course_number
   AND    course_location = :new.course_location
   AND    course_time     = :new.course_time;

   RAISE xLOCATION_CONFLICT;

EXCEPTION
   WHEN NO_DATA_FOUND THEN
        NULL;
END SCHEDULED_CLASSES_ARU;
/
```

This trigger is designed to verify that there are no scheduling conflicts for the class based on time or location. The trigger fails because it must reference its own associated table, **SCHEDULED_CLASSES**, to determine if there is a conflict.

An Exception To This Rule

The before row **INSERT** trigger and the after row **INSERT** trigger are the only types of triggers that can read from or modify a trigger's base table. This may only be done when the **INSERT** statement on the trigger's associated table generated only one new row of data. Consider the trigger in Listing 7.6.

Listing 7.6   A trigger that can read from its associated table.

```
CREATE OR REPLACE
TRIGGER CLASSES_ARI
AFTER INSERT
ON CLASSES
FOR EACH ROW

DECLARE
    xLOCATION_CONFLICT    EXCEPTION;

BEGIN
    SELECT 1
    INTO    nClassConflicts
    FROM    CLASSES
    WHERE   course_number  = :new.course_number
    AND     course_location = :new.course_location
    AND     course_time    = :new.course_time;

    RAISE xLOCATION_CONFLICT;

EXCEPTION
    WHEN NO_DATA_FOUND THEN
        NULL;
END CLASSES_ARI;
/
```

This trigger will not cause a mutating table error as long as only a single class is inserted into the **CLASSES** table at one time. It's possible to insert multiple rows of data using a multiple **INSERT** statement like this one:

```
INSERT
INTO    CLASSES
SELECT *
FROM    IMPORTED_CLASSES;
```

Even if this statement returns only one row, it's still a multiple **INSERT** statement, and a mutating table error will result.

Foreign Key References

Tables that have a foreign key to the trigger's associated table will generate a mutating table error if you attempt to read from or modify any of that table's indexed columns.

The trigger in Listing 7.7 is designed to prevent a course's location and time from being changed if at least one student is scheduled for the course. However, in order to do so, it must make a reference to the **SCHEDULED_CLASSES** table to determine which students are already enrolled in the course. This causes a mutating table error because the act of updating the primary key of the **CLASSES** table impacts the foreign key from the **SCHEDULED_CLASSES** table.

Listing 7.7 Referencing a foreign key column in another table.

```
CREATE OR REPLACE
TRIGGER CLASSES_BU
BEFORE UPDATE OF course_time, course_location
ON CLASSES

DECLARE
    nTotalStudents       number;
    xCLASS_HAS_STUDENTS  EXCEPTION;

BEGIN
    SELECT count (course_number)
    INTO   nTotalStudents
    FROM   SCHEDULED_CLASSES
    WHERE  course_number = :new.course_number;

    IF (nTotalStudents > :new.maximum_enrollment) THEN
       RAISE xCLASS_HAS_STUDENTS;
    END IF;
END CLASSES_BU
/
```

Cascading Deletes

A *cascading delete* occurs when a table with a foreign key reference to another table is given the **ON DELETE CASCADE** constraint. This constraint instructs Oracle to always delete the child rows of deleted parent rows. The use of this constraint is extremely common because it prevents application developers from writing code that leaves leftover children hanging around to muck up the works.

Unfortunately, this can cause problems with database triggers that fire on child tables due to a delete on parent tables. If the **DELETE** trigger attempts to reference the parent table, a mutating table error occurs. The same situation occurs if a **DELETE** trigger on a parent attempts to reference the child table.

This type of mutating table error occurs quite frequently in both statement-level and row-level database triggers, and there is no acceptable workaround using either type of trigger. The only real option is to not use the **ON DELETE CASCADE** constraint.

Working Around The Rules

Enforcing some business rules requires data that is inevitably stored in a trigger's associated table or in tables that have referential integrity constraints with the trigger's associated table. Your best option for working around this problem is to move your processing to an after statement statement-level trigger.

For instance, let's say that when we add a student to the **STUDENTS** table or modify a student's GPA, we want to set a flag in the student's record if the student has the highest GPA. Implementing this with a before statement row-level trigger would cause a mutating table error.

Instead of trying to use a row-level trigger to enforce this rule, we could create an after **INSERT** or **UPDATE** statement-level trigger that reads the **STUDENTS** table to determine the highest GPA and then sets the flag for the appropriate student(s). The trigger in Listing 7.8 shows how this is accomplished.

Listing 7.8   Referencing a trigger's associated table using an after statement trigger.

```
CREATE OR REPLACE
TRIGGER STUDENTS_AIU
AFTER INSERT OR UPDATE OF overall_gpa
ON STUDENTS

DECLARE
   nHighestGPA    number;

BEGIN
   UPDATE STUDENTS
   SET    highest_gpa = 'N';
```

```
    SELECT max (overall_gpa)
    INTO   nHighestGPA
    FROM   STUDENTS;

    UPDATE STUDENTS
    SET .  highest_gpa = 'Y'
    WHERE  overall_gpa = nHighestGpa;
END;
/
```

This approach works very well if your business rules require you to consider all the data in your table every time a modification is made. One concern that you should be aware of with this approach is performance. While this trigger enforces the business rules properly, without the proper indexes in place, this trigger will be a performance hog on all but the smallest of tables.

If your business rules only require certain rows to be touched when processing a new row, you may want to use another approach. This requires you to do one of two things:

- Add a new column to your table to indicate which records have been changed. Then use an after statement statement-level trigger to process rows that are marked as changed.

- Create a new table that stores the key values of rows in the trigger's associated table. We'll call this table a key value lookup table. Use your row-level trigger to store the key values of new or modified rows in the key value lookup table. Implement an after statement statement-level trigger to process the rows that match against the rows in the key value lookup table.

Of these two approaches, the second approach is probably the most performance effective because it utilizes existing indexes on your table. Listing 7.9 is an example of the triggers used in this approach.

Listing 7.9   Implementing a key value lookup scheme to avoid mutating table errors.

```
CREATE OR REPLACE
TRIGGER STUDENTS_ARU
AFTER UPDATE
ON STUDENTS
FOR EACH ROW
```

```
BEGIN
   INSERT
   INTO    TOUCHED_STUDENTS
           (ssn)
   VALUES (:new.ssn);
END STUDENTS_ARU;
/

CREATE OR REPLACE
TRIGGER STUDENTS_AU
AFTER UPDATE
ON STUDENTS

DECLARE
   CURSOR TouchedRecords_cur
   IS
   SELECT ssn
   FOR UPDATE
   FROM    TOUCHED_STUDENTS;

   iFailingClasses    integer := 0;
   iStudentSSN        integer := 0;

BEGIN
   FOR TouchedRecords_rec IN TouchedRecords_cur LOOP
      iStudentSSN := TouchedRecords_rec.ssn;

      SELECT count (*)
      INTO    iFailingClasses
      FROM    SCHEDULED_CLASSES
      WHERE   ssn           = TouchedRecords_rec.ssn
      AND     course_grade > 'D';

      IF (iFailingClasses > 1) THEN
         UPDATE STUDENTS
         SET    probation_flag = 'Y'
         WHERE  ssn = iStudentSSN;
      END IF;

      DELETE
      FROM    TOUCHED_STUDENTS
      WHERE   CURRENT OF TouchedRecords_cur;
   END LOOP;
END STUDENTS_AU;
/
```

These two triggers work together to determine if a student should be put on academic probation every time the student's record is modified—the row-level trigger pitches, and the statement-level trigger catches.

The only significant drawback to this approach is the overhead incurred for each separate transaction through the use of the **INSERT** and **DELETE** statements. If this is a concern, consider implementing the logic for each trigger inside packaged procedures that share access to a PL/SQL table.

In this alternate approach, modified records are written to a global PL/SQL table inside a package by the row-level trigger. The after statement trigger can then reference the data inside the PL/SQL table without performing a read against the database, saving a considerable amount of processing time.

The Data Dictionary And Trigger Source Code

When you create a trigger, Oracle stores the source code for the trigger within the data dictionary. This code is stored in the **ALL_TRIGGERS** view. The structure of the view is shown in Listing 7.10.

Listing 7.10   The structure of the **ALL_TRIGGERS** view.

```
owner                 varchar2 (30)
trigger_name          varchar2 (30)
trigger_type          varchar2 (16)
triggering_event      varchar2 (26)
table_owner           varchar2 (30)
table_name            varchar2 (30)
referencing_names     varchar2 (87)
when_clause           varchar2 (2000)
status                varchar2 (8)
description           varchar2 (2000)
trigger_body          long
```

If you're already familiar with the structure of the **ALL_SOURCE** view (the view that shows you where the source code for procedures, functions, and packages is located), you'll note one significant difference—the source code for a trigger is stored in a **long** variable as a single string and not on a line-by-line basis like procedures, functions, and packages.

Typical Uses For Triggers

Database triggers are an ideal tool for enforcing business rules that are directly related to data. There are many common uses of database triggers, including:

- Enforcing business rules that cannot be enforced with check constraints
- Updating data in other tables
- Marking rows for processing or rows that have been processed
- Signaling that an event has occurred

Each of these uses is described in the following text, but keep in mind that this is certainly not an exhaustive list of uses for database triggers. Every business and every system has different rules.

Enforcing Complex Business Rules

The most complicated rule that can be enforced with a check constraint is a simple mathematical expression. If business rules didn't exceed this level of complication, database triggers probably wouldn't exist. In the real world, business rules are often more complicated than simple equations. It's extremely common for application developers to use a database trigger to enforce an extremely complicated rule.

Updating Relevant Data

If related data is kept in multiple tables (a fairly common occurrence in Oracle systems), it's desirable to use a database trigger to keep related data in sync. Care must be taken when dealing with referential integrity constraints, because references to indexed columns can cause mutating table errors if the trigger isn't structured properly.

Marking Rows For Processing

In some instances, a row-level database trigger is used to make certain that new and modified rows of data are distinguishable from rows that have had certain processing performed.

A similar approach assumes that all unmarked rows haven't been processed. A trigger processes each row of data and flags the row to ensure that processing isn't repeated.

Signaling An Event

A trigger can be used to signal that a particular event has occurred. This can be accomplished by using the **DBMS_Alert** package. This package is discussed in Chapter 9.

Trigger Structure

The basic structure of a database trigger consists of the following several distinct components:

- *Trigger declaration*—Defines the name of the trigger.

- *Triggering event*—Defines the types of DML statements that cause a trigger to fire.

- *Associated table*—Defines the table with which the trigger is associated.

- *Trigger level*—Defines whether the trigger fires at the row or statement level.

- *WHEN clause*—Specifies a boolean condition that is evaluated before the trigger is executed.

- *Trigger body*—Specifies to execute a standard block of PL/SQL when the trigger fires.

Each of these components is explained and illustrated in the following text.

Trigger Declaration

The trigger declaration is the portion of the trigger that defines the name of the trigger. The trigger declaration is highlighted in Listing 7.11.

Listing 7.11   A trigger declaration.

```
CREATE OR REPLACE
TRIGGER CLASSES_ARU
AFTER UPDATE
ON CLASSES
FOR EACH ROW
WHEN new.course_number != old.course_number

DECLARE
   xLOCATION_CONFLICT    EXCEPTION;
```

```
BEGIN
   SELECT 1
   INTO   nClassConflicts
   FROM   CLASSES
   WHERE  course_number   = :new.course_number
   AND    course_location = :new.course_location
   AND    course_time     = :new.course_time;

   RAISE xLOCATION_CONFLICT;

EXCEPTION
   WHEN NO_DATA_FOUND THEN
        NULL;
END CLASSES_ARU;
/
```

Triggering Event

The triggering event of a trigger specifies which DML statements (**DELETE**, **INSERT**, and/or **UPDATE** statements) will cause the trigger to be executed. The triggering event is highlighted in Listing 7.12.

Listing 7.12   A triggering event.

```
CREATE OR REPLACE
TRIGGER CLASSES_ARU
AFTER UPDATE
ON CLASSES
FOR EACH ROW
WHEN new.course_number != old.course_number

DECLARE
   xLOCATION_CONFLICT   EXCEPTION;

BEGIN
   SELECT 1
   INTO   nClassConflicts
   FROM   CLASSES
   WHERE  course_number   = :new.course_number
   AND    course_location = :new.course_location
   AND    course_time     = :new.course_time;

   RAISE xLOCATION_CONFLICT;
```

```
EXCEPTION
   WHEN NO_DATA_FOUND THEN
        NULL;
END CLASSES_ARU;
/
```

Associated Table

Each database trigger, whether statement-level or row-level, is associated with a table. This table is often called the trigger's *associated table* or *base table*. A database trigger is fired when a **DELETE**, **INSERT**, and/or **UPDATE** statement modifies data contained in the trigger's associated table. Listing 7.13 illustrates how a trigger's associated table is defined.

Listing 7.13 Defining a trigger's associated table.

```
CREATE OR REPLACE
TRIGGER CLASSES_ARU
AFTER UPDATE
ON CLASSES
FOR EACH ROW
WHEN new.course_number != old.course_number

DECLARE
   xLOCATION_CONFLICT   EXCEPTION;

BEGIN
   SELECT 1
   INTO   nClassConflicts
   FROM   CLASSES
   WHERE  course_number   = :new.course_number
   AND    course_location = :new.course_location
   AND    course_time     = :new.course_time;

   RAISE xLOCATION_CONFLICT;

EXCEPTION
   WHEN NO_DATA_FOUND THEN
        NULL;
END CLASSES_ARU;
/
```

Trigger Level

Each database trigger is defined at the statement-level or the row-level. A statement-level trigger fires once for each statement that causes the trigger to fire. If 10 rows are updated because of a single **UPDATE** statement, the trigger fires once. A row-level trigger fires once for each row of data modified by any given DML statement. If an **UPDATE** statement modifies 10 rows, the row-level trigger will fire 10 times. The definition of a trigger's level is highlighted in Listing 7.14.

Listing 7.14   Declaring a trigger's level.

```
CREATE OR REPLACE
TRIGGER CLASSES_ARU
AFTER UPDATE
ON CLASSES
FOR EACH ROW
WHEN new.course_number != old.course_number

DECLARE
   xLOCATION_CONFLICT   EXCEPTION;

BEGIN
   SELECT 1
   INTO   nClassConflicts
   FROM   CLASSES
   WHERE  course_number  = :new.course_number
   AND    course_location = :new.course_location
   AND    course_time    = :new.course_time;

   RAISE xLOCATION_CONFLICT;

EXCEPTION
   WHEN NO_DATA_FOUND THEN
        NULL;
END CLASSES_ARU;
/
```

WHEN Clause

The **WHEN** clause is a boolean expression that is evaluated by Oracle before the trigger's body is executed. Using the **WHEN** clause allows a developer to improve performance by testing simple conditions before the trigger's body is executed. Listing 7.15 illustrates the use of the **WHEN** clause.

Listing 7.15   Using the **WHEN** clause.

```
CREATE OR REPLACE
TRIGGER CLASSES_ARU
AFTER UPDATE
ON CLASSES
FOR EACH ROW
WHEN new.course_number != old.course_number

DECLARE
   xLOCATION_CONFLICT   EXCEPTION;

BEGIN
   SELECT 1
   INTO   nClassConflicts
   FROM   CLASSES
   WHERE  course_number  = :new.course_number
   AND    course_location = :new.course_location
   AND    course_time    = :new.course_time;

   RAISE xLOCATION_CONFLICT;

EXCEPTION
   WHEN NO_DATA_FOUND THEN
        NULL;
END CLASSES_ARU;
/
```

Trigger Body

The body of a database trigger, with the restrictions that we've already discussed, is a standard block of PL/SQL. The body of a trigger is highlighted in Listing 7.16.

Listing 7.16   A trigger body.

```
CREATE OR REPLACE
TRIGGER CLASSES_ARU
AFTER UPDATE
ON CLASSES
FOR EACH ROW
WHEN new.course_number != old.course_number

DECLARE
   xLOCATION_CONFLICT   EXCEPTION;
```

```
BEGIN
   SELECT 1
   INTO    nClassConflicts
   FROM    CLASSES
   WHERE   course_number   = :new.course_number
   AND     course_location = :new.course_location
   AND     course_time     = :new.course_time;

   RAISE xLOCATION_CONFLICT;

EXCEPTION
   WHEN NO_DATA_FOUND THEN
         NULL;
END CLASSES_ARU;
/
```

Documenting Triggers

Documentation for a trigger is quite similar to the documentation for a procedure, function, or package. However, some differences do come into play, such as:

- Triggers don't have parameters.

- Triggers are always public objects.

- Triggers always fire whenever the conditions are right.

- Triggers often implement unusual code to work around mutating table errors.

The basics of writing good documentation for your code remain the same, regardless of what type of stored PL/SQL object you're writing. The proper use of a header, pseudocode, commenting, and meaningfully named identifiers all contribute to communicating the purpose and functionality of your trigger to the person who must maintain the code. The use of commenting, identifier names, and pseudocode are discussed in detail earlier in this book. So, let's skip those topics here and take a look at the trigger header.

Trigger Header

Your trigger's header must provide certain information about the trigger. The header for a trigger, like the header for a procedure or function, needs to describe the code and its purpose. These are some of the questions that the header should answer:

- With which table is the trigger associated?

- What type(s) of DML statement causes the trigger to fire?

- If the trigger is an **UPDATE** trigger, does it fire for any particular columns?

- What error conditions can be raised from the trigger?

- Through which hoops does the trigger jump to avoid mutating table errors?

Listing 7.17 shows an example of a header that deals with each of these issues.

Listing 7.17   A sample header for a trigger.

```
-- *******************************************************************
-- Description: The ENROLLED_CLASSES_ARIU trigger fires whenever a
--   row is created or modified in the ENROLLED_CLASSES table. The
--   trigger determines the student's current academic level and
--   the minimum academic level for the course. If the minimum level
--   for the course exceeds the student's academic level, the
--   exception xSTUDENT_NOT_QUALIFIED is raised and the transaction
--   is aborted.
--
-- Fires: On an INSERT or UPDATE of the ENROLLED_CLASSES table, for
--        every new or modified row
--
-- REVISION HISTORY
-- Date          Author      Reason for Change
-- ------------------------------------------------------------------
-- 21 APR 1997  J. Ingram    Trigger created.
-- *******************************************************************
```

Step-By-Step: Creating A Trigger

Let's design a trigger from scratch now, based on a simple set of rules that the trigger must enforce. We'll create a trigger that prevents a students from enrolling in courses, unless the student satisfies a minimum student level (freshman, sophomore, junior, senior, master's, or doctoral).

Trigger Requirements

While the final functionality of the trigger is a rule of the university, the design of the trigger must be grounded in the trigger's associated table and any relationships between the associated table and other tables. For each student's classes, a row must exist in the **ENROLLED_CLASSES** table, which has this structure:

```
ssn                    NOT NULL   varchar2 (9)
course_number          NOT NULL   number   (5)
audit_flag                        varchar2 (1)
```

The **ssn** column in the **ENROLLED_CLASSES** table has a foreign key relationship to the **ssn** column in the **STUDENTS** table, as follows:

```
ssn                    NOT NULL   varchar2 (9)
first_name             NOT NULL   varchar2 (10)
last_name              NOT NULL   varchar2 (12)
street_address         NOT NULL   varchar2 (30)
apartment_number       NOT NULL   varchar2 (4)
city                   NOT NULL   varchar2 (30)
state_code             NOT NULL   varchar2 (2)
zip_code               NOT NULL   number   (5)
home_phone             NOT NULL   number   (10)
financing_num          NOT NULL   integer  (9)
student_level          NOT NULL   number   (1)
degree_plan_code                  number   (5)
overall_gpa                       number   (3, 2)
most_recent_gpa                   number   (3, 2)
middle_name                       varchar2 (10)
```

The **course_number** column in the **ENROLLED_CLASSES** table has a foreign key relationship with the **SCHEDULED_COURSES** table, as follows:

```
course_number          NOT NULL   number   (5)
course_credits         NOT NULL   number   (1)
course_hours           NOT NULL   number   (1)
course_time            NOT NULL   varchar2 (2)
course_location        NOT NULL   number   (5)
min_student_level                 number   (1)
credit_flag                       varchar2 (1)
```

This means that our trigger must retrieve information from two different places (the **SCHEDULED_COURSES** and the **STUDENTS** tables) to determine whether the student can enroll in the class.

Now that we've examined the data structures that we'll have to deal with to implement the trigger, let's move on and start examining how the trigger has to work.

Determining The Trigger's Level

One of the most important steps in designing a trigger is making sure the trigger fires at the right time. This is determined by the way the trigger's base table is used in day-to-day operations.

In order for a student to register for a class, a row must be created in the **ENROLLED_CLASSES** table. Because **INSERT** statements are used to create rows, the trigger we create must obviously fire when a new row is inserted into the table.

The real question is whether rows that already exist in the **ENROLLED_CLASSES** table can be updated. It turns out that a student could very well update a row by deciding to take a specific class at a different time or in a different location. This means that the trigger must also fire when an **UPDATE** statement is executed on the **ENROLLED_CLASSES** table.

Because each row in the **ENROLLED_CLASSES** table represents a single class, the trigger must fire for every row in the table.

Pseudocode

We now know that the trigger must accomplish the following tasks whenever a new row is created or an existing row is modified in the **ENROLLED_CLASSES** table:

- Determine a student's level.

- Determine the minimum level of student that can take a course.

- Compare the student's level to the minimum level for a course.

Based on this definition of what the trigger has to do, we can develop some pseudocode for the trigger that clearly illustrates the logical steps necessary to enforce the business rules. This pseudocode is shown in Listing 7.18.

Listing 7.18 Pseudocode for the **ENROLLED_CLASSES_ARIU** trigger.

```
for each row created or updated loop
   get the student's current level;
   get the minimum level for the course;
```

```
    if the student's level is less than the course level then
       raise an error;
    end if;
end loop;
```

Code

Now that we've written some simple procedural descriptions for the trigger, we're ready to take a crack at coding. Listing 7.19 is the code for the **ENROLLED_CLASSES_ARIU** trigger.

Listing 7.19   Code for the **ENROLLED_CLASSES_ARIU** trigger.

```
TRIGGER ENROLLED_CLASSES_ARIU
AFTER INSERT OR UPDATE
ON ENROLLED_CLASSES
FOR EACH ROW

DECLARE
    iStudentLevel          integer;
    iCourseLevel           integer;
    xSTUDENT_NOT_QUALIFIED  EXCEPTION;

BEGIN
    SELECT student_level
    INTO   iStudentLevel
    FROM   STUDENTS
    WHERE  ssn = :new.ssn;

    SELECT nvl (min_student_level, 0)
    INTO   iCourseLevel
    FROM   SCHEDULED_COURSES
    WHERE  course_number = :new.course_number;

    IF (iStudentLevel < iCourseLevel) THEN
       RAISE xSTUDENT_NOT_QUALIFIED;
    END IF;
END;
```

You might have noticed that the final code for the trigger uses the **nvl()** function when retrieving the value of the **min_student_level** column from the **SCHEDULED_COURSES** table. This allows us to have a course that can be taken by any student.

Testing The Trigger

To ensure that mutating table errors are avoided, every test of a database trigger should incorporate the following tasks:

- Create a single new row in the trigger's associated table.

- Create multiple new rows in the trigger's associated table.

- Modify a single row in the trigger's associated table.

- Modify multiple rows in the trigger's associated table.

- Delete a single row in the trigger's associated table.

- Delete multiple rows in the trigger's associated table.

Obviously, not all of these tests will be valid for a single trigger, but one of the principles of testing is to test events that shouldn't cause a response. For instance, if you've created a row-level **INSERT** trigger, executing an **UPDATE** statement against the trigger's associated table shouldn't cause the trigger to fire.

In addition to the previously outlined tests, a test for a database trigger must also account for different sets of conditions that exist in the data. Based on what we know about the trigger that we just wrote, tests such as the following should be run to test the **INSERT** functionality of the trigger:

- Create a new student, John Williams, with a **student_level** of 1 (freshman) and a new course, Psychology 101, with a **min_student_level** of 1. Attempt to register the student for the course by inserting a row into the **ENROLLED_CLASSES** table. No exceptions should be raised from the trigger.

- Create a new student, Martha Delan, with a **student_level** of 1 (freshman) and a new course, Anthropology 210, with a **min_student_level** of 2 (sophomore). Attempt to register the student for the course. The exception **xSTUDENT_NOT_QUALIFIED** should be raised from the trigger.

- Create a new student, Andrea Jones, with a **student_level** of 1 (freshman) and a new course, Arts & Culture 100, without a **min_student_level**. Attempt to register the student for the course. No exceptions should be raised from the trigger.

At this point, we have created three new classes and three new students, and successfully registered two of the three new students for a class. Now, we have to test the

UPDATE functionality of the trigger. We can test the trigger's **UPDATE** functionality by using tests such as the following:

- Create a new course, Computer Science 560, with a **min_student_level** of 5 (master's student). Use an **UPDATE** statement to move student John Williams from Psychology 101 to Computer Science 560. The exception **xSTUDENT_NOT_QUALIFIED** should be raised from the trigger.

- Set the **student_level** for John Williams to 6 (doctoral). Use an **UPDATE** statement to move this student from Psychology 101 to Computer Science 560. No exceptions should be raised from the trigger.

Naturally, other triggers in place on the **ENROLLED_CLASSES** table might cause errors. If there are other triggers for the table, you should test your trigger alone first so that any internal errors can be isolated quickly. Once you are certain that the trigger's logic is sound, test the new trigger with the table's other triggers in place so you can resolve any conflicts among triggers.

Summary

Chapter 7 addresses the concept of database triggers and the most commonly encountered pitfall—the mutating table error. At this point, you should have an understanding of a trigger's structure and how a trigger relates to a table. You should also have an understanding of the limitations placed on database triggers, and how to design and test your own triggers. Chapter 8 discusses debugging compile and runtime errors in stored PL/SQL objects.

Debugging

CHAPTER

8

HIGH PERFORMANCE

Debugging

Preceding chapters have intentionally left out the subject of debugging SQL and PL/SQL code. Debugging is an essential skill for all application developers, including those who use SQL and PL/SQL. This chapter consolidates knowledge gained from the implementation of several approaches to debugging PL/SQL applications.

Many of the techniques illustrated here work most effectively if you plan ahead when writing your code. Because going back and rewriting existing code is seldom an option, there are also some techniques presented that will help out when you are debugging code you didn't design.

This chapter divides errors into two classes: compile errors and runtime errors. Of the two types of errors, compile errors are the easiest to resolve, so we'll cover those first.

Compile Errors

A *compile error* occurs when a statement is being parsed. The following are all examples of problems in code that can cause a compile error:

- A missing semicolon at the end of an SQL or PL/SQL statement.

- An SQL statement that references a nonexistent table.

- A reference to a variable that hasn't been declared.

- An incorrect **CREATE** command.

This list is by no means exhaustive. Some of these examples are simple mistakes ("Drat, I keep forgetting those darned semicolons."). Others are caused by poor documentation ("This is the table mentioned in the design document, but it has been called something else in the system."). Still others will help you isolate system problems ("I'm referencing this table in my code, but Oracle says the table doesn't exist. I think I need a synonym for the table.").

Fortunately, resolving compile errors is usually very simple. The first step to being able to successfully resolve a compile error is knowing how to find it. Oracle is a big help here, since it reports the position of the compile error if you ask nicely.

Listing Compile Errors

When compiling code inside SQL*Plus, you can show the compile errors for a block of code using the **show errors** command, as follows:

```
show errors
```

Let's assume that you're trying to compile the stored procedure shown in Listing 8.1.

Listing 8.1   A sample stored procedure with compile errors.

```
CREATE OR REPLACE
PROCEDURE Calculate_Student_Grades

IS

    CURSOR Active_Students_cur
    IS
    SELECT ssn
    FROM    STUDENTS
    WHERE   graduation_date IS NOT NULL;

    Active_Student_rec           Active_Students_cur%ROWTYPE;

    vCurrentSSN                  STUDENTS.ssn%ROWTYPE;
    nNewGPA                      STUDENTS.gpa%TYPE;

BEGIN
    FOR Active_Student_rec IN Active_Student_cur LOOP
        nNewGPA := Calculate_GPA (vSSN => vCurrentSSN);
    END LOOP;
END Calculate_Student_Grades;
/
```

When trying to compile this procedure in SQL*Plus, the message

```
Warning: Procedure created with compilation errors.
```

is received. In order to identify the compile errors, you must execute the **show errors** command, as shown in Figure 8.1.

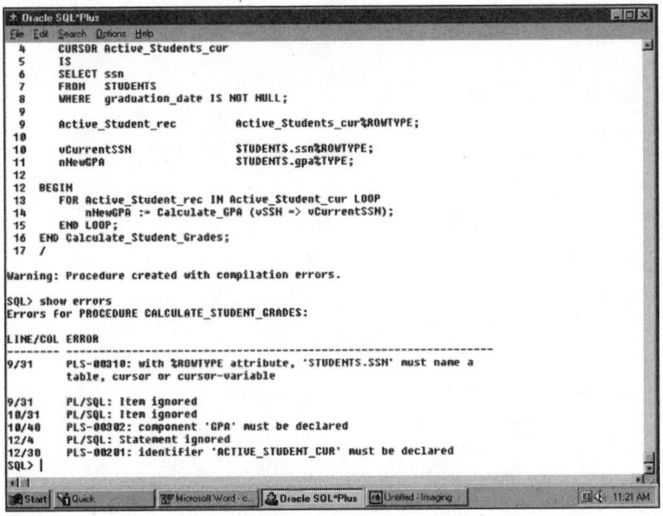

Figure 8.1
Using the **show errors** command.

Figure 8.1 shows the following three compile errors:

- The **vCurrentSSN** variable shouldn't be using a **%ROWTYPE** reference to the **GPA** column in the **STUDENTS** table.

- There is no column named **GPA** in the **STUDENTS** table.

- The reference to the **Active_Students_cur** cursor on line 13 is misspelled. The compiler cannot isolate the reference to the **Active_Student_cur** cursor because it hasn't been declared.

At this point, the **Calculate_Student_Grades**() procedure actually exists within Oracle. The procedure is marked as invalid because it failed to compile, but pulling the source code for the procedure from the **ALL_SOURCE** view will give you the most recently compiled code. Now that you know how to locate compile errors in your code, let's move on to correcting the errors.

Fixing Compile Errors

Now that the compilation errors for the **Calculate_Student_Grades**() procedure have been identified, the source code has to be modified to fix the errors so the procedure can be recompiled. The revised source code that fixes these compile errors is shown in Listing 8.2.

Listing 8.2   The revised **Calculate_Student_Grades()** procedure.

```
CREATE OR REPLACE
PROCEDURE Calculate_Student_Grades

IS

    CURSOR Active_Students_cur
    IS
    SELECT  ssn
    FROM    STUDENTS
    WHERE   graduation_date IS NOT NULL;

    Active_Student_rec            Active_Students_cur%ROWTYPE;

    vCurrentSSN                   STUDENTS.ssn%TYPE;
    nNewGPA                       STUDENTS.overall_gpa%TYPE;

BEGIN
    FOR Active_Student_rec IN Active_Students_cur LOOP
        vCurrentSSN := Active_Student_rec.ssn;
        nNewGPA := Calculate_GPA (vSSN => vCurrentSSN);
    END LOOP;
END Calculate_Student_Grades;
/
```

Figure 8.2 illustrates what happens when we attempt to recompile the procedure now.

Figure 8.2

Compiling the **Calculate_Student_Grades()** procedure after fixing compile errors.

As you can see, there is still at least one compile error in the source code. Once again, we need to issue the **show errors** command to see which compilation errors have occurred. The result of the **show errors** command is shown in Figure 8.3.

Oops! It looks like the **Calculate_GPA()** function doesn't exist. Resolving this compile error requires finding out what happened to the function. Is it in another schema? Does the function even exist?

This process is repeated as necessary to obtain a clean compile for the procedure.

Using Data Dictionary Tables

Errors displayed as a result of using the **show errors** command don't appear out of nowhere. These errors are stored in the **ALL_ERRORS** view, which has the following structure:

```
owner           varchar2 (30)
name            varchar2 (30)
type            varchar2 (12)
sequence        number
line            number
position        number
text            varchar2 (2000)
```

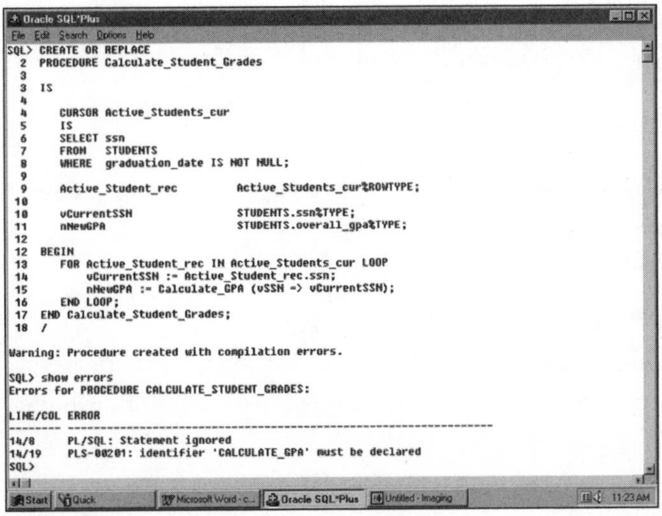

Figure 8.3
Compile errors in the **Calculate_Student_Grades()** procedure.

Since most developers debug one block of code and then move on to another, there's seldom a need to query this table. If you have several blocks of code that all have compile errors, you can query the errors for each object individually from this view using a query like the one shown in Listing 8.3.

Listing 8.3 Pulling error information from the **ALL_ERRORS** view.

```
SELECT line, position, text
FROM   ALL_ERRORS
WHERE  owner = upper ('&1')
AND    name  = upper ('&2')
AND    type  = upper ('&3')
ORDER BY line, position;
```

To use the preceding query, replace **&1** with the schema name that owns the object, **&2** with the name of the object, and **&3** with the type of the object. This query will return the text and position of the error, including a line number.

Line Numbers

Notice that each error is reported with a line number and a position number. SQL*Plus skips over blank lines when compiling code, so you'll need to determine the line of code to which the line number refers. This is done by using the **list** command, as shown in Figure 8.4.

If you like, you can also use the **list** command to display a range of lines. For example,

```
list 10 15
```

displays lines 10 through 15 of your source code. If you specify just one line number, **list** will only display that line. For instance,

```
list 10
```

displays only line 10 of your code. Using the **list** command without specifying a line number instructs SQL*Plus to display the entire contents of the buffer.

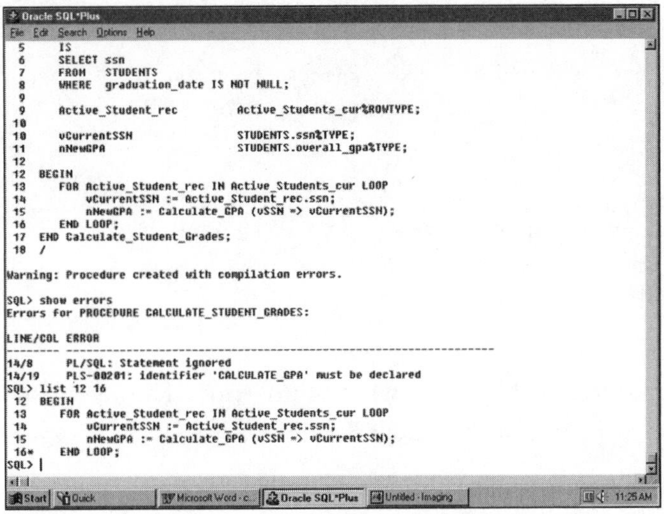

Figure 8.4
Using the **list** command to find a line of code.

When The Line Number Is Wrong

Oracle reports the line number on which an error is detected. It's not uncommon for the reported line number to be incorrect, because you've done something else incorrectly in your code that has no effect until Oracle tries to compile the line number specified in the output of the **show errors** command.

Most of the time, incorrect line numbers are the result of variable and type declaration problems, or as a result of incorrect references to objects or variables. Consider again the code for the **Calculate_Student_Grades()** procedure, presented in Listing 8.4.

Listing 8.4   The **Calculate_Student_Grades()** procedure.

```
CREATE OR REPLACE
PROCEDURE Calculate_Student_Grades

IS

    CURSOR Active_Students_cur
    IS
    SELECT ssn
    FROM    STUDENTS
    WHERE   graduation_date IS NOT NULL;
```

```
    Active_Student_rec          Active_Students_cur%ROWTYPE;

    vCurrentSSN                 STUDENTS.ssn%ROWTYPE;
    nNewGPA                     STUDENTS.gpa%TYPE;

BEGIN
    FOR Active_Student_rec IN Active_Student_cur LOOP
        nNewGPA := Calculate_GPA (vSSN => vCurrentSSN);
    END LOOP;
END Calculate_Student_Grades;
/
```

Attempting to compile this code generates three errors. The line and position numbers of these errors are shown in Table 8.1.

Running the **list** command against line 12 of the code for the procedure shows that the error occurred at the **BEGIN** statement. This isn't really the case. The real cause of the error is the reference on line 13 to the cursor **Active_Student_cur**.

Taking a good look at the variable declarations section makes it pretty clear that line 13 should reference the cursor **Active_Student_cur**. In this instance, debugging by following the line number is a dead end.

As frustrating as compile errors can sometimes be, debugging runtime errors is more frustrating.

Runtime Errors

Runtime errors are errors that occur while code is executing. These errors can arise due to data problems or code problems. For instance, attempting to assign a 31-character string to a **varchar2 (30)** variable will cause a runtime error.

Table 8.1   Compile errors for the **Calculate_Student_Grades()** procedure.

Line Number	Position	Error
9	31	PLS-00310: with **%ROWTYPE** attribute, 'STUDENTS.SSN' must name a table, cursor or cursor-variable
10	40	PLS-00302: component 'GPA' must be declared
12	30	PLS-00201: identifier 'ACTIVE_STUDENT_CUR' must be declared

Most approaches to dealing with runtime errors utilize the **DBMS_Output** package to isolate the location of an error so that a developer can correct the problem. This package provides an excellent debugging tool when used properly.

Using The DBMS_Output Package

The **DBMS_Output** package was first introduced with Oracle7 to allow output to the SQL buffer in SQL*Plus from PL/SQL blocks. The package was intended primarily as a debugging tool, and it has served that purpose admirably (although it is now being supplanted by step-through debuggers available in Oracle's Procedure Builder and several other third-party tools).

In order to use the **DBMS_Output** package for debugging, you must issue the

```
set serveroutput on
```

command in SQL*Plus. This command instructs SQL*Plus to collect the contents of the buffer after executing a PL/SQL block or stored PL/SQL object.

The size of this buffer defaults to 2,000 characters. For practical purposes, this limit is far too low. Fortunately, you can use the

```
set serveroutput on size n
```

command to specify the size of the buffer. In this command, n specifies the buffer size and can range from 2,000 characters to an upper limit of 1 million characters. A million characters is more than sufficient to debug *any* modularized block of code.

Debugging with the **DBMS_Output** package involves mostly calls to the **DBMS_Output.Put_Line()** procedure. This procedure writes a line to the SQL buffer. When a block of PL/SQL code finishes executing, the contents of the SQL buffer are displayed.

Listing 8.5 is an excerpt from the debugging version of the **Build_SUID_Matrix** package (the final version of the package can be found on the CD).

Listing 8.5 An excerpt of debugging code from the Build_SUID_Matrix package.

```
DBMS_Output.Put_Line ('Fetch ObjectSourceCode_cur');

FETCH ObjectSourceCode_cur INTO ObjectSourceCode_rec;
EXIT WHEN ObjectSourceCode_cur%NOTFOUND;

--
-- Initialize variables.
--
iStringLen      := 0;
iStringPos      := 0;

--
-- Clean the line of code before processing it.
--
DBMS_Output.Put_Line ('Call CleanLineOfSource');
vLine      := CleanLineOfSource (ObjectSourceCode_rec.text);
DBMS_Output.Put_Line (vLine);

--
-- If the line contains the string 'DELETE ', this might be a delete
-- operation.
--
DBMS_Output.Put_Line ('Check for DELETE ');
iStringPos := instr (vLine, 'DELETE ');
iStringLen := length (vLine);

--
-- Test the line to determine if the 'DELETE ' string is
--      A) inside a comment
--      B) part of an identifier
--
DBMS_Output.Put_Line ('Is the string inside a comment?');

IF ((instr (vLine, '--') > 0)
    AND
    (instr (vLine, '--') < iStringPos)) THEN
      iStringPos := 0;
END IF;

--
-- Is the string inside a comment?
--
DBMS_Output.Put_Line ('Check for string following a */');
```

```
IF ((instr (vLine, '/*') > 0)
    AND
    (iStringPos > instr (vLine, '/*'))) THEN
        iStringPos := 0;
END IF;


--
-- Is the string inside a comment?
--
DBMS_Output.Put_Line ('Check for */ without a preceding /*');

IF ((instr (vLine, '*/') > 0) AND (instr (vLine, '/*') = 0)) THEN
    iStringPos := 0;
END IF;


--
-- Is the string inside an identifier?
--
DBMS_Output.Put_Line ('Check for part of identifier');
IF ((instr (vLine, '_DELETE ') = (iStringPos - 1))
    AND
    (instr (vLine, '_DELETE ') > 0)) THEN
        iStringPos := 0;
END IF;


--
-- If the delete is beyond the first character of the line,
-- either it is poorly written code or it is a comment.
--
DBMS_Output.Put_Line ('The delete is past the first character');

IF (iStringPos > 1) THEN
    iStringPos := 0;
END IF;


--
-- If the line has passed all the false positive tests, go ahead
-- and display the table name.
--
IF (iStringPos > 0) THEN
    vParsedString := substr (vLine, (iStringPos + 6));
END IF;


--
-- If the line has passed the false positive tests, check to see
-- if it contains a 'FROM' clause.  If so, remove the clause from
-- the string.
```

```
--
IF (iStringPos > 0) THEN
   iStringPos := instr (vParsedString, 'FROM ');

   IF (iStringPos > 0) THEN
      vParsedString := substr (vParsedString, (iStringPos + 5));
   END IF;

   --
   -- Remove the semicolon at the end of the line.
   --
   DBMS_Output.Put_Line ('Replace ; at the end of the line');
   vParsedString := replace (vParsedString, ';', '');

   --
   -- Call the UpdateMatrix procedure to perform the write to the
   -- SUID_MATRIX table.
   --
   UpdateMatrix (vParsedString,
                 vOwner,
                 vObject,
                 'DELETE');
END IF;
```

Each of the calls to the **DBMS_Output.Put_Line()** procedure indicates the progress of the procedure. A string of text is passed as the procedure's lone parameter.

The runtime error must always occur after the last message that was delivered to the buffer. Isolating the error is now a simple matter of determining which statements occurred after the message.

Locating Runtime Errors

Locating a runtime error in a complex piece of code (or one that runs through several pieces of code) is a time-consuming and grueling task. There are two basic ways of isolating a runtime error inside a block of code:

- Ignoring exceptions—allowing errors to rise to the highest level, and debugging based on line number and error text.

- Using a tracepoint variable to keep track of the object's execution.

Each of these methods is discussed in detail in the following sections. Keep in mind that each of these methods is an extreme approach and that these approaches can be blended to best suit your programming style.

Ignoring Exceptions

The basic idea of this approach is that the line and position values returned by Oracle are the most effective method of isolating a problem. Consequently, the developer ignores the use of exception handlers and expects each exception to be raised to the highest possible level.

One significant effect of this approach is that operations are always interrupted if an error occurs while executing a stored PL/SQL object. This error is raised to the highest possible level. Unfortunately, this makes for a very hostile environment for users because every error that occurs interrupts and potentially destroys work.

When an error occurs, the developer collects the error text from the user and begins stepping through the object by hand. The developer must figure out what parameter values were passed to the object and then execute the code to reproduce and isolate the error.

Using Tracepoints

In my opinion, a better method of debugging runtime errors is the use of a *tracepoint* variable to keep track of an object's current location. Listing 8.6 is a sample of code that uses a tracepoint variable.

Listing 8.6   Code using a tracepoint variable.

```
CREATE OR REPLACE
PROCEDURE Calculate_Student_Grades

IS

    CURSOR Active_Students_cur
    IS
    SELECT ssn
    FROM    STUDENTS
    WHERE   graduation_date IS NOT NULL;

    vCurrentSSN             STUDENTS.ssn%TYPE;
    nNewGPA                 STUDENTS.overall_gpa%TYPE;
    iTracePoint             integer;
```

```
BEGIN
    FOR Active_Student_rec IN Active_Students_cur LOOP
        iTracePoint := 1;

        SELECT sum (course_hours),
               sum (decode (course_grade, 'A', 4,
                                          'B', 3,
                                          'C', 2,
                                          'D', 1))
        INTO   iTotalHours, iTotalCredits
        FROM   ENROLLED_CLASSES
        WHERE  ssn = Active_Student_rec.ssn
        AND    nvl (credit_flag, 'Y') = 'Y'
        AND    nvl (audit_flag,  'N') = 'N'
        AND    course_complete <= SYSDATE;

        iTracePoint := 2;

        nNewGPA := iTotalCredits / iTotalHours;

        iTracePoint := 3;

        UPDATE STUDENTS
        SET    overall_gpa = nNewGPA
        WHERE  ssn = Active_Student_rec.ssn;
    END LOOP;

    iTracePoint := 4;

    COMMIT;

EXCEPTION
    WHEN OTHERS THEN
        ROLLBACK;

        INSERT
        INTO    SYSTEM_ERRORS
                (error_time,
                 error_parameters,
                 display,
                 error_text,
                 error_number,
                 error_object)
        VALUES (SYSDATE,
                Active_Student_rec.ssn,
                'N',
```

```
                    SQLERRM || ' at tracepoint ' || to_char (iTracePoint),
                    SQLCODE,
                    'Calculate_Student_Grades');

        COMMIT;
END Calculate_Student_Grades;
/
```

Naturally, this approach takes some time and work to implement, but for complex code the return on investment is exceptionally high. This method has several advantages to its credit:

- You are always aware of an error's location within the object. Each statement has a unique tracepoint value, so when a statement is referenced, it must be the cause of the runtime error—regardless of how innocuous-looking that statement may be.

- You always know which record the object was processing when the error occurred. Spending time looking up the various calls to the object and adding debugging code to determine parameter values wastes time that can be spent fixing the code.

- The error code and message are preserved for reference. Knowing what type of error occurred might save the trouble of even testing the single statement in question.

- You always know the object in which the error occurred. Knowing this can save time when debugging combinations of objects.

Saving these pieces of information is essential if the code is to be repaired quickly. Of course, this approach only works if you don't mind doing extra work up front, but those with the patience and time to implement it properly can save hours of debugging time down the line.

This approach is most effective when your code is designed to handle errors effectively.

Handling Exceptions Cleanly During Execution

Using exceptions thoughtfully can save you a lot of time that you would otherwise spend writing error handling code. Just like many other coding techniques, the best way to use the technique is to design with the technique in mind. While this does add some overhead to the design process, using exception handlers (particularly the **OTHERS** exception handler) is essential to writing effective code.

The OTHERS Exception Handler

The **OTHERS** exception handler serves as a catch-all exception handler, handling any error that falls through any other exception handling that you have in place. This exception handler should always be the last exception handler in your block of code.

This exception handler is a powerful tool if used properly. If used improperly or carelessly, the **OTHERS** exception handler will mask errors and make your debugging work more difficult than it needs to be. Listing 8.7 shows how the **OTHERS** exception handler can be misused.

Listing 8.7   Misusing the **OTHERS** exception handler.

```
CREATE OR REPLACE
PROCEDURE Calculate_Student_Grades

IS

    CURSOR Active_Students_cur
    IS
    SELECT ssn
    FROM    STUDENTS
    WHERE   graduation_date IS NOT NULL;

    vCurrentSSN              STUDENTS.ssn%TYPE;
    nNewGPA                  STUDENTS.overall_gpa%TYPE;
    iTracePoint              integer;

BEGIN
  FOR Active_Student_rec IN Active_Students_cur LOOP
      iTracePoint := 1;

      SELECT sum (course_hours),
             sum (decode (course_grade, 'A', 4,
                                        'B', 3,
                                        'C', 2,
                                        'D', 1))
      INTO   iTotalHours, iTotalCredits
      FROM   ENROLLED_CLASSES
      WHERE  ssn = Active_Student_rec.ssn
```

```
      AND    nvl (credit_flag, 'Y') = 'Y'
      AND    nvl (audit_flag,  'N') = 'N'
      AND    course_complete <= SYSDATE;

      iTracePoint := 2;

      nNewGPA := iTotalCredits / iTotalHours;

      iTracePoint := 3;

      UPDATE STUDENTS
      SET    overall_gpa = nNewGPA
      WHERE  ssn = Active_Student_rec.ssn;
   END LOOP;

   iTracePoint := 4;

   COMMIT;

EXCEPTION
   WHEN OTHERS THEN
        ROLLBACK;
END Calculate_Student_Grades;
/
```

In this example, the exception handler doesn't do anything that will help the developer debug the application if something goes wrong. In fact, the exception handler completely obscures the fact that something is going wrong.

Preventing data from being altered when an error occurs is an admirable goal, but at the end of the semester when grades go out each student will have remarkably maintained the status quo and the developer (or someone who has taken over the responsibilities) will find themselves in a very hot spot. At the very least, the developer in this case should have recorded that an error occurred.

Logging Errors

The best use of the **OTHERS** exception handler is to record that an error has occurred and to prevent damage to the data as a result of the error. The exception handler in Listing 8.8 does that by recording the event to a **SYSTEM_ERRORS** table.

Listing 8.8   Using the **OTHERS** exception handler to log an error.

```
CREATE OR REPLACE
PROCEDURE Calculate_Student_Grades

IS

    CURSOR Active_Students_cur
    IS
    SELECT ssn
    FROM    STUDENTS
    WHERE   graduation_date IS NOT NULL;

    vCurrentSSN               STUDENTS.ssn%TYPE;
    nNewGPA                   STUDENTS.overall_gpa%TYPE;
    iTracePoint               integer;

BEGIN
    FOR Active_Student_rec IN Active_Students_cur LOOP
        iTracePoint := 1;

        SELECT sum (course_hours),
               sum (decode (course_grade, 'A', 4,
                                          'B', 3,
                                          'C', 2,
                                          'D', 1))
        INTO    iTotalHours, iTotalCredits
        FROM    ENROLLED_CLASSES
        WHERE   ssn = Active_Student_rec.ssn
        AND     nvl (credit_flag, 'Y') = 'Y'
        AND     nvl (audit_flag,  'N') = 'N'
        AND     course_complete <= SYSDATE;

        iTracePoint := 2;

        nNewGPA := iTotalCredits / iTotalHours;

        iTracePoint := 3;

        UPDATE STUDENTS
        SET    overall_gpa = nNewGPA
        WHERE  ssn = Active_Student_rec.ssn;
    END LOOP;

    iTracePoint := 4;
```

```
    COMMIT;

EXCEPTION
    WHEN OTHERS THEN
        ROLLBACK;

        INSERT
        INTO    SYSTEM_ERRORS
                (error_time,
                 error_parameters,
                 display,
                 error_text,
                 error_number,
                 error_object)
        VALUES (SYSDATE,
                Active_Student_rec.ssn,
                'N',
                SQLERRM || ' at tracepoint ' || to_char (iTracePoint),
                SQLCODE,
                'Calculate_Student_Grades');

        COMMIT;
END Calculate_Student_Grades;
/
```

Notice the steps taken by the exception handler and the order in which they occur:

1. Roll back any pending changes to the database.

2. Record the error message, location, and any data that could be of use when attempting to resolve the error.

3. Commit the data about the error message.

In this example, the **SYSTEM_ERRORS** table is a custom table implemented to aid in debugging runtime errors. This isn't one of Oracle's data dictionary tables.

Of course, it's possible that there may be other changes pending to the database that didn't originate in this object. In this event, the **OTHERS** exception handler should still record the information about the error before raising the exception to the calling object. The decision about whether or not to roll back the changes can then be made by the calling object.

Your exception handlers will often include calls to some built-in error handling functions in PL/SQL.

Useful Functions

PL/SQL provides two useful functions that allow you to identify errors: **SQLCODE()** and **SQLERRM()**. These functions are specific to PL/SQL and can't be used in your SQL statements; attempting to do so will result in an error. However, the output of these functions can be assigned to variables in your PL/SQL blocks. Let's take a look at each function.

Using The SQLCODE() Function

The **SQLCODE()** function is used to return the number of the most recent Oracle error message during the execution of a PL/SQL block. For instance, a reference to a nonexistent table or view causes Oracle error ORA-00942 to occur. For this error, the **SQLCODE()** function would return:

```
-00942
```

Listing 8.9 illustrates how the **SQLCODE()** function can be used in your exception handlers.

Listing 8.9   Calling the **SQLCODE()** function in an exception handler.

```
EXCEPTION
   WHEN OTHERS THEN
      IF (SQLCODE = -942) THEN
         RAISE xMISSING_TABLE;

      ELSE
         ROLLBACK;

         INSERT
         INTO   SYSTEM_ERRORS
                (error_time,
                 error_parameters,
                 display,
                 error_text,
                 error_number,
                 error_object)
```

```
        VALUES (SYSDATE,
                Active_Student_rec.ssn,
                'N',
                SQLERRM || ' at tracepoint ' || to_char (iTracePoint),
                SQLCODE,
                'Calculate_Student_Grades');

        COMMIT;
    END IF;
END;
```

The error numbers returned by this function are always negative.

Using The SQLERRM() Function

The **SQLERRM**() function returns the complete text of the last Oracle error message to occur during the execution of a block of PL/SQL code. Calling this function is quite simple:

```
vErrorText := SQLERRM;
```

Calling this function when no errors have occurred returns:

```
ORA-0000: normal, successful completion
```

Summary

Debugging is a skill that relies heavily on a developer's experience and familiarity with the code. Debugging is the largest part of a developer's job and probably the most tedious aspect. This chapter covers several techniques that can ease the burden of debugging your code if you plan ahead when you're writing the code.

Special Packages

CHAPTER

9

Special Packages

Oracle provides several packages that allow you to accomplish a wide range of tasks, from interprocess communication to file I/O to dynamically creating and executing SQL statements inside a PL/SQL block. All of these packages are owned by the **SYS** user—one of the two users that exist when Oracle is first installed. The most important of these packages include:

- **DBMS_Alert**
- **DBMS_DDL**
- **DBMS_Describe**
- **DBMS_Job**
- **DBMS_Output**
- **DBMS_Pipe**
- **DBMS_SQL**
- **DBMS_Utility**
- **UTL_File**

This chapter discusses these packages in detail and describes some common uses for each package.

DBMS_Alert

The **DBMS_Alert** package is used to implement synchronous, event-driven interprocess communication via *signals*. This package is often used in conjunction with database triggers in systems that process data based on individual transactions.

The basic processing of an implementation using signals is fairly simple, as you can see in the following steps:

1. An event occurs, typically a row being written to a table.

2. A database trigger calls the **DBMS_Alert.Signal**() procedure.

3. The process that inserted the row into the table issues a **COMMIT**.

4. The signal is sent.

5. All processes that have registered for the signal are notified that the event indicated by the signal has occurred.

The importance of the **COMMIT** in this scheme can't be overlooked. A **COMMIT** must be issued for the signal to be sent.

The processes that receive the signal must first register for the signal by calling the **DBMS_Alert.Register**() procedure.

The **DBMS_Alert** package contains the following procedures:

- The **Register**() procedure

- The **Remove**() procedure

- The **RemoveAll**() procedure

- The **SetDefaults**() procedure

- The **Signal**() procedure

- The **WaitAny**() procedure

- The **WaitOne**() procedure

These procedures and the parameters needed to call each procedure are explained in the following sections.

The Register() Procedure

The **Register**() procedure is used by a PL/SQL block to indicate that it would like to receive a particular signal. This procedure accepts a single parameter, as follows:

```
PROCEDURE Register (name IN     varchar2)
```

The **name** parameter is the name of the signal for which the PL/SQL block is registering. This parameter must have a length of 30 characters or less.

The Remove() Procedure

The **Remove**() procedure is used by a PL/SQL block when receiving a registered signal is no longer appropriate. This procedure accepts a single parameter, as follows:

```
PROCEDURE Remove (name IN    varchar2)
```

The **name** parameter is the name of the signal for which the PL/SQL block has no further need.

The RemoveAll() Procedure

The **RemoveAll**() procedure is used by a PL/SQL block when no further signals should be received. This procedure does not accept any parameters and appears as follows:

```
PROCEDURE RemoveAll
```

The Set_Defaults() Procedure

The **Set_Defaults**() procedure is used by a PL/SQL block to determine the time that will pass between checks to see if a signal has occurred. This procedure accepts a single parameter, as follows:

```
PROCEDURE Set_Defaults (sensitivity IN    number)
```

The **sensitivity** parameter indicates the number of seconds that should pass between checks for the signal. This value can be specified to a precision of hundredths of a second (two decimal positions).

The Signal() Procedure

The **Signal**() procedure is used by a PL/SQL block to send a signal. The procedure accepts two parameters:

```
PROCEDURE Signal (name    IN    varchar2,
                  message IN    varchar2)
```

The **name** parameter is the name of a specific signal. The **message** parameter is a string of text that is received by all objects that receive the specific signal.

It's worth noting that consecutive signals will overwrite the message from a previous signal. Thus, unless you can guarantee that a signal will be processed immediately, it is unwise to pass data to a routine via the **message** parameter because the data could be overwritten by a later alert. Figure 9.1 illustrates how this could happen.

If you need to pass data when an event occurs, you should consider the use of the **DBMS_Pipe** package instead of the **DBMS_Alert** package (more about **DBMS_Pipe** later in this chapter). Alternately, you can mark data that has been affected by an event so that the code on the receiving end of the signal can identify rows that need to be processed.

The WaitAny() Procedure

The **WaitAny()** procedure is used by a PL/SQL block to wait for any of its registered signals to occur. The procedure has four parameters and appears as follows:

```
PROCEDURE WaitAny (name      OUT varchar2,
                   message   OUT varchar2,
                   status    OUT integer,
                   timeout IN    number DEFAULT MAXWAIT)
```

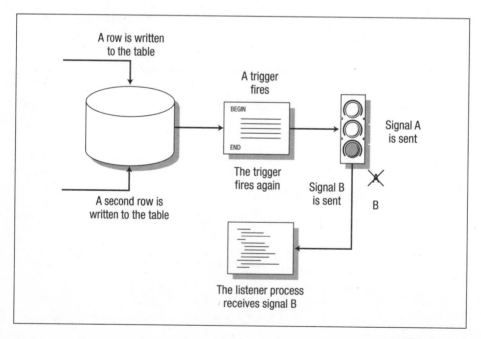

Figure 9.1
Conflicting alerts.

The **name** parameter for this procedure is the name of the signal that has occurred while waiting for an event. It's possible for a signal to have already occurred at the time of the call to the **WaitAny()** procedure. If this is the case, the procedure will return the name of the first signal that is found to have occurred.

The WaitOne() Procedure

The **WaitOne()** procedure is used by a PL/SQL block to wait for a particular signal to occur. The procedure has four parameters: **name**, **message**, **status**, and **timeout**.

```
PROCEDURE WaitOne (name     IN      varchar2,
                   message     OUT varchar2,
                   status      OUT integer,
                   timeout IN      number DEFAULT MAXWAIT)
```

The **name** parameter is the name of the signal for which the PL/SQL block is waiting. The **message** parameter returns any text that is passed with the signal when it occurs. The **status** parameter returns 0 if the signal was received or 1 if the procedure timed out while waiting for the signal. The **timeout** parameter indicates the interval (in seconds) that the **WaitOne()** procedure will wait for the specified signal. If no value for this parameter is specified, it defaults to the value of the **DBMS_Alert.MAXWAIT** constant. The value of this constant is 1,000 days (86,400,000 seconds).

Using Signals

Let's look at an example of some code that uses signals for interprocess communication. Presume we have an order entry system that must be tied to a legacy system. Data is input into the legacy system via a Pro*C program. The trigger in Listing 9.1 is implemented on the **ORDERS** table.

Listing 9.1   Using a trigger to send a signal.

```
TRIGGER ORDERS ARIU
AFTER INSERT OR UPDATE
ON ORDERS
FOR EACH ROW

    CHANGED_ORDER_SIGNAL   CONSTANT varchar2 (10) := 'Changed order';
    NEW_ORDER_SIGNAL       CONSTANT varchar2 (10) := 'New order';
```

```
BEGIN
   IF INSERTING THEN
      DBMS_Alert.Signal (NEW_ORDER_SIGNAL,
                          'A new order has been submitted.');

   ELSIF UPDATING THEN
      DBMS_Alert.Signal (CHANGED_ORDER_SIGNAL,
                          'An order has been changed.');
   END IF;
END ORDERS_ARIU;
```

The Pro*C program is initiated by the system whenever the order entry form is run. This code makes a call to the **DBMS_Alert.Register()** procedure, as follows:

```
DBMS_ALERT.Register ('New order')
```

After registering for the signal, the Pro*C program goes into a loop. During each loop cycle, the program calls the **DBMS_Alert.WaitOne()** procedure:

```
DBMS_Alert.WaitOne (name    => 'New order',
                    message => alert_message,
                    status  => alert_return_value,
                    timeout => 1);
```

This instructs the **WaitOne()** procedure to wait for one second. If no alert has occurred before the end of that second, the procedure returns a value of 1 for the **status** parameter.

Figure 9.2 illustrates how this implementation works.

DBMS_DDL

The **DBMS_DDL** package contains only two procedures—**Alter_Compile()** and **Analyze_Object()**—neither of which performs traditional DDL commands like **CREATE TABLE**:

- The **Alter_Compile()** procedure is used to recompile procedures, functions, packages, and package bodies.

- The **Analyze_Object()** procedure is used to calculate statistics for use by the cost-based optimizer.

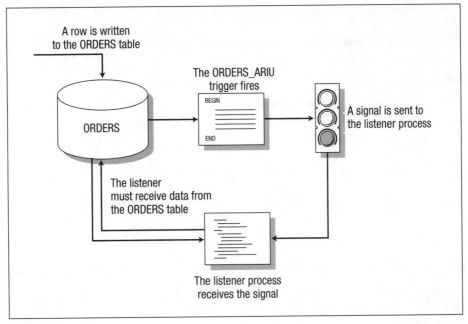

Figure 9.2
Using the **DBMS_Alert** package.

Each of these procedures is described in the following sections, with definitions of the types and numbers of parameters.

The Alter_Compile() Procedure

The **Alter_Compile()** procedure is called to recompile a specific stored PL/SQL object. The procedure accepts three parameters: **type**, **schema**, and **name**.

```
PROCEDURE Alter_Compile (type    IN    varchar2,
                         schema  IN    varchar2,
                         name    IN    varchar2)
```

The **type** parameter indicates if the object is a procedure, function, package body, or package spec. The **schema** parameter indicates the name of the schema that owns the specified object. The **name** parameter is the name of the object that should be recompiled.

The Analyze_Object() Procedure

The **Analyze_Object()** procedure is called to estimate or calculate statistics for a table, cluster, or index. The statistics generated are used by the cost-based optimizer to determine the optimal execution path for DML statements. The procedure accepts six parameters: **type**, **schema**, **name**, **method**, **estimate_rows**, and **estimate_percent**.

```
PROCEDURE Analyze_Object (type              IN    varchar2,
                          schema            IN    varchar2,
                          name              IN    varchar2,
                          method            IN    varchar2,
                          estimate_rows     IN    number := NULL,
                          estimate_percent  IN    number := NULL)
```

The first three parameters identify the object for which statistics will be generated:

- **type**—Indicates the type of the object for which statistics will be generated. This must be 'CLUSTER', 'INDEX', or 'TABLE'.

- **schema**—Indicates the owner of the specified object.

- **name**—Indicates the name of the object.

The remaining parameters instruct the procedure about how to generate statistics for the object:

- **method**—Must either be **NULL** or contain the string 'ESTIMATE'. If the parameter isn't **NULL**, then one of the next two parameters must contain a value that indicates the sampling to be performed so that statistics can be estimated for the object. If the parameter is **NULL**, statistics will be computed.

- **estimate_rows**—Specifies the number of rows from the object that should be used to estimate statistics for the object.

- **estimate_percent**—Specifies the percentage of rows from the object that should be used to estimate statistics.

DBMS_Describe

The **DBMS_Describe** package contains a single procedure, **Describe_Procedure()**, which returns information about the parameters of stored procedures and functions.

The **Describe_Procedure**() procedure has 15 separate parameters, as shown in the following definition:

```
PROCEDURE DBMS_Describe (object_name     IN      varchar2,
                         reserved1       IN      varchar2,
                         reserved2       IN      varchar2,
                         overload            OUT number_table,
                         position            OUT number_table,
                         level               OUT number_table,
                         argument_name       OUT varchar2_table,
                         datatype            OUT number_table,
                         default_value       OUT number_table,
                         in_out              OUT number_table,
                         length              OUT number_table,
                         precision           OUT number_table,
                         scale               OUT number_table,
                         radix               OUT number_table,
                         spare               OUT number_table)
```

The **object_name** parameter identifies the procedure or function that the **DBMS_Describe**() procedure should investigate. The **reserved1** and **reserved2** parameters aren't currently used and should be passed as **NULL** values.

The remaining parameters are PL/SQL tables that hold information about the parameters:

- **overload**—Holds an integer value that indicates to which overloaded procedure or function the parameter corresponds. For instance, a function might be over-loaded three times, so the parameter might contain the values 0, 1, and 2.

- **position**—Holds an integer value that indicates the position of a parameter with the argument list for the object. Position 0 is reserved for a function's return value.

- **level**—Indicates how deep an individual parameter is nested.

- **argument_name**—Indicates the name of an individual parameter.

- **datatype**—Holds an integer value that indicates the datatype of an individual parameter. A complete list of these values can be found in Table 9.1.

- **default_value**—Holds the given default for a parameter.

- **in_out**—Indicates an integer value. 0 indicates the parameter is an **IN** param-eter, 1 means the parameter is an **OUT** parameter, and 2 means the parameter is an **IN OUT** parameter.

- **length**—Indicates the length of **varchar2** or **char** arguments.

- **precision**—Indicates the number of significant digits for a numeric parameter.

- **scale**—Indicates the number of significant digits beyond the decimal point for a numeric parameter.

- **radix**—Indicates the base of a numeric value (decimal, binary, octal, and so forth).

- **spare**—Is not used.

DBMS_Job

The **DBMS_Job** package allows developers to schedule execution of PL/SQL code at a later time. Using the **DBMS_Job** package requires your DBA to set up some parameters in the init.ora file; consult with your DBA to determine if the database is set up for the use of this package.

Table 9.1 Values for the datatype parameter of the **DBMS_Describe.Describe_ Procedure( )** procedure.

Parameter Value	Datatype
1	varchar2
2	number
3	binary_integer
8	long
11	ROWID
12	date
23	raw
24	long raw
96	char
106	mlslabel
250	PL/SQL record
251	PL/SQL table
252	boolean

The package contains the following 10 procedures:

- The **Broken**() procedure
- The **Change**() procedure
- The **Interval**() procedure
- The **ISubmit**() procedure
- The **Next_Date**() procedure
- The **Remove**() procedure
- The **Run**() procedure
- The **Submit**() procedure
- The **User_Export**() procedure
- The **What**() procedure

The simplest sequence of events for running a job is very straightforward. The developer calls the **Submit**() procedure. The developer doesn't have to do any further tasks. At the scheduled time, Oracle will execute the specified job.

Unfortunately, things don't always work as expected. For instance, a job becomes *broken* if an error occurs while the job is executing. It's possible that a job that has already been submitted needs to be altered or canceled entirely. When these things happen, the other procedures within the package come into play.

The Broken() Procedure

The **Broken**() procedure is used to update the status of a job that has already been submitted, typically to mark a broken job as unbroken. The procedure has three parameters: **job**, **broken**, and **next_date**.

```
PROCEDURE Broken (job       IN    binary_integer,
                  broken    IN    boolean,
                  next_date IN    date := SYSDATE)
```

The **job** parameter is the job number that uniquely identifies the job in question. The **broken** parameter indicates whether or not the job will be marked as broken— **TRUE** means that the job will be marked as broken, and **FALSE** means that the job will be marked as unbroken. The **next_date** parameter indicates the time at which the job will be run again. This parameter defaults to the current date and time.

The Change() Procedure

The **Change**() procedure is used to alter the settings for a specific job. The procedure has four parameters: **job**, **what**, **next_date**, and **interval**.

```
PROCEDURE Change (job        IN     binary_integer,
                  what       IN     varchar2,
                  next_date  IN     date,
                  interval   IN     varchar2)
```

Once again, the **job** parameter is the integer value that uniquely identifies the job. The **what** parameter is a block of PL/SQL code that is to be run by the job. The **next_date** parameter indicates when the job will be executed. The **interval** parameter indicates how often a job will be re-executed.

The Interval() Procedure

The **Interval**() procedure is used to explicitly set the amount of time between re-executions of a job. The procedure has two parameters: **job** and **interval**.

```
PROCEDURE Interval (job       IN     binary_integer,
                    interval  IN     varchar2)
```

The **job** parameter identifies a specific job. The **interval** parameter indicates how often a job will be re-executed.

The ISubmit() Procedure

The **ISubmit**() procedure is used to submit a job with a specific job number. The procedure has five parameters: **job**, **what**, **next_date**, **interval**, and **no_parse**.

```
PROCEDURE ISubmit(job        IN     binary_integer,
                  what       IN     varchar2,
                  next_date  IN     date,
                  interval   IN     varchar2,
                  no_parse   IN     boolean := FALSE)
```

The only difference between this procedure and the **Submit**() procedure is that the **job** parameter is passed as an **IN** parameter and includes a job number specified by the developer. If the specified job number is already used, an error will occur.

The Next_Date() Procedure

The **Next_Date**() procedure is used to explicitly set the execution time for a job. The procedure accepts two parameters: **job** and **next_date**.

```
PROCEDURE Next_Date (job      IN      binary_integer,
                     next_date IN     date)
```

The **job** parameter identifies an existing job. The **next_date** parameter specifies the date and time when the job should be executed.

The Remove() Procedure

The **Remove**() procedure is used to remove a job that is scheduled to run. The procedure accepts a single parameter:

```
PROCEDURE Remove (job IN      binary_integer);
```

The **job** parameter uniquely identifies a job. The value of this parameter is the value of the **job** parameter returned by the call to the **Submit**() procedure for the job.

Jobs that are already running cannot be removed by calling this procedure.

The Run() Procedure

The **Run**() procedure is used to immediately execute a specified job. The procedure accepts only one parameter:

```
PROCEDURE Run (job IN      binary_integer)
```

The **job** parameter identifies the job that is to be executed immediately.

The Submit() Procedure

Jobs are normally scheduled using the **Submit**() procedure. The procedure has five parameters: **job**, **what**, **next_date**, **interval**, and **no_parse**.

```
PROCEDURE Submit(job            OUT binary_integer,
                 what       IN      varchar2,
                 next_date  IN      date,
                 interval   IN      varchar2,
                 no_parse   IN      boolean := FALSE)
```

The **job** parameter is a **binary_integer** returned by the **Submit**() procedure. This value is used to uniquely identify a job. The **what** parameter is the block of PL/SQL code that will be executed. The **next_date** parameter indicates when the job will run. The **interval** parameter determines when the job will be re-executed. The **no_parse** parameter indicates whether the job should be parsed at submission time or execution time—**TRUE** indicates that the PL/SQL code should be parsed when it is first executed, and **FALSE** indicates that the PL/SQL code should be parsed immediately.

The User_Export() Procedure

The **User_Export**() procedure returns the command used to schedule an existing job so the job can be resubmitted. The procedure has two parameters: **job** and **my_call**.

```
PROCEDURE User_Export (job     IN     binary_integer,
                       my_call IN OUT varchar2)
```

The **job** parameter identifies a scheduled job. The **my_call** parameter holds the text required to resubmit the job in its current state.

The What() Procedure

The **What**() procedure allows you to reset the command that is run when the job executes. The procedure accepts two parameters: **job** and **what**.

```
PROCEDURE What (job IN     binary_integer,
                what IN    varchar2)
```

The **job** parameter identifies an existing job. The **what** parameter holds the new PL/SQL code that will be executed.

Scheduling A Job

Now let's look at an example of scheduling a typical job using the **DBMS_Job** package. Assume that we have an **Hourly_Tracking**() procedure that we want to run every hour. We schedule this procedure to be run using a call to the **Submit**() procedure, as follows:

```
DBMS_Job.Submit (job        => biJobNumber,
                 what       => 'Hourly_Tracking;',
                 next_date  => SYSDATE,
                 interval   => 'SYSDATE + 1/24',
                 no_parse   => FALSE);
```

This call schedules a job that will be executed immediately and then every hour on the hour. The string passed to the interval parameter equates to "the current date and time plus 1 day divided by 24."

If an error occurs while the **Hourly_Tracking**() procedure is executing, the procedure will halt, and the job will be marked as broken. To restart the job, call the **Broken**() procedure, as follows:

```
DBMS_Job.Broken (job        => biJobNumber,
                 broken     => FALSE,
                 next_date  => SYSDATE);
```

By passing **FALSE** for the **broken** parameter, the job is marked as unbroken and will be executed again at the specified **next_date**.

At the end of the day, we want to stop the hourly execution of the procedure before beginning our nightly backups. This is accomplished by calling the **Remove**() procedure, as follows:

```
DBMS_Job.Remove (job => biJobNumber);
```

DBMS_Output

The **DBMS_Output** package is more familiar to PL/SQL developers than any other package provided by Oracle. The routines contained in this package are often used when debugging stored PL/SQL objects. Consequently, this package is discussed in Chapter 8.

DBMS_Pipe

The **DBMS_Pipe** package is used for asynchronous communication between processes. The basic concepts behind the use of pipes are illustrated in Figure 9.3.

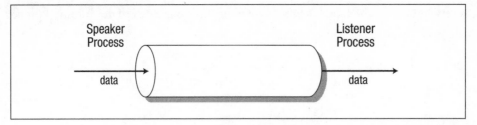

Figure 9.3
The concepts behind the use of pipes.

Like alerts, pipes are often implemented through the use of database triggers. The basic processing of a pipe-based implementation is straightforward:

1. Data is modified or created in a table.

2. A trigger on the table packs data into the pipe using the **DBMS_Pipe.Pack _Message**() procedure.

3. The trigger sends the message using the **DBMS_Pipe.Send_Message**() procedure.

4. The listener module waits for a message using the **DBMS_Pipe. Receive_Message**() procedure. The message is stored in the local buffer.

5. The listener module unpacks the message using the **DBMS_Pipe.Unpack_ Message**() procedure.

6. The listener module processes the data contained in the message.

7. The listener module resets itself to read another message.

This implementation allows multiple messages to be sent to the listener module with no loss of data sent with individual messages. Messages are received by the listener module (or modules) in the same order in which the messages are sent.

The **DBMS_Pipe** package contains several procedures and functions intended for use by application developers:

- The **Create_Pipe**() function
- The **Next_Item_Type**() function
- The **Pack_Message**() procedure
- The **Purge**() procedure

- The **Receive_Message**() function

- The **Remove_Pipe**() function

- The **Reset_Buffer**() procedure

- The **Send_Message**() function

- The **Unique_Session_Name**() function

- The **Unpack_Message**() procedure

Each of these procedures and functions is discussed in the following sections. There is also an example of a simple pipes implementation.

The Create_Pipe() Function

A *public pipe* is accessible to any user who knows the name of the pipe. A *private pipe* is accessible only to its creator, to stored PL/SQL objects run by the creator, and to the certain system user IDS accessible to the DBA. Private pipes are often used when the security of data is of paramount importance.

Public pipes are created implicitly through the use of the **Send_Message**() function. The **Create_Pipe**() function can be used to create a private pipe. This function accepts three parameters: **pipename**, **maxpipesize**, and **private**.

```
FUNCTION Create_Pipe (pipename      IN     varchar2,
                      maxpipesize IN       integer := 8192,
                      private      IN      boolean := TRUE)
RETURN integer
```

The **pipename** parameter is a character string that identifies the pipe. The value for this parameter should not exceed 30 characters and cannot begin with the string **ORA$** (this string is reserved for use by Oracle).

The **maxpipesize** parameter is the maximum size of the pipe in bytes. The value of the **private** parameter indicates whether the function creates a public or private pipe— **TRUE** indicates that the newly created pipe should be private.

The function will return 0 if the new pipe is successfully created. If the specified pipe already exists and you are able to access it, the function returns 0 and the existing pipe is not affected. Otherwise, an error is raised by the function.

Functions created through the use of the **Create_Pipe**() function must be removed using the **Remove_Pipe**() function.

The Next_Item_Type() Function

The **Next_Item_Type**() function is used when unpacking a pipe that can contain different types of values in the same positions. For instance, a message might contain either a company name or a company ID number in the same position. Depending on the value returned from this function, the next portion of the message will be placed into a **character** or **number** variable.

This function returns an integer value that indicates the datatype of the next section of the message. These values are listed in Table 9.2.

This function does not have any parameters.

The Pack_Message() Procedure

The **Pack_Message**() procedure is used to add information to a message. The procedure is overloaded. The different implementations of the procedure are as follows:

```
PROCEDURE Pack_Message (item IN    varchar2)
PROCEDURE Pack_Message (item IN    date)
PROCEDURE Pack_Message (item IN    number)
PROCEDURE Pack_Message (item IN    raw)
PROCEDURE Pack_Message (item IN    ROWID)
```

Each implementation of this procedure is designed to add data of a specific type to the message that will be sent over the pipe.

Table 9.2   Return values for the **Next_Item_Type( )** function.

Return Value	Datatype Of Next Message Section
0	There are no more values in the message
6	number
9	varchar2
11	ROWID
12	date
23	raw

The Purge() Procedure

The **Purge**() procedure is used to completely empty the pipe, thus freeing the memory used by the pipe when it is removed from the SGA. Pipes are not removed from the SGA if they contain messages. Therefore, it is critical that unnecessary pipes are emptied using this procedure.

The procedure accepts a single parameter:

```
PROCEDURE Purge (pipename IN     varchar2)
```

The **pipename** parameter holds the name of an existing pipe.

This procedure empties the pipe by calling the **Receive_Message**() function repeatedly. Therefore, the values in the local buffer will probably change if you use the **Purge**() procedure.

The Receive_Message() Function

The **Receive_Message**() function is used to receive a message from the pipe and place the message in a local buffer. The function has two parameters: **pipename** and **timeout**.

```
FUNCTION Receive_Message (pipename IN     varchar2,
                          timeout  IN     integer := MAXWAIT)
RETURN integer
```

The **pipename** parameter holds the name of the pipe. The **timeout** parameter indicates the period of time that the process will wait for a message to be sent. This parameter defaults to the value of the **DBMS_Pipe.MAXWAIT** constant (86,400,000 seconds).

The **Receive_Message**() function returns an integer value indicating its result. The return values for the function are listed in Table 9.3.

The Remove_Pipe() Function

The **Remove_Pipe**() function is called to destroy a pipe created by a call to the **Create_Pipe**() function. The **Remove_Pipe**() function has one parameter:

```
FUNCTION Remove_Pipe (pipename IN     varchar2) RETURN integer
```

Table 9.3   Return values for the **Receive_Message( )** function.

Return Value	Meaning
0	A message was received.
1	No message was received.
2	The message in the pipe was too large for the buffer.
3	An error occurred.

The **pipename** parameter holds the name of the pipe that is to be deleted. The function will return 0 if the pipe is successfully deleted or if the specified pipe does not exist.

The Send_Message() Function

The **Send_Message**() function is used to send a message through a pipe. The function accepts one parameter:

```
FUNCTION Send_Message (pipename IN     varchar2) RETURN integer
```

The **pipename** parameter holds the name of the pipe through which the packed message is sent. The function will return one of the integer values shown in Table 9.4.

The Unique_Session_Name() Function

The **Unique_Session_Name**() function returns an integer value that uniquely identifies a particular session connected to Oracle. Each session has its own ID number. Calling this function multiple times from the same session will always yield the same result.

Table 9.4   Return values of the **Send_Message( )** function.

Return Value	Meaning
0	The message was successfully sent.
1	The message was not sent due to a timeout.
3	An error occurred while sending the message.

This function is often used to generate a pipename that is specific to a given session. For instance, both session 18 and session 23 might want to create the same pipe, but each session has a unique listener. The **Unique_Session_Name**() function is called and the resulting value is appended onto the pipe's name, yielding a uniquely named pipe for each session.

This function has no parameters.

The Unpack_Message() Procedure

The **Unpack_Message**() procedure is used to extract information from a message. This procedure, like the **Pack_Message**() procedure, is overloaded. The implementations of the procedure are as follows:

```
PROCEDURE Unpack_Message (item    OUT varchar2)
PROCEDURE Unpack_Message (item    OUT date)
PROCEDURE Unpack_Message (item    OUT number)
PROCEDURE Unpack_Message (item    OUT raw)
PROCEDURE Unpack_Message (item    OUT ROWID)
```

Each implementation of the procedure extracts data of a specific type from the message.

Using Pipes

Let's go back to the order entry system example that we discussed for the **DBMS_Alert** package. When an order is created or modified, data in a legacy system must be created or modified as well. A trigger is implemented on the **ORDERS** table that packs a message and sends the message over a pipe. A Pro*C program is implemented to interface with the legacy system and to receive messages over the pipe. Listing 9.2 illustrates how a message can be sent over a pipe.

Listing 9.2 Using a trigger to send a message over a pipe.

```
TRIGGER ORDERS_ARIU
AFTER INSERT OR UPDATE
ON ORDERS
FOR EACH ROW

    ORDERS_PIPE    CONSTANT varchar2 (30) := 'ORDER';
    iMessageStatus integer;
```

```
BEGIN
   DBMS_Pipe.Pack_Message (:new.order_number);
   DBMS_Pipe.Pack_Message (:new.customer_number);
   DBMS_Pipe.Pack_Message (:new.order_cost);

   iMessageStatus := DBMS_Pipe.Send_Message (ORDERS_PIPE);
END ORDERS_ARIU;
```

The Pro*C program is still started by the system when the order entry form is run. This program makes calls to the **DBMS_Pipe.Receive_Message()** function:

```
iMessageReceived := DBMS_Pipe.Receive_Message (ORDERS_PIPE);
```

When **iMessageReceived** holds a 0 after this call, the program begins calling the **DBMS_Pipe.Unpack_Message()** procedures to extract individual pieces of data from the message:

```
IF (iMessageReceived = 0) THEN
   DBMS_Pipe.Unpack_Message (item => iOrderNumber);
   DBMS_Pipe.Unpack_Message (item => iCustomerNumber);
   DBMS_Pipe.Unpack_Message (item => nOrderValue);
END IF;
```

In this implementation, the Pro*C program does not have to make a reference back to the **ORDERS** table to retrieve data. The **ORDERS_ARIU** trigger can send several messages, and the listener program will process each order in succession, with no loss of data. To implement this type of functionality using signals, the Pro*C program has to refer back to the **ORDERS** table to query information.

Figure 9.4 illustrates the high-level processing of this implementation.

DBMS_SQL

The **DBMS_SQL** package allows developers to write stored PL/SQL code that is capable of generating and executing data-specific DDL and DML statements without using hard-coded data values. There are three different types of dynamic SQL that can be built:

- DDL commands
- Nonquery DML statements (**DELETE**, **INSERT**, or **UPDATE** statement)
- DML queries (**SELECT** statement)

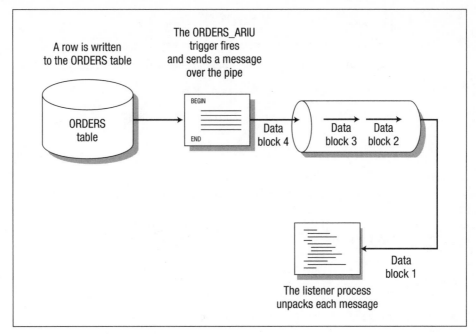

Figure 9.4
High-level processing of a pipe-based implementation.

Each of these operations has separate calls to procedures and functions contained in the **DBMS_SQL** package. In the end, the single steps can be broken down into a generic set of steps:

1. Build a command by concatenating strings together.

2. Open a cursor.

3. Parse the command.

4. Bind any input variables.

5. Execute the command.

6. Fetch the results (in the case of queries).

7. Close the cursor.

There are a number of procedures and functions contained within the **DBMS_SQL** package.

The Bind_Variable() Procedures

The **Bind_Variable**() group of procedures is used to associate values with bind variables in the command that is being built. There are several implementations of this functionality:

```
PROCEDURE Bind_Variable (c      IN      integer,
                         name   IN      varchar2,
                         value  IN      number)

PROCEDURE Bind_Variable (c      IN      integer,
                         name   IN      varchar2,
                         value  IN      varchar2)

PROCEDURE Bind_Variable (c                IN      integer,
                         name             IN      varchar2,
                         value            IN      varchar2,
                         out_value_size   IN      integer)

PROCEDURE Bind_Variable (c      IN      integer,
                         name   IN      varchar2,
                         value  IN      date)

PROCEDURE Bind_Variable (c      IN      integer,
                         name   IN      varchar2,
                         value  IN      mlslabel)
```

There are several other implementations of the **Bind_Variable**() procedure with slightly different names—**Bind_Variable_Char**(), **Bind_Variable_Raw**(), and **Bind_Variable_ROWID**:

```
PROCEDURE Bind_Variable_Char (c      IN      integer,
                              name   IN      varchar2,
                              value  IN      char)

PROCEDURE Bind_Variable_Char (c                IN      integer,
                              name             IN      varchar2,
                              value            IN      char,
                              out_value_size   IN      integer)

PROCEDURE Bind_Variable_Raw (c      IN      integer,
                             name   IN      varchar2,
                             value  IN      raw)
```

```
PROCEDURE Bind_Variable_Raw (c                IN      integer,
                             name             IN      varchar2,
                             value            IN      raw,
                             out_value_size   IN      integer)

PROCEDURE Bind_Variable_ROWID (c      IN      integer,
                               name   IN      varchar2,
                               value  IN      ROWID)
```

While each of these procedures has a slightly different name, each of them accomplishes the same task—namely, storing a value in a bind variable.

The Close_Cursor() Procedure

The **Close_Cursor**() procedure is called to free up the resources used by a cursor. The procedure accepts a single parameter:

```
PROCEDURE Close_Cursor (c IN OUT integer)
```

The **c** parameter is a cursor ID number. The parameter returns from the procedure as **NULL**.

The Column_Value() Procedures

Like the **Bind_Variable**() procedure, there are several implementations of the **Column_Value**() procedure:

```
PROCEDURE Column_Value (c          IN      integer,
                        position   IN      integer,
                        value          OUT number)

PROCEDURE Column_Value (c          IN      integer,
                        position   IN      integer,
                        value          OUT varchar2)

PROCEDURE Column_Value (c          IN      integer,
                        position   IN      integer,
                        value          OUT date)

PROCEDURE Column_Value (c          IN      integer,
                        position   IN      integer,
                        value          OUT mlslabel)
```

```
PROCEDURE Column_Value (c                IN      integer,
                        position         IN      integer,
                        value            OUT number,
                        column_error     OUT number,
                        actual_length    OUT number)

PROCEDURE Column_Value (c                IN      integer,
                        position         IN      integer,
                        value            OUT varchar2,
                        column_error     OUT number,
                        actual_length    OUT number)

PROCEDURE Column_Value (c                IN      integer,
                        position         IN      integer,
                        value            OUT mlslabel,
                        column_error     OUT number,
                        actual_length    OUT number)

PROCEDURE Column_Value_Char (c      IN      integer,
                        position IN      integer,
                        value        OUT char)

PROCEDURE Column_Value_Char (c           IN      integer,
                        position         IN      integer,
                        value            OUT char,
                        column_error     OUT number,
                        actual_length    OUT number)

PROCEDURE Column_Value_Raw (c       IN      integer,
                        position IN      integer,
                        value        OUT raw)

PROCEDURE Column_Value_Raw (c            IN      integer,
                        position         IN      integer,
                        value            OUT raw,
                        column_error     OUT number,
                        actual_length    OUT number)

PROCEDURE Column_Value_ROWID (c     IN      integer,
                        position IN      integer,
                        value        OUT ROWID)

PROCEDURE Column_Value_ROWID (c          IN      integer,
                        position         IN      integer,
                        value            OUT ROWID,
                        column_error     OUT number,
                        actual_length    OUT number)
```

All of these procedures return the value of a column that was fetched using a call to the **Fetch_Rows**() function. The column's value is stored in the **value** parameter.

The Define_Column() Procedures

The **Define_Column**() procedures are used to define the datatype and size of the variables that will receive data from the **Fetch_Rows**() function:

```
PROCEDURE Define_Column (c          IN    integer,
                         position IN    integer,
                         column   IN    number)

PROCEDURE Define_Column (c            IN     integer,
                         position   IN     integer,
                         column     IN     varchar2,
                         column_size IN     integer)

PROCEDURE Define_Column (c          IN    integer,
                         position IN    integer,
                         column   IN    date)

PROCEDURE Define_Column (c          IN    integer,
                         position IN    integer,
                         column   IN    mlslabel)

PROCEDURE Define_Column_Char (c            IN     integer,
                             position   IN     integer,
                             column     IN     char,
                             column_size IN     integer)

PROCEDURE Define_Column_Raw (c            IN     integer,
                            position   IN     integer,
                            column     IN     raw,
                            column_size IN     integer)

PROCEDURE Define_Column_ROWID (c          IN     integer,
                              position IN     integer,
                              column   IN     ROWID)
```

The Execute() Function

The **Execute**() function has two purposes, depending on the type of command being executed. For a simple statement, the function executes the statement and returns the number of rows processed. For a query, the function executes the statement. This call must be followed by a call to the **Fetch_Rows**() function to retrieve data for an individual row. Following is the definition of the **Execute**() function:

```
FUNCTION Execute (c IN     integer) RETURN integer
```

The Execute_And_Fetch() Function

The **Execute_And_Fetch**() function allows developers to combine a call to the **Execute**() function and the first subsequent call to the **Fetch_Rows**() function. All rows beyond the first row must still be fetched using the **Fetch_Rows**() function. Following is the definition of the **Execute_And_Fetch**() function:

```
FUNCTION Execute_And_Fetch (c     IN     integer,
                           exact IN     Boolean := FALSE)
RETURN integer
```

The **exact** parameter instructs Oracle to raise an exception if the query returns more than one row. Even if the exception is raised, the first row of the result set is returned, and the remaining rows can be retrieved normally using the **Fetch_Rows**() function.

The Fetch_Rows() Function

The **Fetch_Rows**() function fetches a single row of data into the local buffer. This data can then be stored in local variables by using the **Column_Value**() procedure. Following is the definition of the **Fetch_Rows**() function:

```
FUNCTION Fetch_Rows (c IN     integer) RETURN integer
```

The Open_Cursor() Function

The **Open_Cursor**() function is called to create a cursor that will be used when parsing and executing the dynamic statement. The function has no parameters and returns an integer value that uniquely identifies the cursor.

The Parse() Procedure

The **Parse**() procedure is called to send a statement to the database server to check for syntax and semantic errors. If necessary, Oracle also determines an execution plan for the statement. Following is the definition of the **Parse**() procedure:

```
PROCEDURE Parse (c             IN      integer,
               statement      IN      varchar2,
               language_flag  IN      integer)
```

The c parameter is the integer value that identifies the cursor opened by the call to the **Open_Cursor()** function. The **statement** parameter holds the dynamic command that will be parsed. The **language_flag** parameter holds an integer value. The valid values for this parameter are shown in Table 9.5.

The Variable_Value() Procedures

The **Variable_Value()** procedures are used to determine the new values for bind variables that are modified by a dynamic SQL statement. The definitions of these procedures are as follows:

```
PROCEDURE Variable_Value (c      IN      integer,
                         name   IN      varchar2,
                         value     OUT number)

PROCEDURE Variable_Value (c      IN      integer,
                         name   IN      varchar2,
                         value     OUT varchar2)

PROCEDURE Variable_Value (c      IN      integer,
                         name   IN      varchar2,
                         value     OUT date)

PROCEDURE Variable_Value (c      IN      integer,
                         name   IN      varchar2,
                         value     OUT mlslabel)

PROCEDURE Variable_Value_Char (c      IN      integer,
                              name   IN      varchar2,
                              value     OUT char)

PROCEDURE Variable Value_Raw (c      IN      integer,
                             name   IN      varchar2,
                             value     OUT raw)

PROCEDURE Variable_Value_ROWID (c      IN      integer,
                               name IN      varchar2,
                               value     OUT ROWID)
```

Table 9.5 Valid values for the **language_flag** parameter of the **DBMS_SQL.Parse( )** procedure.

DBMS_SQL Constant	Integer Value	Description
V6	0	Oracle6 behavior
V7	2	Oracle7 behavior
NATIVE	1	Behavior appropriate to the current database version

Using The DBMS_SQL Package

A common request from users is the ability to change their password. Unfortunately, Oracle does not allow a user to change an account password without having the **ALTER USER** privilege. This privilege also allows users to change information other than the password and for any user. So, unless you want to grant this level of access to users, the DBA has the responsibility of assigning and changing passwords.

Let's use the **DBMS_SQL** package to create a **Change_Password()** function, which the DBA can compile and make accessible to all users. This function can be called from a system's front end, usually via a button on a form or a menu item, to allow the user to change a password (and *only* a password). The **Change_Password()** function is shown in Listing 9.3.

Listing 9.3   The **Change_Password()** function.

```
CREATE OR REPLACE
FUNCTION Change_Password (vUsername IN    varchar2,
                          vPassword IN    varchar2)

RETURN integer

IS

    iCursorID          integer;
    vCommand           varchar2 (80);
    iReturned          integer;

    xMISSING_PARAMETER  EXCEPTION;

BEGIN
    IF (vUserName IS NULL OR vPassword IS NULL) THEN
        RAISE xMISSING_PARAMETER;
```

```
    END IF;

    vCommand := 'ALTER USER '   ||
               vUsername        ||
               'identified by ' ||
               vPassword;

    iCursorID := DBMS_SQL.Open_Cursor;
    DBMS_SQL.Parse (iCursorID,
                    vCommand,
                    DBMS_SQL.v7);

    iReturned := DBMS_SQL.Execute (iCursorID);
    DBMS_SQL.Close_Cursor (iCursorID);

    RETURN 1;

EXCEPTION
    WHEN OTHERS THEN
        RETURN 0;
END Change_Password;
/
```

This function must be run by a user who has the **ALTER USER** privilege. In this implementation, the function allows any user's password to be changed. This particular implementation assumes that you will pass only the login name of the current user as a parameter.

The function first builds the proper SQL*Plus command and stores it in the **vCommand** string. The function then calls functions and procedures in the **DBMS_SQL** package to parse and execute the command.

This function requires a username and password to be passed as parameters. If the user's password is successfully changed, the function returns 1. Otherwise, the function returns 0.

DBMS_Utility

There is one especially useful function in the **DBMS_Utility** package that merits attention. This is the **Get_Time()** function, which returns the current time in hundredths of seconds. If you use this function to implement time-sensitive code, make sure you are prepared for the value to roll over to 0.

UTL_File

The **UTL_File** package, implemented with Oracle 7.3, provides server-side file I/O to text files. There are several basic steps required to do file I/O with the package:

1. Open one or more files for reading or writing using the **FOpen()** function.

2. Read data from a file using the **Get_Line()** procedure *or* write data to a file using the **Put_Line()**, **PutF()**, **Put()**, and/or **New_Line()** procedures.

3. Close files using the **FClose()** or **FClose_All()** procedures.

The package contains the following 10 procedures and functions:

- The **FClose()** procedure
- The **FClose_All()** procedure
- The **FFlush()** procedure
- The **FOpen()** function
- The **Get_Line()** procedure
- The **Is_Open()** function
- The **New_Line()** procedure
- The **Put()** procedure
- The **PutF()** procedure
- The **Put_Line()** procedure

Each of these procedures and functions is described in detail in the following sections. There is also a brief example of using the **UTL_File** package.

The FClose() Procedure

The **FClose()** procedure is provided to close a text file after you have finished reading data. The procedure definition is as follows:

```
PROCEDURE FClose (file_handle IN OUT FILE_TYPE)
```

The **file_handle** parameter is a pointer to an open file. This parameter is of type **FILE_TYPE**, a user-defined datatype in the package spec for the **UTL_File** package.

The FClose_All() Procedure

The **FClose_All**() procedure is used to close all files that are currently open. This is commonly used for cleaning up during error handling or shutdown operations. The procedure accepts no parameters.

All changes to a file are flushed from the buffer before the file is closed.

The FFlush() Procedure

The **FFlush**() procedure is used to force all buffered changes to files to be written to the files immediately. The procedure definition is as follows:

```
PROCEDURE FFlush (file_handle IN    FILE_TYPE)
```

The FOpen() Function

The **FOpen**() function is used to open a text file so that data can be read from or written to the file. The function definition is as follows:

```
FUNCTION FOpen (location  IN    varchar2,
               filename  IN    varchar2,
               open_mode IN    varchar2)
```

The **location** parameter identifies the directory where the file is located or where the file is to be created. The values for this parameter are constrained by an init.ora parameter. Check with your DBA to find out precisely which directories you can use with this parameter.

The **open_mode** parameter determines how the package will handle contents of an existing file. The values for this parameter are shown in Table 9.6.

The Get_Line() Function

The **Get_Line**() function reads the next line of text from an open file and writes that text to a local buffer. The text can then be processed like any local text variable. The function definition is as follows:

```
FUNCTION Get_Line (file_handle IN    FILE_TYPE,
                   buffer       OUT varchar2)
```

Table 9.6   Values for the **open_mode** parameter of the **FOpen( )** function.

Parameter Value	Interpretation
a	Append text to an existing file.
r	Read text from an existing file.
w	Write text to a new file, or write over an existing file.

The **buffer** parameter indicates the name of the local text variable that will hold the line of text that is read. When there are no more lines of text to read in an open file, a **NO_DATA_FOUND** exception is raised.

The Is_Open() Function

The **Is_Open**() function is a boolean function that returns **TRUE** if the specified file is currently open for processing and **FALSE** if the specified file isn't open for processing. The function definition is as follows:

```
FUNCTION Is_Open (file_handle IN     FILE_TYPE) RETURN boolean
```

The New_Line() Procedure

The **New_Line**() procedure is used to write a specified number of new line characters to a file. The procedure definition is as follows:

```
PROCEDURE New_Line (file_handle IN     FILE_TYPE,
                    lines       IN     natural)
```

The **lines** parameter indicates the number of new line characters that should be written to the specified file.

The Put() Procedure

The **Put**() procedure writes a string to a file. The procedure definition is as follows:

```
PROCEDURE Put (file_handle IN     FILE_TYPE,
               buffer      IN     varchar2)
```

The **buffer** parameter can be either a text variable or a character literal.

The PutF() Procedure

The **PutF()** procedure is used to write text to a file in a specified format. The procedure definition is as follows:

```
PROCEDURE PutF (file_handle IN    FILE_TYPE,
               format       IN    varchar2,
               arg1         IN    varchar2 := NULL,
               arg2         IN    varchar2 := NULL,
               arg3         IN    varchar2 := NULL,
               arg4         IN    varchar2 := NULL,
               arg5         IN    varchar2 := NULL)
```

The **format** parameter is used to specify a format model for the output. This string can include two special formatting characters: **%s** and **\n**. Each **%s** is replaced with one of the five optional arguments; thus, there can be up to five **%s** characters in the **format** parameter. All occurrences of **\n** are replaced with a new line character. There can be any number of **\n** characters in the **format** parameter.

The Put_Line() Procedure

The **Put_Line()** procedure writes a specified string to a file and starts a new line in the file. The procedure definition is as follows:

```
PROCEDURE Put_Line (file_handle IN    FILE_TYPE,
                    buffer      IN    varchar2)
```

Using The UTL_File Package

Let's put together a simple example of using the **UTL_File** package to access a file. This procedure will read data from a text file that contains customer information and then write the information to the **CUSTOMERS** table. Listing 9.4 illustrates how this procedure might call the **UTL_File** package.

Listing 9.4   A procedure that uses the **UTL_File** package.

```
PROCEDURE Read_Customer_Data

IS

    FILE_HANDLE        UTL_FILE.FILE_TYPE%TYPE;
```

```
        DIRECTORY CONSTANT     varchar2 (100) := '/users/imports/';

        FILENAME  CONSTANT     varchar2 (10) := 'Customers';
        DELIMITER CONSTANT     varchar2 (1) := '^';
        vLineOfText            varchar2 (2000);

        bMoreText              boolean := TRUE;
        vCustomerName          varchar2 (50);
        vCustomerPhone         varchar2 (20);

BEGIN
    FILE_HANDLE := UTL_File.FOpen (location  => DIRECTORY,
                                   filename  => FILENAME,
                                   open_mode => 'r');

    WHILE (bMoreText) LOOP
        BEGIN
            UTL_File.Get_Line (file_handle => FILE_HANDLE,
                               buffer      => vLineOfText);

            iDelimiterPos  := instr (vLineOfText, DELIMITER);
            vCustomerName  := substr (vLineOfText, 1, (iDelimiterPos - 1));
            vCustomerPhone := substr (vLineOfText, iDelimterPos + 1);

        EXCEPTION
            WHEN NO_DATA_FOUND THEN
                bMoreText := FALSE;
        END;
    END LOOP;

    FClose (file_handle => FILE_HANDLE);
END Read_Customer_Data;
```

Summary

This chapter covers the basics of using many of the packages provided by Oracle; however, a complete examination of the packages could be a book in itself! Use the examples provided here as a basis to set up and investigate problems that you need to handle. As with any language, PL/SQL has nuances that are best experienced rather than described.

Performance Tuning

CHAPTER

10

Performance Tuning

Probably sooner than later, you'll come across a block of code that performs very poorly. As an application developer, part of your job will be to improve the performance of code that doesn't perform well. This chapter provides information about tuning SQL statements and PL/SQL blocks. Most of the material here is geared towards the use of the cost-based optimizer. Materials related to the use of the rule-based optimizer are clearly marked.

The bulk of your performance tuning work will be the analysis and modification of DML statements, but there are also some important tips presented for tuning PL/SQL as well.

Tuning SQL

DML statements (**DELETE, INSERT, SELECT**, and **UPDATE**) are the most common cause of performance problems in stored PL/SQL objects. There are a number of potential reasons why a given DML statement could perform poorly, including:

- Failure to use the proper indexes in a **SELECT, UPDATE**, or **DELETE** statement.

- Number and/or types of indexes degrading the performance of an **INSERT, UPDATE**, or **DELETE** statement.

- Statistics for the tables haven't been updated recently (if using the cost-based optimizer).

- Lack of indexes usable by the **SELECT** or **UPDATE** statement (i.e., the index should not be used by the DML statement).

- The DML statement attempts to modify the value of an indexed column for a **WHERE** clause comparison.

Of course, there are other situations that can cause performance problems, but these are the most common reasons for DML statements to perform poorly.

In many instances, resolving a performance problem first requires that the performance bottleneck be identified. The **EXPLAIN PLAN** statement is an excellent tool for identifying SQL statements that perform poorly.

Using The EXPLAIN PLAN Statement

The **EXPLAIN PLAN** SQL statement is used to illustrate the steps that Oracle goes through to execute a specific DML statement. The use of the **EXPLAIN PLAN** statement is illustrated in Listing 10.1.

Listing 10.1 Using the **EXPLAIN PLAN** SQL statement.

```
EXPLAIN PLAN
SET statement_id = <statement_name>
INTO <plan_table>
FOR <SQL_statement>;
```

In this example, **statement_name** is a unique identifier for the SQL statement, **plan_table** is the name (possibly prefaced with a schema reference) of the table that holds the results (typically **PLAN_TABLE**), and **SQL_statement** is the SQL statement for which the **EXPLAIN PLAN** is being generated.

On a Unix system, the **PLAN_TABLE** table can be created by running the utlxplan.sql file from the $ORACLE_HOME/rdbms/admin directory.

This is the structure of the **PLAN_TABLE** table:

```
statement_id        varchar2 (30)
timestamp           date
remarks             varchar2 (80)
operation           varchar2 (30)
options             varchar2 (30)
object_node         varchar2 (30)
object_owner        varchar2 (30)
object_name         varchar2 (30)
object_instance     varchar2 (30)
object_type         varchar2 (30)
search_columns      number
id                  number
```

```
parent_id          number
position           number
other              long
```

The results of the **EXPLAIN PLAN** statement are written to this table and can be retrieved using the query in Listing 10.2.

Listing 10.2 Getting an **EXPLAIN PLAN** from the **PLAN_TABLE** table.

```
SELECT lpad (' ', 2 * (level - 1)) ||
       operation   || ' ' ||
       options     || ' ' ||
       object_name || ' ' ||
       decode (id, 0, 'Cost = ' || position) "EXPLAIN PLAN";
FROM   PLAN_TABLE
START WITH id = 0
AND    statement_id  = <statement_name>
CONNECT BY PRIOR id = parent_id
AND    statement_id  = <statement_name>;
```

To use the code in this example, replace **statement_name** with the same value that was used for **statement_name** when generating the **EXPLAIN PLAN**. The query produces output that looks like this:

```
EXPLAIN PLAN
--------------------------------------------------------------------
SELECT STATEMENT    Cost = 13
  MERGE JOIN
    TABLE ACCESS FULL STUDENTS
    TABLE ACCESS BY ROWID STUDENTS
      INDEX UNIQUE SCAN STUDENTS_SSN
```

This output shows the series of operations performed by Oracle to resolve the statement and the total cost of those operations. High cost values are extremely undesirable.

Using EXPLAIN PLAN With The Rule-Based Optimizer

Running an EXPLAIN PLAN on a statement that uses the rule-based optimizer will always show a cost of zero. However, you can still use the statement to identify poorly performing SQL statements by examining the operations that Oracle performs to resolve the query.

While using **EXPLAIN PLAN** alone can isolate performance bottlenecks, using **TKPROF** and **EXPLAIN PLAN** together will provide even more insights into how SQL statements perform.

Using TKPROF

TKPROF is a utility provided by Oracle that provides detailed statistics about the execution of a DML statement. The first step involved with running **TKPROF** is setting up a trace file.

Setting Up A Trace File

Before using **TKPROF**, you must create a trace file. You can create a trace file by executing the following command in SQL*Plus:

```
ALTER SESSION SET SQL_TRACE = TRUE;
```

This command instructs SQL*Plus to set up a trace file for all SQL statements and PL/SQL blocks that you execute. When you have finished executing the statements that you wish to examine, execute the following command to stop writing to the trace file:

```
ALTER SESSION SET SQL_TRACE = FALSE;
```

Keep in mind that **ALTER SESSION** is not a DML statement and cannot be run from inside your PL/SQL blocks. Also keep in mind that disconnecting from SQL*Plus or connecting as another user via the **CONNECT** statement will also cause SQL*Plus to stop writing to the trace file.

The location of your trace file depends on how the DBA has set the **USER_DUMP_DEST** parameter in the init.ora file for your database. Consult your DBA to determine the location of the trace files, or look at the init.ora file yourself. Each trace file is given a specific ID number by Oracle (in Unix, this is the system process ID for the SQL*Plus session) and has a .trc extension. Trace files are named according to this convention:

```
ora_ + <id> + .trc
```

Thus, a valid trace file name might be:

```
ora_09213.trc
```

By listing the files in the directory specified by the **USER_DUMP_DEST** parameter, you can easily determine which trace file is yours by simply taking the most recent trace file (the trace file with the highest ID number). Once you've created a trace file for the statement(s) that you want to tune, exit SQL*Plus and run the **TKPROF** utility.

Running TKPROF

TKPROF is an executable that is run at the operating system level. This utility should be stored in the same place as the other Oracle executables. The syntax for running **TKPROF** is as follows:

```
TKPROF trace_file output_file
SORT=sort_options
PRINT=num_statements
EXPLAIN=username/password;
```

Only the first line of this command is required. **trace_file** specifies the name of the trace file that you created using the **ALTER SESSION** command. **output_file** specifies the name of the file generated by **TKPROF**. The other lines of the command are used to instruct **TKPROF** of your preferences for the output file. Each of these lines is explained in the following text.

The **SORT** option instructs **TKPROF** about how SQL statements and PL/SQL blocks will be ordered in the output file. If no sort option is specified, statements will appear in the same order as in the trace file. A complete list of valid sort options is presented in Table 10.1.

If you want to use multiple sort options, use the following syntax:

```
SORT=(option1, option2,...optionN);
```

Now let's return to the command used earlier to run **TKPROF**. If the **PRINT** option is used in the command, only the specified number of statements will be included in the output file. **TKPROF** will create the output file with the specified number of statements after any **SORT** option has been performed.

Table 10.1   Valid **SORT** options for the **TKPROF** utility.

Sort Option	Description
EXECNT	Number of executions.
EXECPU	Amount of CPU time used during statement execution.
EXECU	Number of current block reads during statement execution.
EXEDSK	Number of physical disk reads during statement execution.
EXEELA	Elapsed time during statement execution.
EXEQRY	Number of consistent block reads during statement execution.
EXEROW	Number of rows processed during statement execution.
EXEMIS	Number of library cache misses during statement execution.
FCHCNT	Number of fetches.
FCHCPU	Amount of CPU time used by the fetch.
FCHCU	Number of current block reads while fetching data.
FCHDSK	Number of physical reads while fetching data.
FCHELA	Elapsed time while fetching data.
FCHQRY	Number of consistent block reads while fetching data.
FCHROW	Number of rows fetched by the statement.
PRSCNT	Total number of parses.
PRSCPU	Amount of CPU time used while parsing the statement.
PRSCU	Number of current block reads while parsing the statement.
PRSDSK	Number of disk reads while parsing the statement.
PRSELA	Elapsed time while parsing the statement.
PRSMIS	Number of library cache misses while parsing the statement.
PRSQRY	Number of consistent block reads while parsing the statement.

If the **EXPLAIN** option is used, a username and password are specified with the option. **TKPROF** creates the **PLAN_TABLE** table (and only this table) under the specified schema, generates an explain plan for each DML statement, and then drops the **PLAN_TABLE**.

If you can't find the **TKPROF** executable on your system, ask your DBA to help you find it.

An Example Of Using TKPROF

Let's assume that we have generated a trace file, ora_90213.trc, containing the following DML statement:

```
SELECT last_name, first_name, middle_name
FROM   STUDENTS
WHERE  ssn = '999999999';
```

We'll run **TKPROF** against the trace file using this command:

```
TKPROF ora_90213.trc ora_90213.out EXPLAIN=jschmoe/boogieman;
```

TKPROF generates an output file, ora_90213.out, containing this text:

```
SELECT last_name, first_name, middle_name
FROM   STUDENTS
WHERE  ssn = '999999999';
```

call	count	cpu	elapsed	disk	query	current	rows
Parse	1	0.00	0.00	0	0	0	0
Execute	1	0.00	0.00	0	0	0	0
Fetch	1	0.00	0.00	0	1	1	1
total	3	0.00	0.00	0	1	1	1

```
Misses in library cache during parse: 0
Optimizer hint: CHOOSE
Parsing user id: 3
```

```
Rows     Explain Plan
------   -------------------------------------------------------
     0   SELECT STATEMENT   OPTIMIZER HINT: CHOOSE
     1   TABLE ACCESS (BY ROWID) OF 'STUDENTS'
     1     INDEX (UNIQUE SCAN) OF 'STUDENTS_SSN' (UNIQUE)
```

```
******************************************************************
```

So, how do we read this data?

First, let's look at the explain plan for the **SELECT** statement. By looking at the rightmost operation in the **Explain Plan** column and reading to the left, we can retrace the steps that Oracle took to execute the statement, as follows:

1. First, a scan of the **STUDENTS_SSN** index was performed, which returned one row matching social security number 999-99-9999.

2. The **ROWID** for this row was then used to fetch the values of the **first_name**, **last_name**, and **middle_name** columns from the **STUDENTS** table.

Next, let's look at the statistics that **TKPROF** calculated.

- Zero values for **cpu** and **elapsed** for the statement indicate that it was already parsed in the SGA when the statement was issued.

- The **query** value of 1 indicates that one consistent block read was performed to return the result set for the statement.

- The **current** value of 1 indicates that one current block read was performed to return the result set for the statement.

- The **rows** value of 1 indicates that one row was returned from the statement.

That was pretty simple. A lot of the time, you won't need this level of detail about the performance of your statements, but there will be times when you need this information to determine the source of a problem. For instance, high **disk** values would indicate that performance problems might be stemming from a slow or overworked hard disk drive.

SQL*Plus statements generally perform very well. However, there are some tuning tips with which you should be familiar in the event that one of your statements doesn't meet your performance expectations.

Other Tuning Tips

This section discusses some situations that commonly require performance tuning, including several stumbling blocks that confuse new PL/SQL developers. One of the most common pitfalls by new developers is scanning too many records (often whole tables of records).

Full-Table Scans

Oracle uses a *full-table scan* of a table when it cannot use any of the indexes for the table. A full-table scan retrieves every row of data from a table. In large tables, this process can take a long time to execute and can considerably diminish performance of your applications.

If you haven't quite grasped the inefficiency of using a full-table scan, try imagining that you're running a video store and someone returns a movie. In order to make the returned movie accessible for other customers to rent, it has to be put back in the proper place.

If you have to walk around your store and check all the movies to find the proper place, you're performing the equivalent of a full-table scan. To avoid full-table scans in your DML commands, you should *not:*

- Compare the values of two columns within the same table.

- Pass any columns to a predefined or a stored function.

- Use the **IS NULL** and **IS NOT NULL** comparisons against any column.

- Use **NOT IN** comparisons against any column.

- Use the **LIKE** operator against any column.

- Use subqueries against nonindex columns.

- Make comparisons against nonindexed columns.

There are several instances in which a full-table scan is as quick (or quicker) than the use of indexes. These occurrences include the following:

- A DML statement must return more than 20 percent of the rows in a table.

- The functionality of a statement requires that every row of a table will be processed.

- The table is extremely small. It's difficult to put an exact size on a table, but if a table has more than 500-1,000 rows, a full-table scan will probably be less effective than an indexed reference to the table. You'll need to do some ad hoc testing to determine which approach is best.

A related performance problem occurs when the **WHERE** clause of a statement is incomplete, causing Oracle to scan too many rows of data. While this isn't as expensive as performing an unnecessary full-table scan, it still requires Oracle to waste resources.

Going back to the returned movied metaphor, knowing that the newly returned movie goes in the "Adventure" section is better than knowing only that it belongs somewhere in the store. However, you'll be able to replace the film much more quickly if you also happen to know the name of the movie.

In a **SELECT** statement, the category and name of the movie would be included in the **WHERE** clause.

WHERE Clause Tips

While most of these tips are generalizations, each of them has been proven to be effective much of time. In general, it's best to write your code according to these tips (making necessary allowances to meet your required functionality) and then differentiate from the tips as necessary to improve performance. These tips all apply to the **WHERE** clause for your **SELECT, DELETE,** and **UPDATE** statements:

- Use the first column of the index. If necessary, use several columns of the index to assure that Oracle selects the index that you want to use. Knowing how to identify and use the indexes on a table is a very important skill.

- If your statement references more than one table, make sure that each column is referenced with a table name or table alias. This avoids overhead required for Oracle to determine the table of each column.

- If you're using **AND** conditions, make sure that the condition most likely to cause the query to fail is tested first. This will save processing time by avoiding comparisons that will later be invalidated by a frequently occurring condition.

- If you're using **OR** conditions, make sure that the condition most likely to cause the query to fail is tested last. This will save processing by avoiding comparisons that are more likely to fail in favor of comparisons that are likely to succeed.

- Don't join against unnecessary tables.

- Join only columns of the same datatype and length.

- Avoid the use of implicit datatype conversions.

- Don't use any functions (whether built-in or user-defined) on the left side of an expression.

- Try to avoid the use of the **IN, ANY, ALL, BETWEEN,** and **NOT** operators.

- Use the >= operator instead of the **LIKE** operator wherever possible. If the **LIKE** operator must be used, try to avoid the use of **%string%** conditions with the **LIKE** operator. Using the **LIKE** operator is expensive because Oracle must step through each position in a string of text, which takes a considerable amount of processing time.

Remember, each of these tips is a generalization based on many individual statements. Successful performance tuning is the result of many hours of tedious work to wring out every bit of performance; these tips will only start you along that road.

There are some additional tuning tips that apply when you're using Oracle's rule-based optimizer, which attempts to execute every SQL statement using the same method.

Rule-Based Optimizer

The tips outlined in this section are relevant only when using the rule-based optimizer. Most Oracle installations now predominantly use the cost-based optimizer, but use of the rule-based optimizer is still far from uncommon.

There are two primary conditions that you should be aware of when using the rule-based optimizer in your queries.

- Indexed columns referenced in the **WHERE** clause of your query should be listed in the same order as the columns are included in the index. If your code doesn't follow this pattern, Oracle might use a less effective index to execute your query.

- If you are joining multiple tables in your query, list the tables in the **FROM** clause in order from the largest to the smallest. This will allow Oracle to cache data from smaller tables so conditions can be evaluated against the data in larger tables.

If it seems like using the rule-based optimizer requires more work, that's because it does. Using the rule-based optimizer requires you to be much more conscious of the conditions that exist in your data and the indexes in place on your tables.

While tuning SQL statements is the most common type of performance tuning, there are some general guidelines that can significantly improve the performance of your PL/SQL code as well.

Tuning PL/SQL

There's very little call for tuning a properly designed block of PL/SQL. When performance tuning is necessary, most (if not all) of the work goes into tweaking performance improvements out of individual SQL statements. Still, there are several important design considerations for PL/SQL blocks that can have a significant impact on performance, most notably in the areas of using cursors and exception handling. The use of cursors allows you to significantly reduce the overhead required by your **SELECT** statements.

Using Cursors

In PL/SQL terms, a cursor is best described as a defined **SELECT** statement that can be referenced in your code as a variable. Most PL/SQL blocks contain at least one **SELECT** statement. This statement is often included inside the body of the PL/SQL block, as shown in Listing 10.3.

Listing 10.3 A **SELECT** statement inside the body of a PL/SQL block.

```
DECLARE
    vLastName   varchar2 (20);

BEGIN
    SELECT last_name
    INTO   vLastName
    FROM   STUDENTS
    WHERE  ssn = '999999999';
END;
```

This query returns a single row (at least, we're assuming that there is one distinct social security number per student). While there's nothing wrong with the **SELECT** statement itself, there is a performance problem associated with its use inside the PL/SQL block.

Oracle executes two fetches to return this single row of data. The first fetch returns the row of data returned by the query. The second fetch is performed to make sure that there are no more rows that satisfy the conditions of the query. Any **SELECT** statement inside a PL/SQL block will always perform an extra fetch for this purpose.

This extra fetch can be avoided if the **SELECT** statement is implemented by using a cursor, as shown in Listing 10.4.

Listing 10.4 Implementing **SELECT** statement functionality by using a cursor.

```
DECLARE
    CURSOR StudentName_cur
    IS
    SELECT last_name
```

```
   FROM    STUDENTS
   WHERE   ssn = '999999999';

BEGIN
   OPEN StudentName_cur;
   FETCH StudentName_cur INTO StudentName_rec;
   CLOSE StudentName_cur;
END;
```

The same **SELECT** statement, when implemented with a cursor, requires one less fetch than a standalone **SELECT** statement within the PL/SQL block. However, there are a couple of "gotchas" lurking behind the use of a cursor in this way:

- Using a cursor like this always returns only the first row of a result set. If the query could potentially return more than one row, using a cursor like this may cause you to overlook data that you need to process or an error condition that you should be handling.

- Unless you've used a meaningful identifier to name your cursor, you'll find that debugging your routine is difficult because you must keep jumping to the top of your code to look at your cursor declaration again.

Probably more important than the use of cursors is the wise use of exception handling. Careful use of exceptions can reduce the amount of conditional logic (**IF-THEN** statements, etc.) used in your code, thus reducing the number of instructions that the CPU must process.

Exception Handling

It's very common for developers to flag error conditions and handle the condition through the use of **IF-THEN** logic. Listing 10.5 illustrates the use of this approach.

Listing 10.5   Using **IF-THEN** logic to flag errors.

```
DECLARE
   bAidAmountOk   boolean;
   vLastName      varchar2 (20);
   vFirstName     varchar2 (20);
   nGPA           number   (3,2);
   nSemesterGPA   number   (3,2);
   vSSN           varchar2 (9);
   nFinanceNum    number   (5);
   nTotalAid      number   (7,2);
```

```
    CURSOR Students_cur
    IS
    SELECT ssn, first_name, last_name, financing_num,
           overall_gpa
    FROM   STUDENTS
    WHERE  overall_gpa < 2.5;

BEGIN
    FOR Students_rec IN Students_cur LOOP
        bAidAmountOk := FALSE;

        vFirstName   := Students_rec.first_name;
        vLastName    := Students_rec.last_name;
        nGPA         := Students_rec.overall_gpa;
        nFinanceNum  := Students_rec.financing_num;
        vSSN         := Students_rec.ssn;

        SELECT total_aid
        INTO   nTotalAid
        FROM   STUDENT_FINANCIAL_AID
        WHERE  financing_num = nFinanceNum;

        IF (nTotalAid < $1000) THEN
            bAidAmountOk := TRUE;
        END IF;

        IF NOT bAidAmountOk THEN
            nSemesterGPA := Get_Semester_GPA (vStudentSSN => vSSN);

            IF (nSemesterGPA > 3.0) THEN
                bAidAmountOk := TRUE;
            END IF;
        END IF;
    END LOOP;
END;
```

This example uses the boolean variable **bAidAmountOk** to keep track of a condition throughout the processing of each student record. The highlighted statements deal directly with keeping track of this condition throughout the loop.

This approach does have an impact on performance. Multiple instructions are used to test for the error condition. Each instruction requires CPU cycles to complete. A much better approach involves the use of exceptions to avoid wasting CPU cycles, as shown in Listing 10.6.

Listing 10.6   Using exception handlers to improve performance.

```
DECLARE
    vLastName       varchar2 (20);
    vFirstName      varchar2 (20);
    nGPA            number   (3,2);
    nSemesterGPA    number   (3,2);
    vSSN            varchar2 (9);
    nFinanceNum     number   (5);
    nTotalAid       number   (7,2);
    xAID_AMOUNT_OK EXCEPTION;

    CURSOR Students_cur
    IS
    SELECT ssn, first_name, last_name, financing_num,
           overall_gpa
    FROM   STUDENTS
    WHERE  overall_gpa < 2.5;

BEGIN
    FOR Students_rec IN Students_cur LOOP
        BEGIN
            vFirstName   := Students_rec.first_name;
            vLastName    := Students_rec.last_name;
            nGPA         := Students_rec.overall_gpa;
            nFinanceNum  := Students_rec.financing_num;
            vSSN         := Students_rec.ssn;

            SELECT sum (total_aid)
            INTO   nTotalAid
            FROM   STUDENT_FINANCIAL_AID
            WHERE  financing_num = nFinanceNum;

            IF (nTotalAid < $1000) THEN
                RAISE xAID_AMOUNT_OK;
            END IF;

            nSemesterGPA := Get_Semester_GPA (vStudentSSN => vSSN);

            IF (nSemesterGPA > 3.0) THEN
                RAISE xAID_AMOUNT_OK;
            END IF;

        EXCEPTION
            WHEN xAID_AMOUNT_OK THEN
                NULL;
```

```
        END;
    END LOOP;
END;
```

In this example, the **xAID_AMOUNT_OK** exception is explicitly raised inside the loop to allow execution to skip the instructions that occur after the student's GPA is checked. This probably results in a gain of several CPU cycles being freed up. The highlighted statements in the example are used for this exception handling.

PL/SQL's exception handling is very performance efficient. When an exception is raised, all subsequent instructions within the block are bypassed so the exception can be handled by an exception handler. You can utilize this built-in performance boost by thinking about the organization of your code before you write it and planning to use user-defined exceptions to skip code that you don't need to execute.

Summary

Performance tuning is one of the most grueling aspects of any Oracle developer's job. Often, it will take hours to achieve acceptable performance from a complex query. The tips presented in this chapter will provide a starting point for this type of work, which you *will* have to do at some point in your career.

Using Built-In
SQL And PL/SQL
Functions

APPENDIX

A

HIGH PERFORMANCE

Using Built-In SQL And PL/SQL Functions

One of the nice things about SQL and PL/SQL is the number of built-in functions that Oracle provides. This appendix provides explanations and examples for the most commonly used built-in functions. (You'll also find some other useful functions that Oracle didn't take the time to include.)

Single-Row SQL Functions

This is the largest and most varied group of SQL functions. Functions within this group can operate only on the values contained within a single-row. Single-row functions can be sorted by functionality and the datatype of their parameters. In most aspects, single-row functions closely resemble stored functions. For purposes of this appendix, I've divided the most commonly used single-row SQL functions into five groups: conversion, alphabetic, date, numeric, and miscellaneous.

Examples of each function are included. In some instances, the functions are illustrated like this:

```
chr (97)
```

This is a call to the function that can appear in one of two places:

- Inside a DML statement:

  ```
  SELECT chr (97)
  FROM   <table>;
  ```

In this instance, **<table>** can be the name of any table to which you have access. You can also use **DUAL** here. **DUAL** is a dummy table recognized by the system for the express purpose of retrieving a value.

- On the right side of an expression in a PL/SQL block:

```
vDelimiter := chr (25);
```

In this instance, the output of the function will be assigned to the variable **vDelimiter**.

In other instances, the examples utilize a DML statement or excerpt from a PL/SQL block. This indicates that the function calls must be used in the context shown in the example.

Conversion Functions

Oracle provides conversion functions so values of one datatype can be easily converted to another datatype. While Oracle will perform implicit conversions of datatypes for you, this could lead to performance problems in your applications and to compatibility problems in future versions of Oracle. I strongly recommend that you use these conversion functions instead of relying on Oracle's implicit conversions.

to_char()

The **to_char**() function is probably the most commonly used conversion function. The function converts both numerical data and date data to datatype **varchar2**.

The simplest way of using **to_char**() to convert date information is as follows:

```
to_char ('02/14/97')
```

This converts the date into a character string in the default date format (numerical month, numerical day, and a two-digit year, separated by slashes). However, the most common use of **to_char**() is to convert dates to type **varchar2** in a specific format, as shown in this example,

```
to_char ('14-FEB-97', 'DD-MON-YYYY')
```

which returns the following string:

```
14-FEB-1997
```

Using **to_char()** with numerical data is very similar to using the function with dates. One common use is to simply convert data from a numerical datatype to type **varchar2**. For example,

```
to_char (25000)
```

returns

```
25000
```

When converting numerical data, **to_char()** can also take a second argument, a format model for the output of the function. For example,

```
to_char (25000, '$99,999.99')
```

returns

```
$25,000.00
```

Chapter 3 lists the elements that can be used in format models for numerical and date data.

to_date()

The **to_date()** function is used to convert character data to the **date** datatype. Like **to_char()**, this function can be called with a single parameter, much like

```
to_date ('02-MAY-97')
```

which returns a value of type **date**. **to_date()** may also be called with a second parameter, which instructs the function to convert the specified string from the specified format into a standard date. For example,

```
to_date ('02 May 1997', 'DD MONTH YYYY')
```

returns

```
02-MAY-97
```

Valid elements of the format model are discussed in Chapter 3. The examples provided here have all used the default Oracle date format.

to_number()

The **to_number**() function converts data of type **char** or **varchar2** to type **number**. The function can accept a single parameter. For example,

```
to_number ('25000')
```

returns

```
25000
```

The function can also accept a format model as the second parameter, like the **to_char**() and **to_date**() functions. For example,

```
to_number ('25000', '$99,999.99')
```

returns

```
$25,000.00
```

Valid elements of the format model are discussed in Chapter 3.

Alphabetic Functions

The alphabetic group of functions deals primary with operations on strings but also provides some other interesting functions, such as functions that deal with converting characters to and from their ASCII equivalents.

ascii()

The **ascii**() function returns the ASCII value of a specified character. For example,

```
ascii ('a')
```

returns

97

If you call **ascii**() using a string longer than a single character, only the ASCII value of the first character will be returned. For example,

```
ascii ('abcdefg')
```

returns

97

chr()

The **chr**() function is the counterpart of the **ascii**() function. **chr**() returns the character associated with a specific ASCII value. For example,

```
chr (97)
```

returns

a

initcap()

The **initcap**() function accepts a string as a parameter and returns the string with the first letter of each word in the string capitalized. For example,

```
initcap ('the quick brown fox...')
```

returns

```
The Quick Brown Fox...
```

instr()

The **instr**() function is one of the most useful character functions. In its simplest incarnation, the function accepts two parameters: a string to be searched (let's call this *string1*) and a string to be searched for (let's call this *string2*) within string1. The syntax for **instr**() is as follows:

```
instr ('JELLY BEANS AND APPLE TREES', 'E')
```

The **instr()** function returns an **integer** value. In our example, the result of the function call is

2

indicating that the first occurrence of string2 in string1 occurs at the second character.

The function can accept a third parameter (let's call this parameter *x*), which is used to indicate the starting position for the search within string1. For example,

```
instr ('JELLY BEANS AND APPLE TREES', 'E', 3)
```

returns

8

X can be negative, which instructs Oracle to count backwards from the end of string1 by x characters before starting the search. For example,

```
instr ('JELLY BEANS AND APPLE TREES', 'E', -3)
```

returns

25

As you can see, the value returned by this call to **instr()** is the position of string2 based on the total length of string1 and not on the starting position for the search.

But wait, there's more! **instr()** can also accept a fourth parameter (let's call this parameter y), which tells Oracle which occurrence of the string2 should be returned. For example,

```
instr ('JELLY BEANS AND APPLE TREES', 'E', 3, 2)
```

returns

21

The values of the x and y parameters default to 1 (which means the values start with the first character in string1 and find the first occurrence of string2).

length()

The **length()** function accepts a string as a parameter and returns an **integer** value. For example,

```
length ('HORSES')
```

returns

```
6
```

lower()

The **lower()** function accepts a string and converts each character in the string to its lowercase equivalent. For example,

```
lower ('APPLE')
```

returns

```
apple
```

lpad()

The **lpad()** function accepts two parameters: a string (let's call this *string1*) and an integer value that represents the desired width of the string. Using this information, the function returns the value of string1 padded on the left side until string1 has the desired length. For example,

```
lpad ('apple', 10)
```

returns

```
    apple
```

lpad() can also accept a third parameter, string2, which should be used to pad string1 to the desired width. For example,

```
lpad ('apple', 10, '*')
```

returns

```
*****apple
```

The third parameter of **lpad()** defaults to a single space (' ').

ltrim()

In its simplest incarnation, the **ltrim**() function removes all spaces from the left side of a specified string. For example,

```
ltrim ('       apple')
```

returns

```
apple
```

The **ltrim**() function can also accept a second parameter, a set of characters that should be trimmed from the left side of the string. The string is trimmed until the function reaches the first character not appearing in the specified set. For example,

```
ltrim ('apple', 'ap')
```

returns

```
le
```

The second parameter of **ltrim**() defaults to a single space (' ').

replace()

In its simplest form, **replace**() accepts two parameters: a string to be searched (let's call it *string1*) and a string that should be removed from string1 (let's call it *string2*). For example,

```
replace ('applesauce and marinara sauce', 'sauce')
```

returns

```
apple  and marinara
```

replace() can also accept a third parameter (let's call it *string3*). When string3 is provided, all occurrences of string2 are replaced with string3. For example,

```
replace ('applesauce and marinara sauce', 'sauce', ' tree')
```

returns

```
apple tree and marinara  tree
```

The third parameter of **replace**() defaults to **NULL**.

rpad()

The **rpad**() function is identical to the **lpad**() function, with the exception that string1 is padded on the right side instead of the left.

rtrim()

The **rtrim**() function is identical to the **ltrim**() function, with the exception that the string is trimmed on the right side instead of the left.

substr()

The **substr**() function is another extremely useful function for parsing strings. Most calls to **substr**() use three parameters. For example,

```
substr ('apples and oranges', 1, 6)
```

returns

```
apples
```

The call to **substr**() in this example instructs the function to start with the first character of the specified string and return the first six characters of the string. The third parameter can be left out, in which case, the function starts reading at the position indicated by the second parameter and reads until the end of the string is reached.

The value of the second parameter can be negative, which instructs the function to read backwards from the end of the string to find the starting position.

translate()

The **translate**() function accepts three parameters. For example,

```
translate ('xyz', 'x', 'w')
```

returns

```
wyz
```

Every occurrence of the second parameter within the string is replaced with the third parameter. A common use of this is function is to remove nonprinting or special characters from a string. For example,

```
replace (<string variable>, chr (9), NULL)
```

removes all the tabs from a string of text.

upper()

The **upper**() function is identical to the **lower**() function, with the exception that every character in the string is converted to its uppercase equivalent.

Date Functions

There aren't very many commonly used date functions. However, the one function that is commonly used—**SYSDATE**()—is, perhaps, the most commonly used function provided by SQL*Plus.

SYSDATE()

The **SYSDATE**() function returns the current date and time in the default Oracle date format. The default format for the date returned is

```
MM-DD-YY
```

It's very common to use **SYSDATE**() in conjunction with **to_char**(). For example,

```
to_char (SYSDATE, 'MM-DD-YYYY HH:MI:SS');
```

returns a string containing not only the current date, but also the current time down to the second. The most common uses of **SYSDATE**() don't use a date format model:

```
dStartDate := SYSDATE;
```

Numeric Functions

The following functions all accept numeric values as parameters and return numeric values. Each of the functions listed in this section is accurate to 38 significant digits.

abs()

The **abs**() function accepts a single number as a parameter and returns the absolute value of that number. For example,

```
abs (-9.37)
```

returns

```
9.37
```

mod()

The **mod**() function accepts two numbers as parameters, x and y, and returns the remainder of x divided by y. For instance, calling the function to get the remainder of 5 divided by 2,

```
mod (5, 2)
```

returns

```
1
```

If y is zero, the function returns x. For instance,

```
mod (5, 0)
```

returns

```
5
```

power()

The **power**() function accepts two numbers as parameters, x and y, and returns the value of x raised to the power of y. For instance, calling the function to get the value of 10 raised to the 6th power,

```
power (10, 6)
```

returns

```
1000000
```

If the value of x is negative, the value of y must be an integer. For instance,

```
power (-3.54, 2)
```

returns

```
12.5316
```

round()

The **round**() function accepts a single number, x, as a parameter and rounds that number to the nearest integer value. For instance, calling the function with a value of 15.37,

```
round (15.37)
```

returns

```
15
```

The function can also take an integer parameter, y, following the number parameter. This parameter tells the function how many significant digits should be left in place. Using the same value as the previous example while passing 1 for the y parameter,

```
round (15.37, 1)
```

returns

```
15.4
```

If y is a negative value, the function rounds backwards from the decimal. For example,

```
round (153.17, -1)
```

returns

```
150
```

which has been rounded at the ones position in the final value.

The function can be called with only one parameter. In this case, y defaults to 0, and the function returns an integer value.

sqrt()

The **sqrt()** function accepts a single number as a parameter and returns the square root of that number. For instance, passing 4 to the function,

```
sqrt (4)
```

returns

```
2
```

This function can't accept a negative value as a parameter, but the function can return a decimal value. For example,

```
sqrt (5.25)
```

returns

```
2.29128785
```

trunc()

The **trunc()** function accepts a single number, x, as a parameter and returns that number truncated to 0 decimal places. For instance,

```
trunc (15.37)
```

returns

```
15
```

The function's second parameter, y, tells the function how many digits of the number should be left intact. This second parameter defaults to 0 and must be an integer value. Using the same value as the previous example, but passing 1 for y,

```
trunc (15.37, 1)
```

returns

```
15.3
```

Miscellaneous Functions

There are some commonly used functions that don't fall neatly into any of the other categories—namely, **decode()** and **nvl()**.

decode()

Of all the functions provided by SQL*Plus, **decode()** is perhaps the most useful. A call to **decode()** can accept up to 255 parameters. Calls to **decode()** must follow this basic syntax:

```
decode (expression, value, new value, default value);
```

The **decode()** call can only have one expression and one default value. Value and new value must be a pair of parameters. Consider the following call to **decode()**:

```
SELECT decode (course_grade, 'A', 4,
                             'B', 3,
                             'C', 2,
                             'D', 1, 0)
FROM    SCHEDULED_CLASSES
WHERE   ssn           = '999999999'
AND     course_number = 2103;
```

This function is the closest equivalent to a **case** statement that can be found in SQL. The value and new value parameters don't have to be literal values; however, they can be expressions such as mathematical operations and function calls.

In the event that you try to port SQL statements between Oracle and another relational database, you should be aware that **decode()** is not an ANSI standard SQL function.

nvl()

The **nvl()** function is used to substitute a **NULL** value with another value. The most common example of a call to **nvl()** looks like this:

```
SELECT nvl (base_salary, 20000)
FROM    EMPLOYEES;
```

This would replace any **NULL** value retrieved by the query with the number 20000.

Multi-Row SQL Functions

Multi-row SQL functions (also called *group* or *aggregate* functions) work with groups of rows. These functions ignore **NULL** values, except where noted in this section. The most commonly used multi-row SQL functions fall into the numeric group. All functions listed in this section are numeric functions.

avg()

The **avg()** function returns the average value of a numeric field from a group of rows. For example,

```
SELECT avg (base_salary)
FROM   EMPLOYEES;
```

returns the average salary of all employees.

count()

The **count()** function counts the number of rows in a group of rows. This function counts all rows in the group, including those for which a **NULL** value is present. There are two ways of calling **count()**, as follows:

```
SELECT count (*)
FROM   EMPLOYEE_HISTORY
WHERE  employee_number = 90213
AND    warning          = 'Y';

SELECT count (married)
FROM   EMPLOYEE_HISTORY
WHERE  employee_number = 90213
AND    warning          = 'Y';
```

The first example returns the total number of rows that match the query's **WHERE** clause. The second example returns the total number of rows that have a non-**NULL** value in the specified column.

max()

The **max()** function returns the highest value of a specified column from a group of rows. For example,

```
SELECT max (base_salary)
FROM    EMPLOYEES;
```

returns the salary of the highest paid employee.

min()

The **min()** function returns the lowest value of a specified column from a group of rows. For example,

```
SELECT min (base_salary)
FROM    EMPLOYEES;
```

returns the salary of the lowest paid employee.

sum()

The **sum()** function returns the total of all values for a specified column in a group of rows. For example,

```
SELECT sum (vacation_days_used)
FROM    EMPLOYEES;
```

returns the total number of vacation days taken by employees this year.

PL/SQL Functions

PL/SQL provides two important error reporting functions that are not provided by SQL: **SQLCODE()** and **SQLERRM()**.

SQLCODE()

The **SQLCODE()** function provides the number of the latest Oracle error that has occurred. Following is an example of calling the **SQLCODE()** function:

```
vErrorCode := SQLCODE;
```

SQLERRM()

The **SQLERRM**() function provides the complete text of the most recent Oracle error that has occurred, including the error number provide by the **SQLCODE**() function. Following is an example of calling the **SQLERRM**() function:

```
vErrorText := SQLERRM;
```

Special Functions Used To Convert Numbers

The following functions aren't provided by Oracle, but I've chosen to include them because they are useful in certain situations or are cleverly written examples of the types of work that a function can do.

Converting Numbers Between Bases

Projects that involve the conversion of data from legacy systems may have to deal with numerical data in a nondecimal base. The stored functions described in this section were designed to handle these conversions.

> **Author's Note:** The following functions were contributed by Shawn Ramsey of AT&T Wireless Services in Seattle, Washington. Many thanks to Shawn for allowing me to include these functions here.

Converting Base10 Numbers To Another Base

The **Decimal_2_Any_Base**() function converts numbers from base10 to any base between base2 and base36 (inclusive). Listing A.1 shows the complete source code for the function.

Listing A.1 The **Decimal_2_Any_Base()** function.

```
FUNCTION Decimal_2_Any_Base

  (p_DecNo IN    integer,
   p_Base  IN    integer)

RETURN varchar2 IS
```

```
-- ****************************************************************
-- DESCRIPTION: Takes a decimal number and converts the base to
--              any base from 2 to 36
--
-- Parameters:  p_DecNo = Decimal Number to convert.
--              p_Base  = Base to convert the number to.
--
-- Returns:     Character string of the number converted to the
--              desired base. NULL if invalid conversion or
--              a conversion error occurs.
--
-- AUTHOR:      Shawn M. Ramsey
--
-- REVISION HISTORY
-- Date          Reviser     Change
-- ----------------------------------------------------------------
-- 28 JAN 1997  S. Ramsey    Function creation.
--
-- ****************************************************************

---- Characters for conversion
v_AnyNo varchar2(36) := '0123456789ABCDEFGHIJKLMNOPQRSTUVWXYZ';

---- Variables for conversion
n_DecNo  integer         := p_DecNo;
n_Base   integer         := p_Base;
v_Return varchar2 (100) := NULL;
n_Cnt    integer         := 0;
n_Val    integer         := 0;

BEGIN
    ---- Check Base Number and Number to convert
    IF (NOT n_Base BETWEEN 2 AND 36) OR (n_DecNo < 0) THEN
       RETURN NULL;

    ELSIF (n_DecNo = 0) THEN
       RETURN '0';
    END IF;

    ---- Initialize Variables
    v_Return := '';
    n_Cnt    := 0 ;

    ---- Loop and convert
    WHILE (n_DecNo <> 0) LOOP
```

```
    n_Val     := mod (n_DecNo,
                    (n_Base**(n_Cnt+1)))/(n_Base**n_cnt);
    n_DecNo  := n_DecNo - (n_Val * (n_Base**n_Cnt));
    v_Return := substr (v_AnyNo, n_Val+1, 1) || v_Return;
    n_Cnt     := n_Cnt + 1;
  END LOOP;

  RETURN v_Return;

EXCEPTION
  WHEN OTHERS THEN
      RETURN NULL;
END;
```

Converting Numbers Of Odd Bases To Base10

The **Any_2_Base10**() function can be used to convert a number in any base between base2 and base36 to its base10 equivalent. Listing A.2 shows the complete source code for the function.

Listing A.2   The **Any_2_Base10()** function.

```
FUNCTION ANY_2_Base10()

  (p_Conv   IN varchar2,
   p_Base   IN integer)

RETURN varchar2 IS

-- ****************************************************************
-- DESCRIPTION: Takes a number in any base from 2 to 36 and
--              converts it to an integer number.
--
-- Parameters:  p_Conv  = Number to convert.
--              p_Base  = Base to convert the number from.
--
-- Returns:     Number converted to the decimal. NULL if invalid
--              conversion or a conversion error occurs.
--
-- AUTHOR:      Shawn M. Ramsey
--
-- REVISION HISTORY
-- Date          Reviser     Change
-- ---------------------------------------------------------------
-- 28 JAN 1997  S. Ramsey   Function creation.
--
-- ****************************************************************
```

```
---- Characters for conversion
v_AnyNo    varchar2 (36) := '0123456789ABCDEFGHIJKLMNOPQRSTUVWXYZ';

---- Exception
e_BadData exception;

---- Variables for conversion
v_Conv     varchar2 (200) := upper (p_Conv);
v_ValChar  varchar2 (200) := NULL;
n_Base     integer        := p_Base;
n_Return   integer        := NULL;
n_Cnt      integer        := 0;
n_Val      integer        := 0;

BEGIN
   ---- Check Base Number and Number to convert
   IF (NOT n_Base BETWEEN 2 AND 36) OR (v_Conv IS NULL) THEN
      RETURN NULL;
   END IF;


   ---- Initialize Variables
   n_Return  := 0;
   n_Cnt     := 0;
   v_ValChar := substr (v_AnyNo, 1, n_Base);

   ---- Validate String
   FOR n_Cnt IN 1..length (v_Conv) LOOP
       IF (v_ValChar NOT LIKE '%' ||
           substr(v_Conv, n_Cnt, 1) || '%') THEN
              RAISE e_BadData;
       END IF;
   END LOOP;


   ---- Loop and convert
   FOR n_Cnt IN 1..length (v_Conv) LOOP
       IF (v_ValChar NOT LIKE '%' ||
           substr (v_Conv, n_Cnt, 1) || '%') THEN
              RAISE e_BadData;
       END IF;
   END LOOP;


   ---- Convert Number
   FOR n_Cnt IN REVERSE 1..length (v_Conv) LOOP
       n_Val    := instr (v_ValChar, substr (v_Conv, n_Cnt, 1)) - 1;
       n_Return :=  n_Return + (n_Val *
                    (n_Base**(length (v_Conv) - n_Cnt)));
   END LOOP;
```

```
    RETURN n_Return;

EXCEPTION
    WHEN OTHERS THEN
        RETURN NULL;
END;
```

Is_Number()

The **Is_Number**() function is a relatively simple function that depends on an exception being raised to work properly. A function like this can be useful when data occasionally contains characters mixed with numerals. Listing A.3 gives a complete listing for the function.

Listing A.3   The **Is_Number()** function.

```
FUNCTION Is_Number (vValue IN       number) RETURN boolean

IS

   nValue    number;

BEGIN
   nValue := to_number (vValue);
   RETURN TRUE;

EXCEPTION
   WHEN INVALID_NUMBER THEN
        RETURN FALSE;
END Is_Number;
```

Summary

This has been a discussion of the most commonly used SQL and PL/SQL functions. There are several more functions that haven't been discussed, but these functions aren't commonly encountered. If you encounter a call to a function that you don't recognize and you can't locate the source code, it might be a function that wasn't discussed here. Your best bet is to check for the function in the *PL/SQL User's Guide And Reference* provided by Oracle.

DML Command Syntax And Examples

APPENDIX

B

HIGH PERFORMANCE

DML Command Syntax And Examples

For those of you who aren't familiar with the basic format of DML statements in Oracle, I've provided this reference. This reference is by no means a bible of every possible permutation of a statement, but it does cover each statement quite thoroughly. Chances are, the material presented here will be applicable in more than 99 percent of the DML statements you will write. Specifically, this appendix covers the **DELETE**, **INSERT**, **SELECT**, and **UPDATE** statements.

The DELETE Statement

The **DELETE** statement is used to remove one or more rows from a table. The basic format of a **DELETE** statement is as follows:

```
DELETE
FROM    <table>
WHERE   <one or more data conditions>;
```

The use of **FROM** is entirely optional, although the table name must be specified. The use of the **WHERE** clause is also optional, but excluding it will cause all the rows in the table to be deleted.

If you want to delete all rows in a table, you might consider using the **TRUNCATE** command instead. This command removes the rows in the table without generating rollback information. If you are absolutely positive that you don't want the data, **TRUNCATE** is much faster than **DELETE**.

Be careful, though! Once you empty a table in this way, its contents are gone. If you later need the data, you will have to have your DBA recover the data from a backup.

The INSERT Statement

The **INSERT** statement is used to add a new row of data to a table. The basic format of an **INSERT** statement is as follows:

```
INSERT
INTO    <table>
        (<column listings>)
VALUES (<column values>);
```

If you are inserting column values in the order in which the table's columns are defined, you may omit the column listing. Otherwise, you must include the column listings so Oracle will place the new data values in the proper columns.

It is possible to create multiple rows with a single **INSERT** statement. This is called a *multiple insert*. The format of a multiple insert is as follows:

```
INSERT
INTO    <destination table>
        <destination table column listings>
SELECT <source table column listings>
FROM    <source table>;
```

You may use an asterisk in place of the source table column listings to indicate that all of the source table's columns should be selected. If this is the case, the layout of the source and destination tables must be exactly alike.

Multiple inserts are commonly used to copy data within a table back into the table with different primary key values. This is very useful when creating test data.

The SELECT Statement

The **SELECT** statement is used to retrieve data from a table. The basic format of a **SELECT** statement is as follows:

```
SELECT <column listing>
FROM    <source table> <source table alias>
WHERE  <one or more data conditions>;
```

If you wish to select all the columns that match your **WHERE** clause, you may use an asterisk instead of naming all the columns from your source table. The use of the

WHERE clause is optional, but excluding the clause will cause all the rows of data to be retrieved from the table.

The use of a table alias is optional, but it is quite common in queries that join two or more tables to return data. The basic format when using a table alias is as follows:

```
SELECT <column listing>
FROM    <source table> <source table alias>,
        <source table> <source table alias>
WHERE   <one or more data conditions>;
```

A table alias is most often used to abbreviate a table's name so that columns in the **WHERE** clause may be referenced with the abbreviation instead of the table name. When two columns in different tables share the same name, the desired column must be identified using either a table name or table alias.

The use of an optional **ORDER BY** clause is quite common, as well. The basic format of an **ORDER BY** clause is as follows:

```
SELECT <column listing>
FROM    <table> <table alias>
WHERE   <one or more data conditions>
ORDER BY <column>;
```

The **ORDER BY** clause instructs Oracle to gather the data and then sort it according to one or more conditions. Use of this clause adds overhead to the performance of the statement.

The UPDATE Statement

The **UPDATE** statement is used to modify data that already exists in a table. The basic format of an **UPDATE** statement is as follows:

```
UPDATE <table>
SET    <column> = <value>,
       <column> = <value>
WHERE  <one or more data conditions>;
```

You may specify as many columns as you like in the **SET** clause. The use of the **WHERE** clause is (once again) optional, but excluding the clause will cause every row in the table to be updated.

Getting In Touch With Other Oracle Professionals

APPENDIX

C

HIGH PERFORMANCE

Getting In Touch With Other Oracle Professionals

While I've been writing this book, I've been perusing the Web frequently, looking for information about Oracle. Information about anything can be found on the Web, and Oracle is no exception. Keyword searches on "oracle" will turn up hundreds of hits. Here are some of the best resources that I've found for getting the answers to Oracle questions.

Frequently Asked Questions And White Papers

There are several Web sites, both commercial and individual, that provide white papers and answers to Oracle questions. You'll probably want to bookmark at least one of these sites.

- The Cobb Group has set up the Exploring Oracle Developer/2000 and Designer/2000 page (**www.cobb.com/eod**).

- JCC's Oracle Home Page (**www.jcc.com/oracle.html**) has a search engine for Oracle7 topics, as well as links to other resources.

- The Oracle FAQ Contents page (**www.bf.rmit.edu.au/Oracle/contents.html**) breaks down questions into several topics.

- The Oracle User Resource (**www.oracle-users.com**) has several white papers available online.

- Orapub of Earth (**www.europa.com/~orapub**) provides several online papers.

- The RGS Oracle-PL/SQL-WWW interface page (**gserver.grads.vt.edu**) includes PL/SQL blocks to perform useful functions as well as some Java and Perl information.

- Underground Oracle Frequently Asked Questions (**www.onwe.co.za/frank/ faq.htm**) is an excellent online resource for searching through front-line wisdom and answers some very tough questions.

Most white papers available online use Adobe Acrobat format. The Adobe Acrobat reader is available at **www.adobe.com**.

Newsgroups

In the fall of 1996, the **comp.databases.oracle** newsgroup was split into the following newsgroups:

- **comp.databases.oracle.server** deals with server-related issues.

- **comp.databases.oracle.tools** deals with questions regarding the Designer/2000, Developer/2000, and other Oracle products other than the database server.

- **comp.databases.oracle.marketplace** is an excellent place to go looking for a job, if you're an Oracle professional. This newsgroup also serves as a forum for third-party software developers to announce their products.

- **comp.databases.oracle.misc** handles issues that don't belong in the other subgroups.

- **comp.databases.oracle** remains in service as well, but is now lightly used.

These newsgroups are an excellent place to find information about specific Oracle-related topics. If you have access to Usenet newsgroups, do yourself a favor, and subscribe to one or more of these subgroups.

Oracle On Linux

Since 1995, Linux (a free version of Unix for x86 processors) has been gaining popularity. It was inevitable that these users would eventually want Oracle on their systems. Currently, Oracle has no plans to implement a Linux version (nor do I expect that to change). Still, Linux users press ahead by running Oracle for SCO Unix under Linux. There are a few Web pages that provide information about getting Oracle for SCO up and running under Linux.

- Georg Rehfeld (**www.wmd.de/wmd/staff/pauck/misc/oracle_on_linux.html**) provides step-by-step instructions on setting up Oracle on a Linux box using SCO Unix drivers.

- Christopher Browne (**www.conline.com/~cbbrowne/rdbms.html**) provides an overview of database management systems that run on Linux, including Oracle.

Oracle User Groups

The largest user group for Oracle products is the International Oracle Users Group (**www.ioug.org**). In addition to IOUG, there are many smaller user groups in specific geographical regions. The groups listed below are all within the U.S. and Canada.

- The Calgary Oracle Users Group (**www.dbcorp.ab.ca/coug**) serves Oracle users in and around Calgary, in the Alberta province of Canada.

- The Chicago Oracle Users Group (**www.roman.com/coug**) serves Oracle users in and around the city of Chicago.

- The Gulf Coast Oracle Users Group (**www.southwind.com/gcoug**) is dedicated to serving Oracle users along the Gulf Coast in the states of Louisiana, Mississippi, Alabama, and in the Florida Panhandle.

- The Houston Oracle Users Group (**www.cois.com/houg**) serves users in and around the Houston area.

- The Indiana Oracle Users Group (**www.rtt.in.net/inoug**) serves Oracle users in the state of Indiana.

- The Johnstown Oracle Users Group (**homepage.third-wave.com/joug**) serves Oracle users in Cambria and Somerset counties of Pennsylvania.

- The Mid-Atlantic Association of Oracle Professionals (**www.maop.org**) serves users centered around Washington, D.C.

- The Mid-South Oracle Users Group, or MidSoug, (**www.midsoug.org**) serves Oracle users in Memphis and the adjacent areas of Mississippi and Arkansas.

- The Midwest Oracle Users Group (**www.moug.org**) is dedicated to serving Oracle users in Illinois, Indiana, Iowa, Kentucky, Michigan, Minnesota, Missouri, Wisconsin, and Ohio.

- The New Jersey Oracle Users Group (**www.mfgsys.com/njoug.htm**) serves Oracle users in the state of New Jersey.

- The New York Oracle Users Group (**www.nyoug.org/nyoug**) serves users of Oracle products in the New York Metropolitan area and holds at least four meetings each year.

- The Northern California Oracle Users Group (**www.nocoug.org**) is dedicated to serving Oracle users in northern California.

- The Northwest Oracle Users Group (**www.ariscorp.com/nwoug**) is dedicated to serving Oracle users in the Pacific Northwest. Links to several smaller regional groups are provided.

- The Rocky Mountain Oracle Users Group (**www.rmoug.org**) serves Oracle users in and around Colorado.

- The San Diego Oracle Users Group (**www.pubsvc.dsr.com/sdoug**) serves Oracle users in San Diego.

- The South Florida Oracle Users Group (**www.ugn.com/sfoug1.htm**) serves Oracle users in south Florida, notably the Naples/Ft. Myers area.

- The St. Louis Oracle Users Group (**clearperception.com/sloug**) serves Oracle users in St. Louis and neighboring areas of Missouri and Illinois.

- The Twin Cities Oracle Users Group (**www.tcoug.org**) serves Oracle users in the Twin Cities area of Minnesota.

- The Virginia Oracle Users Group (**www.crtnet.com/voug**) serves the users of Oracle products in the state of Virginia.

Many of these groups publish newsletters, some of which are available over the Web. Full details about the organization, including contact names and numbers, can be found on the Web page of each group.

This is not a complete list of regional user groups; it's merely a list of those who have established a Web presence at press time. A complete and more up-to-date listing of regional user groups can be found on the IOUG Web site.

SQL And PL /SQL Coding Standards

APPENDIX

D

SQL And PL/SQL Coding Standards

PL/SQL has become a mature and popular language since its introduction in 1991, yet the language is still relatively young compared to its ancestors (both direct ancestors, like Ada, and indirect ancestors, like COBOL and Fortran). One of the most common questions I am asked is about coding standards for SQL and PL/SQL.

The primary purpose of coding standards has always been to make maintenance easier for developers. In order to satisfy this requirement, PL/SQL coding standards must address several areas of the development process. Table D.1 displays some of the development areas that PL/SQL coding standards address.

The level of specifics contained in a coding standard should be fairly strict. While this may seem to be a burden during the development process, the people who do maintenance down the line will appreciate adherence to the standards.

The best way to ensure adherence to standards is to use structured peer review when a code module is completed. If the code is readable, the peer review process will flow more smoothly, and the reviewers will be able to concentrate their review time on understanding the intimacies of code rather than on deciphering an entry for the obfuscated PL/SQL contest! Peer reviews also provide a last line of defense against "sleeper" bugs (often overlooked by even the best developers), which are found a lot more easily when the code is readable.

If your organization does some or all of its own SQL and PL/SQL training, you should make an effort to incorporate standards training into your course materials.

I hope you find the examples presented in this text easy to read and understand. I also hope that you notice the consistency of style in the way examples appear. Every piece of code on the CD-ROM and in the text conforms to the following coding standard.

Table D.1 Development areas addressed by coding standards.

Development Area	Includes
Vertical spacing	Spacing between statements; spacing between procedures and functions within package bodies.
Horizontal spacing	Spacing between identifiers and operators; number of statements per line; maximum line width.
Procedural calls	Use of positional or named notation when calling stored PL/SQL objects.
Commenting	Type of comments to be used and the frequency, spacing, positioning, and content of comments.
Code reuse/modularity	Contents of procedures and functions; organization of procedures and functions into packages.
Identifiers	Rules for naming identifiers; rules for naming stored PL/SQL objects.
SQL statements	Formatting rules for embedded SQL statements.
Performance	Performance tips (particularly for embedded SQL statements).
Debugging	A standard method of handling exceptions inside PL/SQL objects as well as inside other applications that call stored PL/SQL objects.
Testability	Rules for writing stored PL/SQL objects so that unit testing can be accomplished.
Development environment	Rules determining what tools will be used for application development and what processes must be followed by developers.
Capitalization	Rules determining which keywords will be used in UPPER case, Mixed case, and lower case.
Conformance to standards	Rules designating when it is allowable for code to not agree with the coding standard.
Documentation	Rules that designate whether the coding standards will be applied to design documents and what type of documentation must exist for particular routines.

A Sample SQL And PL/SQL Coding Standard

This document defines the SQL and PL/SQL environment and programming standards and procedures for <insert your company name here>. The standards established in this document apply to all SQL and PL/SQL development efforts.

These PL/SQL coding standards were written to allow for consistency in PL/SQL code written by various developers while allowing for some individual styles and preferences to be expressed. The central purpose of any coding standard for SQL and PL/SQL must deal with database performance, clarity of code, and maintainability of code. This standard should be considered a guideline for developing easily maintainable SQL and PL/SQL applications in a high-performance Oracle database.

Developers should attempt to meet the spirit of this document by applying good judgment, rather than strictly adhering to the letter of the standard. This standard applies to all developer-written SQL and PL/SQL code (including scripts, stored procedures and functions, database triggers, and stored packages). Generated code is not governed by this standard.

This document is a living document that evolves based on the experiences of you, the developer. You should be aware that changes may occur to this document in the future, based on your (or other developers') experiences and insights.

The Development Environment And Processes

This section of the standard is highly dependent on the nature of your organization; therefore, I will only give suggestions on the types of material that should be included in this section of your coding standard. The *Development Environment And Processes* section of the standard should address the following issues:

- *Your version control processes*—A good working knowledge of PL/SQL is important to a developer, but the inability of a single developer to follow version control processes could be disastrous!

- *Standard tools for your development efforts*—If you have a standard configuration for your tools, it should be described in painstaking detail. If your tools support central administration of this configuration, so much the better.

- *Peer review practices*—Many organizations have formal peer review processes in place to validate the quality of design documents, code, and test results. If your organization uses these processes, the coding standard should (at the very least) point developers to your process documents.

- *Documentation*—Describe the documentation required when developers create new code and what documents need to be updated when maintenance is performed. Provide reasonable facsimiles of this documentation (or excerpts from real documents that satisfy your requirements).

- *Testing standards in place*—Provide examples of thorough test scripts and plans. Tests for each aspect of your system (front end, stored procedures and functions, packages, and database triggers) should be discussed in detail.

- *Standard routines*—You should describe whether standard routines, such as error handling, help system calls, and so forth, are available and when these routines should be used. Provide a detailed explanation of each standard call and its interfaces.

These issues can be addressed in appendices to your coding standard or in other documents, as long as your developers receive the necessary information.

References To Other Documents

I personally favor one stop shopping; pack the standard with as much information as possible and reduce the amount of time developers spend tracking down other documents.

Programming Design Standards

Developers should design for modularity. *Black box* is a term often used in conjunction with modules; each module should perform one (and only one) function using a defined interface and produce a predictable result. So long as the interface for a code module is not changed, the code module may be altered without affecting outside code.

Each module contains one or more routines (and the data structures and variables needed to support the routines). PL/SQL allows developers to implement modularity through the use of packages, which can contain procedures and functions as well as global type, variable, and constant declarations.

Stored functions that use parameters of the **IN OUT** and **OUT** types are not allowed. Stored functions should use only the **RETURN** statement to return a value.

Developers are encouraged to identify routines that can be reused. This code can be centralized, tested, and used by other developers to improve the reliability of system code and to reduce development time for more complex modules.

The Modularity Ombudsman

If your organization consists of ten or more people, it might be a good idea to appoint a "Modularity Ombudsman" who has some experience with SQL and PL/SQL. The responsibilities of this position include:

- *Identifying code segments that can be reused*

- *Developing and testing reusable modules*

- *Documenting modules and promoting their use*

The modularity ombudsman should also take part in peer review for new modules to help increase code reuse throughout your project.

Headers

A header should appear at the start of any script, procedure, function, package body, or package spec. Consider this template header:

```
-- ****************************************************************
-- Description: Describe the purpose of the object. If necessary,
-- describe the design of the object at a very high level.
--
-- Input Parameters:
--
-- Output Parameters:
--
-- Error Conditions Raised:
--
-- Author:      <your name>
--
-- Revision History
-- Date         Author        Reason for Change
-- -------------------------------------------------------------
-- 03 JAN 1997 J.Schmoe       Created.
-- ****************************************************************
```

The Usefulness Of Headers

There are some people who dislike headers or feel that a header is a useless burden to place on a developer. I disagree: At no other point in the code are provisions made for documenting the overall purpose, logic, and interface of a module. In my opinion, a header is the most essential documentation for any piece of stored code.

Formatting Guidelines For SQL And PL/SQL Statements

These guidelines are provided to give code a generally consistent appearance, including indentation, horizontal alignment, and vertical alignment. Adherence to these standards will make code more readable and more easily understood when maintenance is necessary.

Alignment Of Operators

These guidelines enhance the readability of code by adding white space and clarifying complex expressions.

- Arrange series of statements containing similar operators into columns whenever it will not cause excessive white space and you have sufficient room to do so.

  Correct:
  ```
  vFirstName := 'Roger';
  vLastName  := 'Smith';
  vSSN       := 999999999;
  ```

  Incorrect:
  ```
  vFirstName := 'Roger';
  vLastName := 'Smith';
  vSSN := 999999999;
  ```

- Always use parentheses in expressions containing more than one identifier or literal. This clarifies code for inexperienced developers who are not familiar with operator precedence and helps eliminate the possibility that you've overlooked something in your equation.

Correct:

```
IF (nSSN < 2.5) THEN
   <statements>
END IF;
```

Incorrect:

```
IF nSSN < 2.5 THEN
   <statements>
END IF;
```

- Align the **IN** and **OUT** keywords in columns when defining the interface for a procedure or function.

Correct:

```
PROCEDURE Days_Between (dStartDate    IN     date,
                        dEndDate      IN     date,
                        nGPA          IN OUT number,
                        nDaysBetween     OUT number)

<procedure declarations and body>
```

Incorrect:

```
PROCEDURE Days_Between (dStartDate IN date,
                        dEndDate IN date,
                        nGPA IN OUT number,
                        nDaysBetween OUT number)

<procedure declarations and body>
```

- When calling a procedure or function, align the parameters into a column. This reduces the visual clutter around the call, making it stand out from the rest of the code.

Correct:

```
DaysBetween (dStartDate   => dEnrolledDate,
             dEndDate     => dGraduationDate,
             nGPA         => nFinalGPA,
             nDaysBetween => nDuration);
```

Incorrect:

```
DaysBetween (dStartDate => dEnrolledDate,
             dEndDate => dGraduationDate,
             nGPA => nFinalGPA,
             nDaysBetween => nDuration);
```

Capitalization

Table D.2 contains a list of keywords that should always be fully capitalized when referenced in code. Some of these keywords are commonly used reserved words; reserved words that do not appear on this list should be capitalized as well.

The keyword **REPLACE** is to be used in uppercase only when used as part of the **CREATE OR REPLACE** clause that is used to create a stored PL/SQL object. Calls to the SQL function **replace()** should not be presented in uppercase.

In addition to the keywords presented in Table D.2, fully capitalize all of the following:

- The names of all standard exceptions (**NO_DATA_FOUND, OTHERS, TOO_MANY_ROWS**), and all user-defined exceptions.

- The names of all constants and all user-defined datatypes.

- All acronyms (**ANSI, ASCII, HUD, NASA, NOAA, YMCA**, and so forth).

Table D.2   Capitalize these keywords.

ALL	FALSE	MINUS	ROWTYPE
AND	FETCH	NOT	SELECT
AS	FOR	NOTFOUND	SET
BEGIN	FOUND	NULL	SQLCODE
BETWEEN	FROM	OPEN	SQLERRM
BODY	FUNCTION	OR	TABLE
CLOSE	GOTO	ORDER BY	THEN
COMMIT	GROUP BY	OUT	TYPE
CONSTANT	HAVING	PACKAGE	UNION
CREATE	IF	PROCEDURE	UNION ALL
DECLARE	IN	RAISE	UPDATE
DELETE	INSERT	REPLACE	VALUES
ELSE	INTERSECT	RETURN	VIEW
ELSIF	INTO	ROLLBACK	WHEN
END	IS	ROWCOUNT	WHERE
EXCEPTION	LIKE	ROWID	WHILE
EXIT	LOOP	ROWNUM	

- The names of all tables, snapshots, and views, as well as the aliases given to these objects in queries.

- The names of all database triggers.

Use mixed case to refer to the names of user-defined procedures and functions (functions provided by SQL*Plus and PL/SQL are still referenced in lower case). For example:

```
Calculate_GPA
DBMS_Output.Put_Line
```

Optionally, use mixed case for user-defined identifiers. If you choose this method, use capital letters to help make the identifier names more meaningful by visually breaking variable names into words; here are some examples:

```
vString
nBaseSalary
nGPA
iTardyDays
iClassNumber
lComments
rStudentPhoto
```

All text not handled by these rules should use lowercase. Consider the following:

```
CREATE OR REPLACE PACKAGE My_Sample_Package AS
PROCEDURE My_Sample_Procedure (nParameter1 IN      number,
                               nParameter2    OUT number)

IS

   YES    CONSTANT    char (1) := 'Y';

BEGIN

   IF (some expression) THEN
      replace (vString, chr (9), '    ');
   END IF;

END My_Sample_Procedure;
END My_Sample_Package;
```

Comments

As much as some developers dislike the task, commenting code is essential if the code is going to be maintained. There are a number of steps that can be taken to make comments less necessary:

- Use meaningful identifiers for variables, constants, and parameters. If you use abbreviations to compose identifiers, use the abbreviations consistently (e.g., don't use both **ADDR** and **ADRS** to signify **ADDRESS**).

- Use the named parameter style of executing procedures and functions. This is especially effective if both the parameters and the variables passed to the stored PL/SQL object have meaningful identifiers.

- Comments about revisions belong in the prologue, not in the body of the module.

Commenting Changes And Problem Tracking

If you're using a problem-tracking system on your project, it's better to reference a particular report from that system and provide a brief summary of the changes made to solve that problem. Don't attempt to include all the information about the problem in the prologue; that's why you bought a problem tracking system!

- Break complex equations and formulas into several smaller statements.

- Reuse existing functions and procedures to accomplish your tasks. Identify code that can be reused.

There are a number of locations in PL/SQL code where comments should almost always be used, including the following instances:

- Before each loop structure.

- Before each **BEGIN...END** sub-block.

- Before each conditional logic expression (**IF** <condition> **THEN**).

- Before any other logically significant statements.

Do not comment each line of code! Only comment important parts of your code, explaining why the code is written in a particular way. Explain business rules if possible. Never use a comment to restate the actions of a piece of code.

PL/SQL supports the following two styles of commenting:

```
/* We need to determine which students are in academic trouble. */
-- We need to determine which students are in academic trouble.
```

PL/SQL does not support the nesting of C-style comments; you cannot comment out a C-style comment using other C-style comments. For this reason, it is strongly recommended that only the double-dash (--) style of commenting be used except when commenting out blocks of code.

The exception to this rule is inside 3GL programs that use the Oracle Precompilers. The Oracle Precompilers don't support single line comments. On these occasions, use the commenting style most appropriate to the 3GL.

If a comment is required, place the comment on the line immediately preceding the line of code. Do not append comments to the end of code; if a comment is warranted by the complexity of the code and you have used meaningful identifiers, the comment should be complicated enough that you need to explain the situation using more than one or two words.

Correct:
```
--
-- Determine which students might be in trouble academically. We want
-- to help them perform better in school.
--
IF (some condition) THEN
```

Incorrect:
```
IF (some condition) THEN -- who's got bad grades?
```

All comments should use proper grammar, punctuation, and spelling. Comments should be complete, coherent sentences.

Volume Of Comments

As a general rule, about one-third of your final code should be comments. This figure often varies depending on the size and complexity of the code, but is an excellent rule of thumb.

Indentation

The most important element in readable code is consistent indentation, which illustrates clearly the logic flow of a procedure. Consider these blocks of code:

```
IF (x < 7) THEN
IF (y < 0) THEN
<statements>
END IF;
ELSIF (x > 10) THEN
<statements>
ELSE
<statements>
END IF;


IF (x < 7) THEN
   IF (y < 0) THEN
      <statements>
   END IF;
ELSIF (x > 10) THEN
   <statements>
ELSE
   <statements>
END IF;
```

Horizontal alignment in the second block of code makes it much easier to follow, even though it is syntactically and functionally identical to the first block of code.

You should not use more than three or four levels of indentation in any block of code. If this many levels of indentation become necessary, consider breaking the code into smaller modules. Too many levels of indentation is almost as bad as no indentation at all.

- Code should always be indented consistently, using three spaces for each level of indentation. Variable, type, and constant declarations should all be indented to the first level of indentation. Do not use tab characters.

```
IF (some expression) THEN
   IF (some expression) THEN
      IF (some expression) THEN
         <statements>
      ELSIF (some expression) THEN
         <statements>
      END IF;
```

```
    END IF;
END IF;

<statements>
```

- Statements following the **WHEN** clause of an exception handler should be indented five spaces, in order to create a column-like effect within the exception handler.

  Correct:
  ```
  EXCEPTION
     WHEN OTHERS THEN
          DBMS_Output.Put_Line (SQLERRM);
  ```

  Incorrect:
  ```
  EXCEPTION
     WHEN OTHERS THEN
        DBMS_Output.Put_Line (SQLERRM);
  ```

Horizontal Spacing

You've probably heard of the obfuscated C contest, where the entrants attempt to cram as much code as possible onto a single line that does some type of work while remaining completely unreadable. If you have any experience maintaining code, you've probably seen more than a few pieces of code that have a good chance of winning a contest like this. The guidelines presented in this section are an attempt to guide you away from writing hard-to-read code.

- One of the most important elements in creating readable code is the spacing placed around operators. Table D.3 shows common operators and keywords that need to be preceded and followed by a space when they are used in expressions.

  Often more than one of the operators and keywords shown in Table D.3 will be adjacent to each other inside an expression. In this instance, it is recommended that only one space lie between the two operators/identifiers. For example:

  ```
  IF (vMajor IS NOT NULL) THEN
  ```

- Spaces should precede and follow character (') literals.

Table D.3   Operators and keywords to be preceded and followed by a space when used in expressions.

+	-	*	/
&	<	>	=
!=	<=	>=	:=
=>	||	..	:
<>	IN	OUT	AND
OR	NOT	NULL	

```
SELECT first_name || ' ' || middle_name || ' ' || last_name
       'student_name'
FROM   STUDENTS
WHERE  ssn = 999999999;
```

- Do not leave any blank spaces preceding or following the ** operator.

```
nRaisedNum := nNum**nPower;
```

- Do not leave blank spaces before or after the plus (+) and minus (-) signs when used as unary operators.

```
nNumber := -nSecondNumber;
nNumber := +nSecondNumber;
```

- Do not use spaces between multiple parentheses or semicolons (;). Always precede the first opening parenthesis of a set with a space.

```
AND (((x < 5) AND (y < 5))
OR   ((x > 5) AND (y > 5)));
```

Vertical Spacing

Vertical spacing helps distance elements in the code from one another, reducing the visual clutter above and below statements. To create appropriate vertical spacing for your code, place a blank line in the locations described in the following list:

- Before lines containing the keywords **IF**, **ELSE**, **ELSIF**, and **EXCEPTION**. If the line is preceded by a comment, place the blank line before the comment instead of before the line of text.

```
--
-- If the student's grade point average meets the criteria for
-- mandatory academic counseling, add the student's name and social
-- security number to the list.
--
IF (nRealGPA < 1.5) THEN
   <statements>


--
-- We also want to consider students who are failing two or more
-- classes, even if their GPA is above 1.5.
--
ELSIF Has_Two_Fails (nForSSN => nSSN) THEN
   <statements>

ELSE
   <statements>
END IF;
```

- Before any line containing the **LOOP** keyword. Do not place a blank line before source code containing the **END LOOP** keyword. (As with lines of code containing the **IF** keyword, keep the comments for a line of code with the comment by placing a blank line before the comment.)

```
--
-- For each student returned by the query, add the student's social
-- security number to the PL/SQL table.
--
FOR Students_rec IN Students_cur LOOP
   <statements>
END LOOP;
```

- Before each exception after the first declared within the **EXCEPTION** section of a PL/SQL block.

```
EXCEPTION
   WHEN NO_DATA_FOUND THEN
        <statements>

   WHEN TOO_MANY_ROWS THEN
        <statements>

   WHEN OTHERS THEN
        <statements>
```

- Before and after the variable, constant, and type declarations for a PL/SQL block.

```
PROCEDURE Update_Student_GPA (nSSN IN      number)
IS

    <declaration>
    <declaration>

BEGIN
    <statements>;
END Update_Student_GPA;
```

- Following the declaration of the procedure and its parameters.

```
PROCEDURE Update_Student_GPA (nSSN IN      number)

IS
```

- Do not place an empty line before a line containing the **END IF** keyword. Do place blank lines after the last line of code containing the **END IF** keyword.

```
IF (some expression) THEN

    IF (some expression) THEN

        IF (some expression) THEN
            <statements>
        END IF;
    END IF;
END IF;

<statements>
```

Named Vs. Positional Notation

Procedures and functions should always be called using named notation for their parameters. This helps identify the data that is being passed to the stored PL/SQL object (assuming that the identifiers chosen for the parameters are meaningful). Place only one parameter on each line of the call:

```
DaysBetween (dStartDate    => dEnrolledDate,
             dEndDate      => dGraduationDate,
             nGPA          => nFinalGPA,
             nDaysBetween  => nDuration);
```

Statements Per Line And Line Width

Place only one statement (or part thereof) per line of code. Break compound statements over multiple lines. Do not exceed a maximum line width of 80 characters (including indentation). Due to space limitations, the lines in this book are limited to a maximum of 70 characters.

If your code has a complex equation or formula that is expressed using a single statement or operation, consider breaking the code into several smaller statements to make the operations less intimidating. The equation will be much easier to debug; in addition, the process of breaking the equation into subsections will increase your awareness of any mistakes that you make.

SQL Statement Formatting Rules

The formatting of SQL statements is one of the few areas in which this standard can be "the law." All SQL statements should conform precisely to these standards to the maximum extent possible; even slight deviations can have a performance impact on an Oracle database.

Oracle caches individual SQL statements within its shared global area (SGA). When a new statement is issued, Oracle does a block comparison of the statement against statements in the SGA. If a match is found, Oracle re-executes the stored version of the statement, rather than parsing the new statement and then executing it.

For instance, presume that the SGA contains the following SQL statement:

```
SELECT name, ssn, grade
FROM   STUDENT_GRADES
WHERE  grade > 90;
```

Now presume that someone executes this statement:

```
SELECT name, ssn, grade
  FROM STUDENT_GRADES
 WHERE grade > 90;
```

The second statement, although functionally identical to the statement already existing in the SGA, would not find a match in the SGA and would be parsed to determine the proper execution plan for the statement, thus increasing the overhead of the statement and slowing the response to the user.

To make matters worse, the first (and the correct) statement might be pushed out of the SGA to make room for the new statement, further impacting the processing of code that does follow the standard. The placement of a single space or shifting the case of a single character will force an SQL statement to be parsed and placed in the SGA instead of finding a matching statement in the SGA, due to the nature of the block comparison algorithm that Oracle uses.

Admittedly, the time required to parse a single statement to determine an execution plan is very small, but with tens or hundreds of users hitting the database at the same time, those milliseconds add up very quickly. Performance improvements are sometimes achieved in one fell swoop, but a lot of performance tuning work is the result of painstakingly wringing small improvements out of a lot of different pieces of code.

A number of examples are listed in the following sections. In each section, one example is labeled *Correct* and the other examples are labeled *Incorrect*. The example labeled correct is the *only* acceptable format for statements of the type, even though the other statements shown (and many variations not shown) are functionally equivalent to the "correct" statement.

DELETE Statements

Correct:
```
DELETE
FROM    STUDENTS
WHERE   ssn = 999999999;
```

Incorrect:
```
DELETE
  FROM STUDENTS
 WHERE ssn = 999999999;
```

Incorrect:
```
DELETE STUDENTS WHERE ssn = 999999999;
```

INSERT Statements

Correct:
```
INSERT
INTO    STUDENTS
        (ssn,
         first_name,
         last_name,
```

```
        ...
        most_recent_gpa)
VALUES (999999999,
        'Roger',
        'Smith',
        ...
        NULL);
```

Incorrect:
```
INSERT
INTO STUDENTS (ssn, first_name, last_name,... most_recent_gpa)
VALUES (999999999, 'Roger', 'Smith',...NULL);
```

Incorrect:
```
INSERT INTO STUDENTS
VALUES (999999999, 'Roger', 'Smith', ... NULL);
```

Incorrect:
```
INSERT INTO STUDENTS VALUES (999999999, 'Roger', 'Smith',...NULL);
```

SELECT Statements

Correct:
```
SELECT last_name, first_name, middle_name, ssn, most_recent_gpa
FROM    STUDENTS
WHERE   ssn = 999999999;
```

Incorrect:
```
SELECT last_name, first_name FROM STUDENTS
WHERE
ssn = 999999999;
```

Incorrect:
```
SELECT ssn, most_recent_gpa
FROM STUDENTS
WHERE most_recent_gpa < 2.0;
```

UPDATE Statements

Correct:
```
UPDATE STUDENTS
SET     apartment_number = 'H',
        street_address   = '16 Northwest Main Street'
WHERE   ssn = 999999999;
```

Incorrect:
```
UPDATE STUDENTS
SET apartment_number = 'H',
street_address = '16 Northwest Main Street'
WHERE ssn = 999999999;
```

Incorrect:
```
UPDATE STUDENTS
SET    apartment_number = 'H', street_address = '16 Northwest Main
Street'
WHERE ssn = 999999999;
```

PL/SQL Naming Conventions

Using a set of naming conventions for PL/SQL objects tends to create more meaningful identifiers. This section of the standard will come into play most often when creating identifiers (variables and constants) inside blocks of code.

It is common to utilize abbreviations to shorten identifiers. When doing so, the abbreviations should be meaningful and used consistently (e.g., do not use both **ADDR** and **ADRS** as an abbreviation for **ADDRESS**).

Database Triggers

Database triggers are named using this convention:

```
table_name + trigger_type_extension
```

In this example, **table_name** is the name of the trigger's base table, and **trigger_type_extension** represents one of the four types of database triggers listed in Table D.4, plus one or more of the letters shown in Table D.5 to indicate which DML statements cause the trigger to fire.

Thus, a **BEFORE INSERT** or **UPDATE** row level trigger on the **STUDENTS** table would be named **STUDENTS_BRIU**.

If the length of the trigger name exceeds 30 characters when following this standard, abbreviate the name of the trigger's base table to create the name of the trigger. Under no circumstances should the trigger type extension be abbreviated.

Table D.4 The four types of database triggers.

Trigger Type	Extension	Fires
Before statement	_B	Once, before the DML statement acting on the table.
Before row	_BR	Once for each row affected by the DML statement, before the DML statement is executed.
After row	_AR	Once for each row affected by the DML statement, after the DML statement is executed.
After statement	_A	Once, after the DML statement has finished executing.

Table D.5 Modifications to **trigger_type_extension** to indicate DML statements handled by the trigger.

Trigger Type Extension	DML Statement
D	The trigger fires when a **DELETE** statement modifies the base table.
I	The trigger fires when an **INSERT** statement modifies the base table.
U	The trigger fires when an **UPDATE** statement modifies the base table.

Identifiers

When declaring variables and constants, the developer should preface a meaningful identifier with one of the prefixes shown in Table D.6.

Identifiers should always use mixed-case and capital letters to indicate separation of elements within an identifier. Thus, a variable of type **varchar2** that holds a student's first name would be **vStudentFirstName**.

The identifiers used for explicitly declared cursors should be meaningful; the suffix **_cur** should be appended to the identifier. For example:

```
CURSOR Students_cur
IS
SELECT first_name, middle_name, last_name, overall_gpa, most_recent_gpa
FROM   STUDENTS;
```

Table D.6 Datatype prefixes for use in identifiers.

Datatype	Prefix	Example
binary_integer	bi	biArrayIndex
boolean	b	bStudentQualifiesForAid
char	c	cYesOrNo
date	d	dEnrolledDate
exception	x	xTABLE_DOES_NOT_EXIST
integer	i	iCoursesCarried
long	l	lComments
longraw	lr	lrStudentPhoto
natural	na	naArrayIndex
number	n	nRemainingBalance
raw	r	rStudentPhoto
rowid	row	rowStudent
varchar2	v	vStudentFirstName

Identifiers declared using **%TYPE** should still include a datatype prefix as part of the identifier name:

```
nStudentSSN    STUDENTS.ssn%TYPE;
```

Identifiers declared using **%ROWTYPE** should be named like the object that is lending the variable its structure. These identifiers should always include the **_rec** suffix as part of the identifier:

```
Students_rec          STUDENTS%ROWTYPE;
FailingStudents_rec   FailingStudents_cur%ROWTYPE;
```

Procedures And Functions

Stored procedures and functions should be named first by the type of action the object performs and then by the object of that action. For instance, a procedure that calculates interest on a student's remaining balance would be named **Calculate_Balance_Interest**.

Packages

Packages should be named in accordance with the general purpose of the procedures and functions contained within the package. For instance, a package containing routines used to calculate a student's GPA would be named **GPA_Calculations**.

Written Documentation

All documentation pertaining to system design should follow the conventions identified in this standard. This applies especially to pseudocode that is used to document stored PL/SQL objects.

In addition, all written documentation should reference calls to built-in and developer-written procedures and functions using a set of parentheses, as in "will call the **Calculate_Semester_GPA**() procedure". The names of built-in and developer-written code modules should also be referenced in **bold**.

Taking Advantage Of Standardized Code

Oracle stores the source code for PL/SQL objects inside the **ALL_SOURCE** view of the **DBA_SOURCE** table in the **SYS** schema. This allows you to query the most recent source code for a procedure or function from the database.

If the coding standards are followed fairly closely, it's possible to write scripts that work with your source code to assist you in your documentation efforts. Included on the CD-ROM is a script that takes full advantage of the coding standards to collect information about and document source code.

The Build_SUID_Matrix Package

Oracle stores dependencies in the **ALL_DEPENDENCIES** view, but this information exists only at the object-to-object and object-to-table levels. The view cannot, for instance, state precisely which objects perform **INSERT** statements on a specific table.

The **Build_SUID_Matrix** package was designed to locate all references to tables within a specified PL/SQL object. The procedures and functions in the package locate table references and sort the references by type (**SELECT**, **INSERT**, **UPDATE**, **DELETE**, and **%TYPE** or **%ROWTYPE**). The package populates the **SUID_MATRIX** table with this information.

Once the **SUID_MATRIX** table is fully populated, a query can be run to see precisely which objects access a specified table or which tables a specified object references. This is particularly useful when:

- Examining the impact of creating a new index.

- Examining the impact of altering a table's structure.

- Determining which objects perform a particular type of operation against a table.

Improving The Build_SUID_Matrix Package

There are a number of potential improvements that can be made to the **Build_SUID_Matrix** package:

- Improving the level of detail determined to the column level. Knowing which objects modify data in a table is very useful, but if 20 routines update a table and only a few routines update a particular column that has a suspect value, it's even quicker to find the routines that modify the value in that column.

- Recognizing objects within packages. The current implementation of the package only recognizes objects to the package level and doesn't differentiate between procedures and functions within the package.

What's New In Oracle8?

What's New In Oracle8?

As of this writing, Oracle8 is finally in beta and due to be released any day. Chances are that Oracle8 will have been released by the time you read this text. Hopefully, the information contained in this appendix will give you a step up on understanding the drastic changes accompanying Oracle8. You've almost certainly heard by now that Oracle8 supports the object concept, but there are other important changes, as well.

Any rumors you've heard about people seeing this information with glazed eyes are entirely true. In some ways, the changes between Oracle7 and Oracle8 are more radical than the changes that occurred between Oracle6 and Oracle7. This appendix outlines some of the more striking changes implemented in Oracle8.

New Datatypes

Oracle8 introduces several new datatypes. Some of these datatypes are used to support the *object-relational database* model. In this model, data structures are based on object-oriented techniques for representing the real world. Relational operations are still usable in this model, meaning that all Oracle7 databases are forward compatible with Oracle8.

Several other new datatypes serve a variety of purposes, including:

- **varrays** support the use of multivalue columns.

- Large object (LOB) datatypes are used to support the storage of objects up to four gigabytes in size.

- Nested tables are tables that appear as columns in other tables.

Obviously, these are radical new types of constructs for an Oracle database. We'll discuss each new type individually. In addition to these new datatype definitions, the concept of a **ROWID** has been altered, as well.

The object Datatype

In Oracle8, an *object* is a self-contained construction that holds information about real-world data and the operations that can be performed on the data. Information about the data is stored in attributes, while the operations that can be performed on the data are methods.

An *attribute* is simply a declaration of an element of data using one of Oracle8's recognized datatypes (**include** objects, **varray**s, and large object datatypes). A *method* is a code module that operates against one or more attributes of the object.

For instance, let's say you're trying to represent a student as an object. There are certain characteristics common to every student. Some of these characteristics might be as follows:

- First, middle, and last names
- Social security number
- Address and phone number
- Application date and acceptance date
- Graduation date
- GPA
- Degree plan or course of study
- Parents
- Amount of tuition and fees owed
- Dormitory assignment

Obviously, this isn't a complete list, but it will do for the sake of this example. All of these elements would be attributes of a student object. Looking at the preceding list, it's likely that some attributes can be broken down further, like the address. An address has the following components:

- Street name or route
- Box number
- City

- State

- ZIP code

Each individual student object will also have certain operations that have to be performed, such as:

- Calculating a GPA

- Calculating the financial aid for which a student qualifies

- Calculating interest on a student's unpaid tuition and housing costs

This list could go on forever. But, at this point, we have enough information to present Listing E.1, which shows what a complex object declaration for a student might look like in Oracle8.

Listing E.1   A complex object declaration in Oracle8.

```
CREATE TYPE Address_TYPE AS object
(street_name_or_route    varchar2 (40),
 house_or_box_number     integer,
 city_name               varchar2 (30),
 state_code              varchar2  (2),
 zip_code                integer);

CREATE TYPE Degree_TYPE AS object
(department_name         varchar2 (30),
 degree_level            integer,
 degree_name             varchar2 (30),
 degree_field            varchar2 (40));

CREATE TYPE Housing_TYPE AS object
(dormitory_name          varchar2 (30),
 occupancy_code          varchar2  (1),
 room_cost               number (6,2));

CREATE TYPE Student_TYPE AS object
(first_name              varchar2 (20),
 middle_name             varchar2 (20),
 last_name               varchar2 (30),
 ssn                     varchar2  (9),
 address                 Address_TYPE,
 application_date        date,
 acceptance_date         date,
```

```
gpa                     number (3,2),
degree_plan             Degree_TYPE,
father_name             varchar2 (60),
mother_name             varchar2 (60),
mother_maiden_name      varchar2 (20),
account_number          integer,
housing_assignment      Housing_TYPE,
MEMBER FUNCTION Get_SSN                      RETURN varchar2,
MEMBER FUNCTION Calculate_GPA                RETURN number,
MEMBER FUNCTION Award_Financial_Aid          RETURN number,
MEMBER FUNCTION Calculate_Account_Interest RETURN number);
```

Storing this information in a straight relational model would require the definition of several tables. Now, all that's needed is a single **STUDENTS** table with the following definition:

```
CREATE TABLE STUDENTS OF Student_TYPE;
```

Every row created in the **STUDENTS** table is an object of the type **Student_TYPE** and has all of the attributes and methods in Listing E.1. The **INSERT** statement that creates a new student would look like this:

```
INSERT
INTO    STUDENTS
VALUES ('John',
       'Joseph',
       'Doe',
       '999999999',
       address('North Main Street',
               23,
               'Philadelphia',
               'PA',
               '45032'),
       SYSDATE,
       SYSDATE,
       NULL,
       degree_plan(),
       'William Robinson Doe',
       'Jane Elizabeth Doe',
       'Martin',
       ACCOUNT_SEQ.NEXTVAL,
       housing_assignment('Elam Arms',
                          'S',
                          795.43));
```

Every attribute of the defined type can be given constraints (**NOT NULL** constraints, **DEFAULT** value constraints, and so forth). These attributes can also be indexed like a column in a table.

The PL/SQL functions **Get_SSN**(), **Calculate_GPA**(), **Award_Financial_Aid**(), and **Calculate_Account_Interest**() are all methods in this example. Keep in mind that a method isn't restricted to being a PL/SQL procedure or function. Methods can also be calls to a library of objects stored in the database and written in a language like C or C++. The functionality of these methods is defined (or referenced) in the type body.

The varray Datatype

The **varray** datatype enables you to create structures that are essentially arrays, without having to deal with the crude limitations of PL/SQL tables. Like object datatypes, a **varray** is a datatype declaration, not a variable declaration. A declaration of a **varray** might look like this:

```
CREATE TYPE Name_Array_TYPE AS varray (10) OF varchar2 (60)
```

You must declare a maximum size for the datatype when it is declared. As with a PL/SQL table, referencing a **NULL** or nonexistent element of a **varray** variable causes a **NO_DATA_FOUND** exception to be raised. Elements in the variable are referenced like the elements of a PL/SQL table. For instance:

```
Names_array (7)
```

Using a **varray** type, you could easily implement a multivalue column in a single row of a table. For example:

```
CREATE TYPE Courses_Array_TYPE as varray (9) OF number;

CREATE TABLE STUDENTS
(first_name            varchar2 (20),
 middle_name           varchar2 (20),
 last_name             varchar2 (20),
 ssn                   varchar2 (9),
 address               Address_TYPE,
 application_date      date,
 acceptance_date       date,
```

```
gpa                     number (3,2),
degree_plan             Degree_TYPE,
father_name             varchar2 (60),
mother_name             varchar2 (60),
mother_maiden_name      varchar2 (20),
account_number          integer,
housing_assignment      Housing_TYPE,
courses                 Courses_Array_TYPE);
```

This defines a row in the **STUDENTS** table that stores course information. Each student could have as many as nine courses, all contained within a single row in the **STUDENTS** table.

The Large Object Datatypes

Oracle8 implements four new large object datatypes:

- **bfile**—Used to point to a binary file stored in the host operating system's file system.

- **blob**—Used to store unstructured binary data.

- **clob**—Used to store single-byte character data.

- **nclob**—Used to store multi-byte character data.

Each of these datatypes is intended for a specific use, but there are certain characteristics that these datatypes all have in common:

- Columns of these types may be up to four gigabytes in length.

- Tables may contain one or more columns of each of these types.

For instance, the following is a valid table definition in Oracle8:

```
employee_num        number
first_name          varchar2 (20)
middle_name         varchar2 (20)
last_name           varchar2 (20)
photo               bfile
resume              bfile
```

This table—**EMPLOYEES**—contains two columns with a datatype of **bfile**. These files are not stored within the database but reside on the file system at the OS level.

For instance, the **resume** column might always point to an employee's resume that is continually updated in Microsoft Word.

Values of these new datatypes are always populated with a *LOB locator*, which is comparable to a pointer. Actual data is not stored in the table but at another location inside the database. In the case of data with type **bfile**, the actual data is a file maintained outside of Oracle by the host operating system.

With the exception of the **nclob** datatype, you may also include multiples of these datatypes in object types that you create. To manipulate objects of the LOB datatypes, the **DBMS_LOB** package has been provided.

The Nested Table Datatype

A *nested table* is actually a table that is a column in another table. Consider again the sample student object presented earlier in this appendix. Instead of defining the datatype **Address_TYPE**, address information could have been stored in the STUDENTS table like this:

```
CREATE TABLE STUDENTS
(student          Student_TYPE,
 address_list     ADDRESSES_TABLE)
```

Using this table definition, a single student could have multiple addresses. As with the **varray** datatypes, this datatype could be used to implement a multivalue column in a row of data. The nested table method has the advantage of not requiring a maximum number of values for the column.

The New ROWID

Oracle8 has a new pseudocolumn called an *extended ROWID*. This pseudocolumn contains all the elements of the **ROWID** from Oracle7, plus a data object number that uniquely identifies a particular segment. An Oracle7 **ROWID** is now referred to as a *restricted ROWID*.

The DBMS_ROWID Package

Oracle8 introduces the **DBMS_ROWID** package, which contains functions that operate on the **ROWID** and extended **ROWID** pseudocolumns. Among the functions provided in this package are functions that can convert **ROWID** values between the restricted and extended formats.

Changes To SQL*Plus And PL/SQL

Obviously, such drastic changes to the supported datatypes require changes to SQL*Plus and PL/SQL to support the new datatypes. The following sections take a brief look as some of the changes made to SQL*Plus and PL/SQL.

SQL Changes

In addition to allowing columns of the new datatypes to be defined, Oracle has added several commands to be used with the new datatypes:

- ALTER TYPE
- CREATE DIRECTORY
- CREATE LIBRARY
- CREATE TYPE
- CREATE TYPE BODY
- DROP TYPE
- DROP TYPE BODY

In addition to these new commands, Oracle8 offers some new built-in functions and object views. While a complete discussion of the new commands isn't necessary, you may want to know a little more about some new built-in functions and a new type of object called an object view.

New Built-In Functions

Oracle8 has added several new built-in trigonometric functions. These functions are listed in Table E.1.

Object Views

An *object view* is a construct implemented in Oracle8 to ease the migration from the relational database to the object-relational database. Object views allow you to query and manipulate relational data as if the data were object data.

Table E.1   New trigonometric SQL functions.

Function	Purpose
acos( )	Returns the arc cosine of a parameter, n, in radians.
asin( )	Returns the arc sine of a parameter, n, in radians.
atan( )	Returns the arc tangent of a parameter, n, in radians.
atan2( )	Returns the arc tangent of two parameters, x and y, in radians.

PL/SQL Changes

PL/SQL fully supports all the new Oracle8 datatypes. For instance, you may declare **object** and **varray** types in your functions, procedures, and packages just like variables of any other datatype.

Summary

This appendix hasn't covered everything you need to know about Oracle8, nor could it do so without taking an enormous amount of space. Instead, this appendix provides an overview of some of the new concepts contained in Oracle8. Just like Oracle7, Oracle8 promises to revolutionize the way databases are created using Oracle.

4GL, 41

Ada, 58
Alerts
    and pipes, 296
ALTER USER privilege, 311
    and changing passwords, 310
Arrays
    vs. cursors, 52
Associated table, 242, 244

—B—

Base table, 250. *See also* Associated table.
BEGIN statement, 51
Blank lines
    in SQL*Plus, 262
Blocks
    and sub-blocks, 50
    definition, 50
Break
    set of actions, 92
break command
    types of events, 92
Broken job, 295
    definition, 291

—C—

C, 55, 58, 70
Cartesian products. *See* Joins.
Cascading delete
    definition, 236
COBOL, 41
Code, standardizing
    PL/SQL, 27
    SQL, 27
Columns. *See also* Tables.
    definition, 37
Comments
    single-line vs. multi-line, 145
COMMIT statement, 42
Compile error
    definition, 257
Compute command
    types of operations, 97
Constraints
    definition, 28
    types, 29
Continue statement
    lack of in PL/SQL, 186
Conversions
    explicit, 44, 53
    implicit, 44
    reasons for using explicit, 44

Cursors
    definition, 51
    explicit, 52
    implicit, 53
    problems using, 331
    vs. arrays, 52

—D—

Data definition language. *See* DDL.
Data dictionary, 240
Data manipulation language. *See* DML.
Database
    basics, 27–28
Database triggers, 20, 65
    basic structure, 242
    common uses, 241
    and **DBMS_Alert**, 281
    definition, 223
    row-level, 19
    statement-level, 18
    types, 19
    typical uses, 18
    use for row-level, 241
Datatypes
    composite, 55
    most common, 44
    scalar, 55
DBMS_Alert package, 281
    procedures, 282
    vs. **DMBS_Pipe** package, 284
DBMS_DDL package, 286
    procedures, 286
DBMS_Describe package
    prodedure, 288
DBMS_Job package, 290
    procedures, 291
    scheduling a job, 294
DBMS_Output package, 265, 295
DBMS_Pipe package, 295

    procedures, 296
    vs. **DMBS_Alert** package, 284
DBMS_SQL package, 302
    and changing passwords, 310
    procedures, 304
DBMS_Utility package, 312
    especially useful function, 312
DDL, 41, 42
DECLARE statement, 51
Delete, cascading
    definition, 236
DELETE statement, 42
Dependencies
    definition, 121, 163
DML, 42, 48, 49, 60, 67
Documentation
    three basic aspects of the procedure, 141
    trigger vs. function, 247
    trigger vs. package, 247
    trigger vs. procedure, 247

—E—

Elements
    referencing, 56
END statement, 51
Error
    mutating table, 233
Error messages, 137
    and packages, 211
    assigned numbers, 138
Error, compile
    definition, 257
Errors, 269. *See also* Exceptions.
    in Oracle, 58
    useful functions in PL/SQL, 275
Errors, runtime
    better method of debugging, 269
    definition, 264
    locating, 268

most effective method of isolating
problems, 269
Exception handler
importance of using carefully, 272
order of steps, 275
Exceptions
and the **RAISE** statement, 61
handling, 58
importance of creating
user-defined, 138
origin of term, 51
reasons for occurring, 137
user-defined, 61
EXCEPTION statement, 51
Exit and quit commands
values that can be returned, 103
EXIT statement, 64
Extra fetch
avoiding, 330

Fetch, extra
avoiding, 330
Fortran, 41
Forward declaration, 119
Fourth-generation programming
language. *See* 4GL.
Full-table scan
and use of indexes, 327
avoiding, 327
definition, 326
Function declaration
portions, 170
Function documentation
vs. trigger documentation, 247
Functions
and procedures, 14
calling, 167

creating, 160, 183
definition, 157
documenting, 179
dropping, 161
most common uses, 14
packaged vs. standalone, 204
poor programming style for defining
parameters, 165
purity levels, 61
referencing from stored objects, 163
structure of stored, 170
tests, 190

Header, 141

Identifier names
and documenting code, 145
Implementation
processing pipe-based, 296
processing using signals, 281–82
Indexes
ways to create, 33
INSERT statement, 42
Instructions
PRAGMAs, 58

Joins
Cartesian products, 44
definition, 44
outer, 45
simple, 45

—L—

Languages. *See also* 4GL, C, COBOL, Fortran, Pascal, PL/SQL, SQL.
  Ada, 51
  data definition, 41
  data manipulation, 41
Legacy system, 301
Line numbers
  incorrect, 263
Lines, blank
  in SQL*Plus, 262
Listings
  1.1 A generic cold backup script for an Oracle database, 4
  1.2 Logic for a hot backup of an Oracle database, 5
  1.3 A sample script to create a new user in an Oracle database, 7
  1.4 The HTMLCODE.SQL script, 7
  1.5 A script to recompile stored objects that are marked as invalid, 9
  1.6 Generated code to recompile invalid PL/SQL objects, 10
  1.7 A simple script that allows unit testing for a function, 10
  1.8 A simple script to update area codes inside phone numbers, 12
  1.9 A typical stored procedure, 14
  1.10 A typical stored function, 15
  1.11 Use of the **Calculate_GPA** function in a SQL statement, 16
  1.12 A typical package spec, 16
  1.13 A typical package body, 17
  1.14 A typical database trigger, 20
  1.15 An **UPDATE** trigger using a **WHEN** clause, 21
  2.1 A sample table creation script using constraints, 28
  2.2 A revised table creation script using constraints, 30
  2.3 Finding the indexes for a table, 34
  2.4 Finding the existing roles in your database, 35
  2.5 A simple DDL statement, 41
  2.6 A simple DML statement, 42
  2.7 A query that causes a Cartesian product, 44
  2.8 A query using a simple join, 45
  2.9 A query using an outer join, 46
  2.10 A sample PL/SQL block, 50
  2.11 A sample PL/SQL block with a sub-block, 50
  2.12 The declaration of an explicit cursor, 52
  2.13 A **CURSOR FOR** loop, 52
  2.14 A PL/SQL record declaration, 54
  2.15 A PL/SQL table declaration, 55
  2.16 A user-defined exception, 61
  2.17 Using an **EXIT** statement with multiple loops, 64
  2.18 A typical stored procedure, 67
  2.19 A typical stored function, 67
  2.20 A sample package spec, 69
  2.21 Using a stored procedure to simulate a C **continue** statement, 71
  3.1 A generic cold backup script for an Oracle database, 78
  3.2 The DROP_ALL.SQL script, 79
  3.3 A script that grants privileges to roles, 80
  3.4 A script to create an application developer's account, 81
  3.5 An SQL report on code stored in the data dictionary, 82
  3.6 A unit test for the **Calculate_GPA**() procedure, 84

3.7 A documented header for a script, 89

4.1 Embedded SQL within a stored procedure, 113

4.2 Creating a stored procedure, 116

4.3 Declaring a local procedure within a procedure, 118

4.4 Using a forward declaration for a local procedure, 119

4.5 The structure of the **ALL_DEPENDENCIES** view, 121

4.6 Defining parameters for a stored procedure, 122

4.7 Checking the values of parameters, 122

4.8 Defining a parameter using **%TYPE**, 123

4.9 Defining a parameter using **%ROWTYPE**, 123

4.10 Default values for parameters, 124

4.11 An anonymous PL/SQL block that calls a procedure, 125

4.12 Calling a stored procedure from another stored procedure, 126

4.13 Calling a procedure using named notation, 127

4.14 Calling a stored procedure using positional notation, 128

4.15 Mixing named and positional notation, 128

4.16 The procedure declarations portion of a procedure, 130

4.17 The variable declarations portion of a procedure, 131

4.18 The executable declarations portion of a procedure, 133

4.19 The body of a procedure, 134

4.20 The exception handler of a procedure, 136

4.21 Using the **OTHERS** exception handler, 138

4.22 Using **SQLCODE()** and **SQLERRM()** in an **OTHERS** exception handler, 139

4.23 Using the **RAISE** statement in your code, 139

4.24 Using the **Raise_Application_Error()** procedure, 140

4.25 The **Calculate_GPA()** procedure with a header, 141

4.26 Pseudocode for the **Calculate_GPA()** procedure, 143

4.27 Pseudocode for the **Annual_Review()** procedure, 147

4.28 The code for the **Annual_Review()** procedure, 148

4.29 Part of the unit testing scripts for the **Annual_Review()** procedure, 153

5.1 A PL/SQL function that utilizes a DML statement, 158

5.2 A procedure calling the **Raise_Salary()** function, 158

5.3 A testing script for the **Raise_Salary()** function, 159

5.4 Creating a function, 160

5.5 Declaring a local function within a procedure, 161

5.6 The structure of the **ALL_DEPENDENCIES** view, 163

5.7 Use of the **RETURN** statement in a function, 165

5.8 A return value of a user-defined datatype, 165

5.9 Using **%TYPE** definitions for parameters and return values, 167

5.10 Using **%ROWTYPE** definitions

for parameters and return values, 167

5.11 Calling a function within a DML statement, 168

5.12 The **Raise_Salary**() function called in Listing 5.11, 168

5.13 An anonymous PL/SQL block that calls a function, 169

5.14 A stored function calling another stored function, 169

5.15 The function declaration, 171

5.16 The variable declaration section of a function, 172

5.17 The executable declarations of a function, 174

5.18 The body of a function, 176

5.19 The exception handling portion of a function, 178

5.20 The **Parse_String**() function with a header, 180

5.21 Pseudocode for the **Parse_String**() function, 181

5.22 Pseudocode for the **Assign_Instructor**() function, 185

5.23 The code for the new **Assign_Instructor**() function, 188

5.24 A test script for the **Assign_Instructor**() function, 192

6.1 The definition of global constructs in a package spec, 200

6.2 Referencing an object within a package, 201

6.3 Defining a procedure within a package spec, 202

6.4 Defining a function within a package spec, 204

6.5 Defining the purity level of a packaged function, 206

6.6 A package spec containing an overloaded function, 207

6.7 Creating a procedure inside a

package body, 209

6.8 Creating a function inside a package body, 210

6.9 Initializing packaged variables, 211

6.10 Logic for the function **Next_Word**(), 214

6.11 Revised pseudocode for the **Next_Word**() function, 215

6.12 Logic for the **Build_Error**() procedure, 215

6.13 Logic for the **Next_String**() function, 216

6.14 The package spec for the **System_Errors** package, 216

7.1 Using a DML statement inside a database trigger, 223

7.2 Using a **WHEN** clause, 226

7.3 Using boolean functions in a database trigger, 230

7.4 A sample **CREATE TRIGGER** command, 231

7.5 A trigger that causes a mutating table error, 234

7.6 A trigger that can read from its associated table, 235

7.7 Referencing a foreign key column in another table, 236

7.8 Referencing a trigger's associated table using an after statement trigger, 237

7.9 Implementing a key value lookup scheme to avoid mutating table errors, 238

7.10 The structure of the **ALL_TRIGGERS** view, 240

7.11 A trigger declaration, 242

7.12 A triggering event, 243

7.13 Defining a trigger's associated table, 244

7.14 Declaring a trigger's level, 245

7.15 Using the **WHEN** clause, 246

7.16 A trigger body, 246

7.17 A sample header for a trigger, 248

7.18 Pseudocode for the **ENROLLED_CLASSES_ARIU** trigger, 250

7.19 Code for the **ENROLLED_CLASSES_ARIU** trigger, 251

8.1 A sample stored procedure with compile errors, 258

8.2 The revised **Calculate_Student_Grades()** procedure, 260

8.3 Pulling error information from the **ALL_ERRORS** view, 262

8.4 The **Calculate_Student_Grades()** procedure, 263

8.5 An excerpt of debugging code from the **Build_SUID_Matrix** package, 265

8.6 Code using a tracepoint variable, 269

8.7 Misusing the **OTHERS** exception handler, 272

8.8 Using the **OTHERS** exception handler to log an error, 273

8.9 Calling the **SQLCODE()** function in an exception handler, 276

9.1 Using a trigger to send a signal, 285

9.2 Using a trigger to send a message over a pipe, 301

9.3 The **Change_Password()** function, 310

9.4 A procedure that uses the **UTL_File** package, 316

10.1 Using the **EXPLAIN PLAN SQL** statement, 320

10.2 Getting an **EXPLAIN PLAN** from the **PLAN_TABLE** table, 321

10.3 A **SELECT** statement inside the body of a PL/SQL block, 330

10.4 Implementing **SELECT** statement functionality by using a cursor, 330

10.5 Using **IF-THEN** logic to flag errors, 331

10.6 Using exception handlers to improve performance, 333

Local functions
and accessibility, 163

Local procedures
declaring within PL/SQL code, 118

Locks, 47

Loops
CURSOR FOR, 52
FOR, 63
WHILE, 64

LOOP statement, 63

—M—

Many-to-many relationships, 31, 32

Mutating table error, 233
and foreign key, 236
cascading delete, 237

—N—

Notation
named, 127
named vs. positional, 129
positional, 128

NULL statement, 63

—O—

Objects
    private, 16, 17
One-to-many relationships, 31, 32
One-to-one relationships, 31
Operators, 47
Optimizer
    rule-based vs. cost-based, 329
Optimizer, rule-based
    primary conditions, 329
Oracle error ORA-00942, 276
Oracle exceptions
    and confusing the debugging
        process, 140
Outer joins, 45
Overloaded object
    definition, 207

—P—

Package body
    contents, 208
Package documentation
    vs. trigger documentation, 247
Package specification. *See* Package specs.
Package specs, 16, 17
    how to define, 202
    in PL/SQL, 69
    primary purpose, 212
    types of definitions, 199
Packages
    contents, 16
    defining purity levels, 205
    definition, 199
    definition of body, 16
    definition of specification, 16
    in PL/SQL, 69
    testing, 220

Packages, special
    DBMS_Alert, 301
    DBMS_DDL, 286
    DBMS_Describe, 288
    DBMS_Job, 290
    DBMS_Output, 265, 295
    DBMS_Pipe, 295
    DBMS_SQL, 302
    DBMS_Utility, 312
Parameters
    constraining, 122
    definition, 122
    for functions, 164
    references to, 105
    types, 67
    types for stored procedures, 123
Pascal, 55
Passwords
    changing, 310
p-code, 159, 228
Performance problems
    most common causes, 319
pipename parameter
    character length, 297
Pipes
    and alerts, 296
    private, 297
    public, 297
    unique names, 301
Pipes, unnecessary
    importance of emptying, 298
PL/SQL
    deficiencies, 70–72
    select features, 49
    vs. SQL for client/server
        development, 74
PRAGMA. *See also* Instructions.
    definition, 205

Private pipe
  and security, 297
Private synonyms
  definition, 37
Privileges
  definition, 35
  system level, 35
  table level, 35
Pro*C program, 286, 302
Problems, performance
  most common causes, 319
Procedural Logic/Structured Query
  Language. *See* PL/SQL.
Procedure Builder, 232, 265
Procedure declaration
  portions, 129
Procedure documentation
  vs. trigger documentation, 247
Procedures
  and functions, 14
  most useful place to document, 141
  named method, 68
  package vs. standalone, 203
  positional method, 68
  reasons for writing, 13
Prologue. *See* Header.
Public pipe, 297
Public synonyms
  definition, 37

—R—

RAISE statement
  and exceptions, 61
Records, 53
Referential integrity
  definition, 31
  types, 31
Relationships
  many-to-many, 31, 32
  one-to-many, 31, 32
  one-to-one, 31
Roles, 6
  definition, 35
ROLLBACK statement, 42
Rows. *See also* Tables.
  definition, 38
Rule-based optimizer
  primary conditions, 329
  tuning tips, 329
Runtime errors
  better method of debugging, 269
  definition, 264
  locating, 268
  most effective way of isolating
    problems, 269

—S—

Scan, full table
  definition, 326
  avoiding, 327
  and use of indexes, 327
Schemas
  definition, 36
Script development
  dynamic code generation, 7
Scripting
  creating unit testing pieces of code, 10
Scripts
  HTMLCODE.SQL, 7
  importance of storing in version
    control, 90
  important aspects, 90
  tasks performed, 78
Security features. *See* Privileges, Roles.
SELECT statement
  performance problem, 330
Sequences
  definition, 36

SGA, 28, 39, 40, 41, 73
Show command
    and arguments, 99
Signals
    and **DBMS_Alert**, 281
    overwriting previous signals, 284
Simple joins, 45
Snapshots
    benefits of using, 37
    definition, 36
Special packages
    DBMS_Alert, 301
    DBMS_DDL, 286
    DBMS_Describe, 288
    DBMS_Job, 290
    DBMS_Output, 265, 295
    DBMS_Pipe, 295
    DBMS_SQL, 302
    DBMS_Utility, 312
SQL
    vs. PL/SQL for client/server
        development, 74
SQL scripts
    and generating other SQL scripts, 79
SQLCODE(), 275, 276
SQLERRM(), 275, 277
Standardizing code
    PL/SQL, 27
    SQL, 27
Statements
    BEGIN, 51
    COMMIT, 42
    DECLARE, 51
    DELETE, 42
    END, 51
    EXCEPTION, 51
    EXIT, 64
    INSERT, 42
    LOOP, 63
    NULL, 62

RAISE, 61
ROLLBACK, 42
SELECT, 42
UPDATE, 42
Stored function
    vs. stored procedure, 67
Stored objects
    and DML statements, 159
Stored PL/SQL objects
    common traits, 13
Stored procedures
    components, 129
    definition, 113
    reasons for providing performance
        improvements over code, 114
    vs. stored function, 67
Structured Query Language. *See* SQL.
Subqueries
    definition, 49
Substitution variable
    definition, 105
Synonyms
    definition of private, 37
    definition of public, 37
System automation
    backups, 4
    creating new users, 6
    scripting, 4
    testing code, 12
System Global Area. *See* SGA.

— T —

Tables
    aliases, 46
    associated, 242, 244
    base, 250
    definition, 37
    definition of columns, 37

definition of rows, 37
in PL/SQL, 55
Tasks
  conditions indicating automation, 88
  conditions indicating scripting, 88
  deciding whether to perform with a
    script, 87
Tests
  examples of positive and negative, 152
  for functions, 190
TKPROF, 322
Trace file
  creating, 322
Tracepoint variable
  advantages of using, 271
  and debugging runtime errors, 269
Trigger
  pseudocode, 250
  requirements, 249
Trigger body, 242, 246
Trigger declaration, 242
Trigger documentation
  vs. function documentation, 247
  vs. package documentation, 247
  vs. procedure documentation, 247
Trigger header
  questions to answer, 247
Trigger level, 242, 245
Triggering event, 242, 243
Triggers
  and loading data more quickly, 233
  disabling more than one, 233
  single vs. several, 226
  testing **UPDATE** functionality, 253
  vs. other stored PL/SQL objects, 228
Triggers, database
  and **DBMS_Alert**, 281
  basic structure, 242
  common uses, 241

defining to fire, 225
definition, 223
restrictions, 224
row-level, 229
tasks for testing, 252
ttitle command
  actions, 102
Tuning tips
  when using rule-based optimizer, 329

Unit test
  advantages, 87
Unit testing script
  advantages over typical ad hoc
    testing, 82
  tasks of well-written, 84
UPDATE statement, 42
UTL_File package, 107
  procedures, 312
  steps to do file I/O, 312
  using to access a file, 316

Variables
  declaring dynamically, 57
  initializing, 57
Views
  definition, 38
  performance implications, 38

WHEN clause, 242, 245
WHERE clause tips, 328

HIGH PERFORMANCE

NOTES

_____
_____
_____
_____
_____
_____
_____
_____
_____
_____
_____
_____
_____
_____
_____
_____
_____
_____
_____
_____
_____
_____
_____
_____
_____